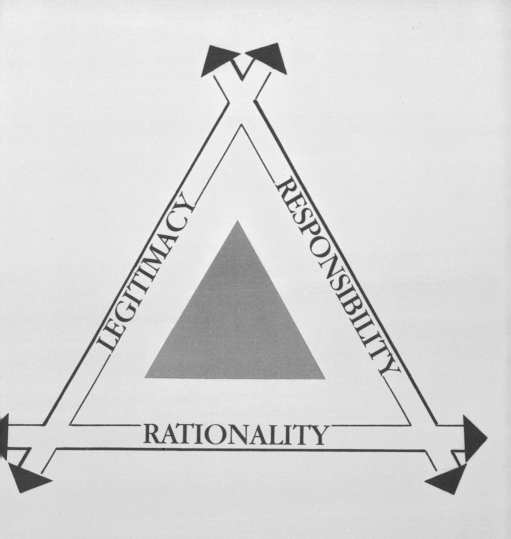

The Search for New Directions
in Business and Society

edited by
EDWIN M. EPSTEIN
DOW VOTAW

Rationality, Legitimacy, Responsibility
Search for New Directions in Business and Society

Rationality, Legitimacy, Responsibility
Search for New Directions in Business and Society

Edited by

EDWIN M. EPSTEIN
University of California, Berkeley

DOW VOTAW
University of California, Berkeley

Goodyear Publishing Company, Inc.
Santa Monica, California

Library of Congress Cataloging in Publication Data

Rationality, legitimacy, responsibility.

  Proceedings of a workshop/conference held at
the School of Business Administration, University
of California, Berkeley, Mar. 23–26, 1975.
  Bibliography: p. 203
  Includes index.
  1. Industry—Social aspects—Congresses.
I. Epstein, Edwin M.   II. Votaw, Dow.
III. California. University. School of Business
Administration.
| HD60.R38 | 301.18'32   78-18302
ISBN 0-87620-807-3

Current printing (last digit):
10 9 8 7 6 5 4 3 2 1

Y-8073-2

Printed in the United States of America

To
the Memory of
Raymond A. Bauer

WORKSHOP/CONFERENCE
"BUSINESS AND SOCIETY: STATE OF THE ART AND PROGRAM FOR THE FUTURE"

Berkeley, March 24–26, 1975

CONTRIBUTORS

Kenneth E. Boulding, Department of Economics, University of Colorado

Howard R. Bowen, Departments of Economics and Higher Education, Claremont Graduate School

Harvey Brooks, School of Engineering, Harvard University

Earl F. Cheit, School of Business Administration, University of California, Berkeley

C. West Churchman, School of Business Administration, University of California, Berkeley

William Letwin, Department of Politics, The London School of Economics and Political Science

Neil J. Smelser, Department of Sociology, University of California, Berkeley

PARTICIPANTS

G. L. Bach, Graduate School of Business, Stanford University

Raymond A. Bauer, Graduate School of Business Administration, Harvard University

Ivar Berg, Department of Sociology and Anthropology, Vanderbilt University

L. Earle Birdzell, General Electric Company

Phillip I. Blumberg, School of Law, The University of Connecticut

Wayne G. Broehl, Jr., The Amos Tuck School, Dartmouth College

Fletcher L. Byrom, Chairman of the Board, Koppers Company

Keith Davis, College of Business Administration, Arizona State University

Melvin A. Eisenberg, School of Law, University of California, Berkeley

Edwin M. Epstein, School of Business Administration, University of California, Berkeley

William M. Evan, Department of Sociology, The Wharton School, University of Pennsylvania

William C. Frederick, Graduate School of Business, University of Pittsburgh

Harold L. Johnson, Graduate School of Business Administration, Emory University

Louis B. Lundborg, Chairman of the Board (retired), Bank of America

Joseph W. McGuire, Graduate School of Administration, University of California, Irvine

R. Joseph Monsen, Jr., Graduate School of Business Administration, University of Washington

Milton Moskowitz, Senior Editor, *Business and Society Review*

Lee E. Preston, School of Management, State University of New York, Buffalo

Theodore V. Purcell, S. J. Jesuit Center for Social Studies, Georgetown University

S. Prakash Sethi, School of Management and Administration, University of Texas, Dallas

Barbara Shenfield, Political and Economic Planning, London, England; and Visiting Professor of Sociology, Rockford College, Illinois

George A. Steiner, Graduate School of Management, University of California, Los Angeles

Frederick Sturdivant, College of Administrative Science, Ohio State University

Dow Votaw, School of Business Administration, University of California, Berkeley

Clarence E. Walton, President, The Catholic University of America

Donald J. Watson, Manager: Public Relations Planning and Research, General Electric Company

Mayer Zald, Chairman, Department of Sociology and Anthropology, Vanderbilt University

Contents

Preface

This volume is the direct outgrowth of a workshop/conference held at the School of Business Administration, University of California, Berkeley, on March 23 to 26, 1975. Although the phrase *business and society* is not very descriptive of the field which it encompasses, it is nonetheless the designation by which the field is most widely known and the title we used to describe the workshop/conference: Business and Society—State of the Art and Program for the Future. Our goals were to provide an opportunity for some leading scholars and business people to come together for a few days of stock-taking and reassessment of developments in a field which has slowly been gaining momentum over a period of some twenty years and to consider what might be the most promising lines of research, study, and teaching during the decade ahead.

Like most new fields of scholarly inquiry, the field of business and society (sometimes known as *business environment* and the *social foundations of business,* among other terms) has undergone growing pains. The "real" world of economic activity, with its press of daily problems, and the more cloistered world of scholarship and theory have experienced their inevitable and often healthy conflict here as elsewhere, but probably with somewhat less vituperation. It was as obvious to people engaged in business as it was to those of us working in the universities that the relationship between economic activity and the society in which it was carried on had undergone rapid and profound changes in the last twenty to twenty-five years. While the tumultuous 1960s subjected all American institutions to close scrutiny, sharp criticism, and, on occasion, great pressures, for no area was this more the case than for the business community. Both its newness and these rapidly changing societal perceptions about the role of business made the business and society field difficult to define. Consequently, much controversy arose over how the field was to be dominated and what was to be included and what excluded from this area of inquiry. The labels which came to be attached to research and teaching in the area are too numerous to list here. It seemed to us and to people in the General Electric Foundation that it was about time to take a look at what had been happening and to try to refine our understanding of what the business and society field really was, of what went on within it, and of where it was going, without worrying excessively about a name.

Obvious to us from the beginning was the fact that *business,* because of its connotations of private economic activity, was too narrow a term to be ideal. Similarly, although many of the issues pertinent to the field are, in the American context, generated by the activities of large corporations, we felt that *corporations and society* narrowed the focus unduly and, hence, was not satisfactory. One of our participants, William Evan, suggested that "organizations" and society was a more appropriate way of describing the field, on the ground that most of the social issues with which we in the field were concerned had to do with organizations in the broad sense, non-business as well as business and noneconomic as well as economic. Although that title is an improvement over *business and society,* we felt that it was, perhaps, too broad, especially at the present stage of development, and that it might diffuse the target and distract attention. For those and other reasons, we decided to stick with the older, more traditional, and less accurate title but one which, because of its widespread usage, in spite of its defects, is still probably the best understood.

As a format for the workshop/conference, we chose to orient each of the discussion sessions around a paper to be prepared in advance by a recognized authority in a particular dimension of the field, the aggregate (which proved to be seven papers and seven discussion sessions) to cover most of the important subdivisions which have come to be identified with the field of business and society. When we had matched our topics with our authors, we discovered that we had selected representatives from at least seven different disciplines, only a few of which were directly related to business: sociology, political science, economics, management, philosophy, natural science, and law. Some of our authors fell into more than one category. Several of the authors, moreover, during various stages of their careers had held positions of considerable administrative responsibility in higher education and have had, accordingly, an opportunity to reflect on the role of the business and society field in the broader context of the range of disciplines and areas of teaching and research inquiry found in the modern university.

One should not be startled when what one "knows" to be the case actually turns out to be so. The field of business and society is not only interdisciplinary, it is multidisciplinary. The choice of topics and authors confirmed that fact, and the workshop discussions added even more disciplines to the list: psychology, anthropology, history, engineering, policy sciences, and even futurology. While this disciplinary mixture adds a good deal of color, richness, and intrigue, it also presents some very serious problems. One of the participants commented during the sessions that while it was comforting to believe that God designed the world in neat compartments so as to help the various disciplinary departments in the university go about their work, that is not the way things are in fact. Employing the tools of many disciplines to the issues at hand may encourage interaction; it probably will not solve many problems, however, until God or some innovative thinker provides a genuine systems theory for the whole society. Moreover, this inherently multi- and interdisciplinary character of business and society inevitably causes some degree of discomfort among scholar-teachers in the field. While it is possible to claim expertise in one discipline and familiarity, perhaps, with a second, none among us has the audacity to profess real competence in the seven (or, more accurately, ten) disciplines which are relevant to the business and society area. In the meantime, however, we will have to make do with what we have. Because of the wide variety of topic and author and of what we learned at the workshop/conference itself, we were confirmed in our view that *business* was a bit too confining. Consequently, the title of this volume was changed to describe more accurately some of the core issues and premises of the field.

Underlying our conception of the workshop/conference from the very beginning, our planning for it, and our assignment of topics for papers, were three basic ideas. First, the context within which our interests and concerns are located is the relationship between economic institutions, on the one hand, and society, or social systems, on the other. Although much "economy" is not "business," the Neil J. Smelser paper devotes itself primarily to the broader arena, and properly so, because it was intended to provide the introductory and encompassing work into which the others were to be fitted. C. West Churchman opens his essay in a still broader arena but focuses on the corporation, a major instrumentality of business. Second, the compelling issues of the economy today (whether they be social policy, government intervention, "post industrial" capitalism, corporate governance, or whatever) cannot be discussed independently of the great philosophical issues of our time. Churchman relates some of these broad issues, such as holism versus reductionism and rationalism versus empiricism, to our attempts to understand the corporation.

Third, as Alvin W. Gouldner has said so well in only a slightly different context, "The criticism and transformation of society can be divorced only at our peril from the criticism and transformation of theories about society." The same can be said about the criticism and transformation of the relationship between economic institutions and social systems and of theories about that relationship. The workshop/conference was essentially an attempt to bring into juxtaposition a quarter of a century's comments about this relationship and theories which have arisen to explain and justify it. While we have all been long on comment and criticism, there has been a rather considerable neglect of theory. Consequently, while the workshop/conference sought to confront the comment with the theory, it sought also to stimulate new and more useful theory-building and to overcome the theoretical apathy pervading the discipline.

The Coming Crisis of Western Sociology (New York: Basic Books, 1970), p. 3.

To explore all of these ideas thoroughly would have required much more than one workshop/conference and many more than seven authors. This problem was resolved by our assigning to three basic ideas a central role in the workshop/conference and in the papers prepared for it. It seemed to us all along that rationality, legitimacy, and responsibility formed an especially important triangular foundation underlying the bridge between economic institutions and other sectors of society and one on which a creative workshop/conference could be built. This approach defined the conceptual boundaries around which the workshop/conference was organized and the theme of this volume. It also supplied some of the criteria which we employed in selecting the conference participants, academic and business alike, primarily a willingness to examine the theoretical as well as the practical issues.

Had our circumstances been utopian and our wits unbounded, the conception and the reality of the workshop/conference might have been somewhat closer together; our ideas might have been communicated more clearly to the willing authors, the papers presented in more appropriate sequence, and the discussion kept always on target. Given the number of individuals involved (some two dozen), their individual personalities and intellectual approaches, the complexities of schedules and geography, and the unfeasibility of a preliminary assembly of authors, the reality came closer to conception than we had a right to expect. The basic concepts, and their research and teaching dimensions, appeared in reasonably good order.

With regard to the three major themes and the scholarly goal of the workshop/conference, the authors' tasks were distributed more or less evenly. Neil Smelser and West Churchman concerned themselves primarily with rationality; Kenneth Boulding (and to some extent Earl Cheit) oriented his paper around issues of legitimacy; Howard Bowen, Harvey Brooks, and William Letwin explored various aspects of the responsibility theme; Cheit considered the educational relevance of all three themes and of the workshop/conference as a whole to the roles played by most of our participants in higher education for business. As editors, we have taken it upon ourselves to integrate and interpret for a general audience the seven papers and the discussions of those papers by the participants and to add some comments of our own. Of course, we assume full responsibility for our portion of what follows and hope that the authors and participants will be rational, as well as tolerant, concerning our comments and interpretations and that they will accept the editors' role as legitimate in the context of what we set out to do and as the fulfillment of our responsibilities both to them and to those who read this volume. We are hopeful this book will serve a useful function not only to faculty and students in business and society courses, but also to other members of business administration and social science faculties who have expressed frequent interest and curiosity—and occasional skepticism—about this field. Similarly, we believe the volume will be of interest and use for practitioners in business (and in other societal institutions) who must frequently deal with and always understand other sectors of our social system.

In addition to our overwhelming debt to the seven authors and to the participants, we owe special thanks to L. Earle Birdzell and Joseph Bertotti and, particularly, Donald J. Watson, all of the General Electric Company. They encouraged the conveners and made possible the generous support of the General Electric Foundation, which saw the need for the workshop/conference and provided the financial and other organizational assistance which was so essential to its successful outcome.

We also owe thanks and appreciation to the following: Thomas M. Jones, Carlyle Johnson, David Palmer and Paul Tiffany, past and present doctoral students in the School of Business Administration, University of California, Berkeley, who handled many of the operating details associated with the workshop and this volume; Mesdames Betty Kendall, Ellen McGibbon, and Helen Way who typed parts of the manuscript; Professor Joseph Garbarino, Director, and Mrs. Virginia Douglas, Adminstrative Assistant, at the Institute of Business and Economic Research at Berkeley, who greatly facilitated such an undertaking in the Berkeley setting; the School of Business Administration which housed and furnished hospitality for the meetings; and, especially, to the then-Dean Richard H. Holton and to Nadine Breed, Administrative Services Officer. Finally, our special thanks to Ms. Dorothy Draper, conference coordinator extraordinaire, whose efficiency, conscientiousness, and constant good humor helped make the workshop/conference an enjoyable as well as a worthwhile experience.

Edwin M. Epstein
Dow Votaw

Rationality, Legitimacy, Responsibility
Search for New Directions in Business and Society

Introduction

Among the great philosophical concepts which have echoed through the corridors of Western society in recent centuries, shaping our beliefs, ideologies, institutions, and values, are rationality, legitimacy, and responsibility. Individually and in various combinations the three frequently have been the focus of public debate about the nature and normative principles of the relationship between economic institutions and social systems, between business and society. At many levels all three concepts have profoundly influenced our thinking, discourse, and public policy concerning the character of the American political economy, the societal role of the great corporation, and the arguments now being made to justify the economic, social, and political structure of advanced industrial capitalism. All three are intimately bound up in the important philosophical conflicts of our time, including the opposition of holism and reductionism, equality and efficiency, liberty and accountability, and many other issues in developing social thought.

Rationality brought an end to the magical character of medieval life and reoriented almost all aspects of society. It had a particularly far-reaching effect upon economic thought and behavior. Rationality became both the philosophical basis and the practical justification for the market society, for capitalism with its systemic dependence upon rational conduct and the rational organization of labor and other productive resources, and for the greatly altered social structure which resulted. Underlying almost all Western economic analysis is some version of rationality predicated on concepts of weighed choices, measured alternatives, and consideration of marginal utility. Regarded once as the basic philosophical and psychological principle—dominating all other considerations—economic rationality is now perceived by investigators also as a variable, as a tool to aid investigation, and as an empirical feature of the economic system itself. Some believe that it is important to all of our thinking about economic institutions and social systems that we consider the consequences of broadening our meaning of economic rationality and the implications of our having to take into account other rationalities and values—for example, the desire to achieve social equality and political democracy—which are not essentially economic in character. There is also increasing recognition that policies and decisions which are economically rational may be disastrous—patently irrational in social and political terms.

Smelser talks of "other rationalities," such as communal or social, which, in certain situations and in certain combinations, actually subordinate economic rationality and properly become regarded as the fundamental forces in social life. This is a crucial observation. Churchman speaks for a "new rationalism" and of the deep concern its disciples have for future generations, but agrees with Smelser in at least one important respect: that the old rationality is an inadequate philosophical and psychological concept with which to investigate, understand, and change society and to do it in such a way as to include the needs and values of future generations. Churchman noted at the workshop, however, that he and other monists cannot tolerate a variety of rationalities, because their very goal in the new rationalism is to put them all together into one. Although Churchman describes his new rationalism as the underlying philosophical tradition of the systems approach, he emphasizes the need for a sound world view that the human intellect can grasp and use to begin to formulate approximate answers to our basic questions. In his analysis, Churchman deals, as it seems one must in this context, with the issues of rationalism versus empiricism and holism versus reductionism, issues over which philosophers have long been at war and about which society has long been confused.

Little more need be said in defense of our decision to include rationality among the three fundamental concepts underlying the relationship between economic institutions and social systems. The "climate of opinion," to use Becker's term,[1] which in any society delineates what can be thought or done from that which cannot, certainly includes in Western society a major component of rationality. This is particularly true of American society with its philosophical grounding on the enlightened notions of humanistic rationalism and on its economic creed based upon Smithian premises of Rational Economic Man. That rational component has been undergoing rapid and profound change, yet much of our thinking, especially in the context of economic behavior, has ignored the changes. While our assumptions are being questioned, few of the competing world views still appear tenable. Part One of this book, an introductiory essay by the authors and the Smelser and Churchman essays, will explore some of the major questions about rationality and suggest tentatively the theories and methodologies that will be necessary if answers are to be found.

Where rationality is primarily philosophical and psychological in its nature, legitimacy is the product of social and political thought. It is much closer to the real world and to real world experience but is not unrelated to rationality. Certainly the test of rationality is a factor in whether society regards a particular social institution, system, or structure as legitimate. The medieval Inquisition, whose basic assumptions were irrational, was probably more the victim of rationality than of any other change in social attitude. In contemporary times, it has frequently been alleged that failure to meet the test of rationality has played a key role in the legitimacy crisis of the modern corporation.

Legitimacy, however, has an existence apart from rationality. Boulding approaches the concept of legitimacy through the avenue of institutional survival. As Smelser's theme is the survival of the economic system and Churchman's is the survival of future generations, Boulding's focus is the survival of the business institution. He concludes that in the decades ahead survival will depend much more upon the nonmarket environment, especially on the ability of the business institution to retain legitimacy, than upon the market environment. If we view legitimacy, as Boulding does, as the belief or perception by society that a particular social institution is appropriate or proper or consistent with the moral foundations of that society, we arrive at some rather interesting propositions. Satisfactory performance, for example, is not the only point. An institution regarded as legitimate by society can survive failure after failure of performance of social tasks without endangering its survival, but even satisfactory performance cannot guarantee survival if legitimacy is lost. Our American Revolution bears witness to that fact with regard to the institution of British rule.

There are many observers who see the low repute in which business generally, and the large corporation in particular, are held today as evidence of a legitimacy crisis. Much of the discourse concerning the relationship between business and society revolves around this issue. Some define the whole corporate social responsibility movement in terms of a response to the perceived crisis of legitimacy. Others, like Irving Kristol, relate the corporate legitimacy crisis to current attacks on capitalism itself.[2] Some of this discourse has been aimless or even self-defeating, owing in large part to the lack of useful theory and methods of analysis concerning legitimacy. Boulding's essay is a promising attempt to fill some of the theoretical and analytical gaps.

Responsibility contains both the philosophical concepts basic to rationality and the sociological and legal/political elements essential to legitimacy. Responsibility is relational, having to do with the expectations held and obligations owed by one party to another with regard to the operations of social institutions. These expectations and obligations are derived from analytical systems predicated on either normatively based values or logically deduced concepts of the universe. In this dependence upon philosophical-psychological concepts to determine duty or obligation, responsibility is akin to rationality. Responsibility, however, like legitimacy, is dependent upon the dynamics of change within the social system which are frequently reflected in developments within the political process and legal system. William Letwin highlights these two sources of responsibility (the philosophical, and the political/legal) by distinguishing two bases of business responsibility, the moral and the legal. The first, often popularized as ethics, springs from a system of normative thought; the second derives from the operations of formal institutions and processes through which social expectations are articulated in democratic societies. Responsibility adheres to all social institutions. Harvey Brooks makes that point abundantly clear in his examination of technology assessment which, at root, is an effort to render technology—and those who develop and utilize technology—responsible to other sectors of society. Moreover, responsibility, is essential, points out Howard Bowen, to rendering business (or any other institution) legitimate within a social system.

Perhaps no phrase has been bandied about more, has generated more heat with less light, and indeed has degenerated into a veritable cliche than "social responsibility of business." In fact, a substantial part of the literature and much of the teaching effort associated with the business and society field has dealt with social responsibility. While the substantial disagreement that exists as to the responsibility of business institutions and their managers is reflected in such areas as (1) business ideology, (2) defining the societal tasks of business institutions, and (3) addressing the thorny problems of evaluating "responsible" versus "irresponsible" behavior, no assessment of the business and society field would be complete without an analysis of the multidimensional concept of responsibility.

As we suggested, the concepts of rationality, legitimacy, and responsibility underlie our understanding of the relationship between business institutions and the rest of the social system. So too, they have been central to the teaching and research which have taken place during the past two decades in the business and society field. One can scarcely pick up a course outline or examine a journal article or monograph without being struck by the importance of this conceptual trend. Earl F. Cheit's essay provides a fitting conclusion to this volume by relating the three to the central purpose of the workshop/conference: an examination of the development of the business and society field in terms of both teaching and research and an attempt to discern the likely—and desirable—directions of the field in the decade ahead. For after all it was our interest in the program for the future as well as the state of the art which brought together the academics and the practitioners in the workshop/conference. Cheit's contribution has the singular virtue of providing valuable perspective on the field as it fits into the historical evolution of university education in the United States and as a bridge between the "useful" and the "liberal" arts. Although, for the reasons suggested above, we have positioned it as the concluding essay in the book, we could just as well have used it as the opening piece (just as we did in the actual format of the workshop/conference) since it provides a context for and establishes the mission both of the actual gathering in March, 1975, and of this volume.

NOTES

1. Carl L. Becker, *The Heavenly City of the Eighteenth-Century Philosophers* (New Haven: Yale University Press, 1932), p. 5; but Becker traces the term to the seventeenth-century by way of Alfred North Whitehead.

2. See Irving Kristol, "When Virtue Loses All Her Loveliness," *The Public Interest,* Fall, 1970, pp. 3–15, and "On Corporate Capitalism in America," *The Public Interest,* Fall, 1975, pp. 124–141.

PART 1

Rationality

The broad context of this volume is the relation between economic activity and its social environment. As the first step toward evaluating some of the more important aspects of that relationship, Neil Smelser considers the parameters of economic activity. Because of his earlier work with Talcott Parsons in this general area,[1] Smelser's paper shows the benefits of long exposure to its subject matter and a perspective gained by reconsideration of a seminal study of more than twenty years standing. Smelser does not revisit the earlier work, however, but, instead, identifies several underlying themes with special importance for the analysis of economic activity. He does so by raising three basic questions:

1. What is the status of the assumption of economic rationality?
2. What is the most appropriate unit to identify as that within which economic activity transpires?
3. What are the relations of economic growth to the political and social structures of society?

Smelser summarizes his conclusion very clearly when he says that

> Our existing answers to these core questions are not satisfactory and are perhaps growing increasingly out of date, and...we have to forge new kinds of answers in the light of contemporary theoretical and empirical developments,[2]

the most important of these developments being the "discovering and pointing out that economic activity is embedded in a network of both economic and noneconomic structures, rationalities, and sanctions."[3]

The first question, it seems to us, is the most important, in that the answers to the others depend to a large extent upon answers to it. The appropriate unit cannot be determined without reference to the kinds of rationality that guide economic behavior. The answer to the third question requires certain assumptions about rationality. But how does one go about forging "new kinds of answers" to these questions? Smelser approaches the task by examining economic behavior in which the traditional economic rationality is minimized or subordinated to some other kind of rationality and the sanctions for controlling the movement of economic goods and services are noneconomic. He talks mostly of communal rationalities, as did Max Weber.[4] C. West Churchman urges the adoption of a "new rationalism" based on modern systems analysis but with roots in classical rationalism and also emphasizes the importance of seeking new kinds of answers to social questions. Assumptions that are no longer tenable, explanations that no longer explain, and values that seem inconsistent with observations in the real world soon produce social static and disturbance, frustration, confusion, disillusionment, and a "tragic mood that might lead us to a kind of anti-rationalism."[5] It might be noted also that inoperable assumptions and explanations and inconsistent values may impair the legitimacy of social institutions, a problem of particular importance in assessing Smelser's third core questions and the subject of the Boulding paper in Part Two.

THE RISE OF RATIONALISM

Although medieval universalism had already begun to weaken by the sixteenth century, European rationalism destroyed it in the seventeenth and eighteenth centuries. Will Durant catches the atmosphere nicely.

> To understand the Middle Ages we must forget our modern rationalism, our proud confidence in reason and science; we must enter sympathetically into the mode of men disillusioned by these pursuits, standing at the end of a thousand years of rationalism, finding all dreams of utopia shattered by war and poverty and barbarism, seeking consolation in the hope of happiness beyond the grave, inspired and comforted by the story and figure of Christ, throwing themselves upon the mercy of God, and living in the thought of His eternal presence.[6]

Philosophical interest shifted rapidly from the supernatural to the natural, and cultural rationalism came to rely on reason rather than on faith in creating a theory of man's destiny. The latter development irrevocably linked rationality with teleology and laid the foundation for another philosophical conflict. (See below.) We should note that *rationality* is not coextensive with such terms as *logic, planning, thinking, calculation,* or *game theory* but is related in diverse ways to all of them. Furthermore, Churchman points out in his essay that the rationalist "has to use other means than an argument from the obvious." The foundations of arithmetic and geometry have been questioned, and utility theory is only just now having its "obvious" premises shaken. The new rationalism, in Churchman's view, is aimed at selecting a *Weltanschauung* that passes certain critical tests, which Churchman describes, but is not obvious.

When rationality overrode the magical, economic rationality became the sine qua non of the growing commercial orientation of life and of the emerging market system. Communal and other rationalities also became consolidated and institutionalized in Western society. The potential conflicts between economic and communal rationalities were minimized by the social mechanism of differentiation. The sphere of private affairs became separated from the sphere of business affairs, and the communal principles of mutual responsibility, solidarity, sharing, and socialization were separated from most economic activity but continued to survive on the communal side, especially in kinship relations. Thus the dichotomy of business and society was also made possible. It is often contended that the separation of management and control is another example of this same structural differentiation at work. (See Smelser's comment on page 00.)

The separation of private affairs from business affairs produced distinct sets of moralities and virtues. As long as these sets appeared to be, or were believed to be, consistent, they provided a powerful justification for the social structure of capitalism. However, when, as Irving Kristol and others observed centuries later, the private virtues of frugality, hard work, reliability, and sobriety were no longer perceived to be consistent with public or business virtues, especially in the dominant corporate sector, the ideological underpinnings of capitalism were eroded.[7] The corporate social responsibility movement was defended by some as an attempt to reconcile these divergent virtues and attacked by others because it confused personal virtues with business virtues. Christopher Stone's *Where the Law Ends* is a good example of an attempt to define corporate social responsibility in terms of responsibility and ethical behavior in personal relationships.[8] Smelser takes a much more basic approach to the issue by seeking to integrate economic rationalities with other rationalities so as to close the gap between private and business affairs, and Churchman pursues a new and still broader rationality, of which the economic dimension is only a part. He defines morality in such a way as to unify the many moralities resulting from structural differentiations.

THE NEW RATIONALISM

New and often countertrends are now at work in society. Constraints of environment and ecology, life-threatening dimensions of technology, modern systems analysis, and a dozen other widely perceived social phenomena are producing a new universalism, a new holism, and a new world view which dramatize the shortcomings and narrowness of economic rationality and produce the powerful social tensions and symptoms of disturbance which are described in the Smelser and Churchman papers.

However, one must be aware that the new principle of "plucking a flower and troubling a star"[9] describes a world system with subsystems, not a universal medieval creed without parts. Yet the values of the rationalistic mastery of the universe are still dominant and must be taken into account.

The cultural values growing out of the Protestant Ethic have now spread worldwide, or have received sustenance from other cultural sources,[10] and include, as Smelser describes them: rationality in the organization of economic and social life, the freedom of people to exploit their natural environment, hard work for its own sake, and mastery, achievement, and personal ambition as desirable human qualities.

> It seems that the headlong and mindless worship of these values constitute a large part of the reason we now face some of our environmental imbalances and threatened shortages of resources. These values have contributed directly to the exploitation, the spoilage, and ultimately the exhaustion of the environment. It is again one of the ironies of history that after centuries of struggle these values have conquered the world, and at precisely the moment of victory, the values themselves have proved to be archaic and outmoded, even burdensome and dysfunctional.

Both Smelser and Churchman address themselves to other and new rationalities which can be used to supplement economic rationality as a tool of social analysis. Many more scholars have sought the same goals along similar paths. Bell urges a "sociologizing mode" to replace the "economizing mode" in the large corporation.[11] David McClelland and others have tried to identify motivations other than material ones in economic behavior.[12] The protagonists in the arena of corporate social responsibility still struggle over what one does about the "bottom line," and, indeed, how the bottom line is to be defined, and the ideological weakness of capitalism is said to be found in its rationality, calculation, and selfishness.[13] In other words, there seems to be a considerable amount of evidence to support Smelser's impression that the answer to the question about the status of the assumption of economic rationality is at present unsatisfactory, the writings of Milton Friedman and other neo-conservative economists notwithstanding. Even new rationalities will not solve all of these dilemmas, however, unless other philosophical controversies are also resolved.

HOLISM AND REDUCTIONISM

Explicit in Churchman's essay and implicit in the background of Smelser's is one of the great philosophical debates of the modern era, with holism or monism, on one side, and reductionism or, as Churchman calls it, pluralism, on the other. The question is whether the world can be perceived or understood as a whole or whether it can only be known by reducing it to its constituent parts. The disagreement is particularly virulent in biology, where the holists argue that the whole is greater than the sum of its parts and that "putting the pieces together again, whether in reality or just in our minds, can yield no complete explanation of the behavior of even the most elementary living system,"[14] while the reductionists deny that the human intellect can grasp enough of the total picture to begin to approximate answers to our basic questions.[15] A below-the-surface issue is the destiny of humankind, which explains the emotion behind the debate. The contest manifests itself in areas far afield from biology, however, and affects our discussion of incrementalism in public policy formation, "zero-based budgeting," and other issues where preoccupations with the whole and with parts come into conflict.[16]

Because it appeared to be, and in many respects was, hostile to medieval universalism, rationality became identified with the reductionist view. Hence the issue of holism versus reductionism is descended in part from classical rationality. Descartes' second rule of logic, for example, required that each problem or difficulty be divided into as many parts as possible, a sharp break with the customary approach of medieval thought. Science also became identified with reductionism and appears finally to have triumphed over the holistic (humanistic) view with which it had been in conflict for centuries, except for an occasional resurgence, as in biology. Only very recently (in various guises, among them general systems analysis and the "new rationalism") has holism made a recovery, and one can believe, with William Bowen, "that in secret recesses of the mind a great many highly educated human beings dimly but incorrigibly cherish notions of man's kinship with stars..."[17] Churchman describes the controversy as a fight "between those who wish to see and design their world in pieces and those who wish to see and design it as a whole."[18]

The teleological dimension has been associated with the debate from the beginning. Again science seems about to impose the conclusion that existence has no purpose. Jacques Monod, for example, wrote that science starts from the postulate that there is no purpose in nature.[19] On one level it is very difficult to argue with that conclusion. On another level Churchman does argue with it and finds his teleonomy in "our expectations concerning the values of future generations." "We are the caretakers of the world of our progeny" he writes. The latter part of his essay considers the implications of this view, including some comments about the corporate scene. Erich Jantsch shares Churchman's view that human beings can give existence its purpose. Jantsch describes his own book, *Design for Evolution,* as an exploration into the acquisition and use of knowledge for human purposes. It elaborates on the theme—not novel to our critical age—that rational knowledge cast into the form of internally consistent, logically constructed and closed models of science constitutes a useful, but by no means sufficient, tool for dealing with matters of human design for a human world. In such matters, the *"know-how"* of ordering and implementing well-perceived, goal-oriented action, the very domain in which the objectivating models of science are helpful, constitutes the lowest level in a hierarchy of knowledge for human purposes.[20]

In his oral presentation preceding the group discussion of his paper, Churchman emphasized the importance of the teleological issue, particularly with regard to the responsibilities of one generation to future generations, and illustrated his point with some comments about the way in which science and technology, the enemies of existential purpose, are actually compelling a teleological approach. How else, he asks, can we deal with some of the long-term problems we are now generating? The literature on the effects of plutonium, for example, estimates that the appropriate time spans may range from 1,200 to 300,000 years. Each generation, according to Churchman, must regard itself as a caretaker with respect to future generations; this is the purpose of each generation and the reason we need a new rationalism and a new world view. One of the discussants (Ivar Berg) found this idea of building a rationalist's image of the world around consensually held values having to do with the well-being of future generations a difficult position to accept, on the ground that it forces one into the jaws of a trap. Either one runs the risk of being "labeled an incrementalist, a vulgar pragmatist, or, even worse, as antitheoretical or anti-intellectual," or one is forced to a level of abstraction which is not much help in trying to run a railroad, a view which Raymond Bauer later endorsed. Needless to say, the issue was not resolved.

RATIONALIST VERSUS EMPIRICIST

There is another philosophical debate of long standing that has practical implications for our assumptions about economic rationality. It is the debate between rationalist and empiricist over the role of reason with regard to data and over the existence of innate ideas. The empiricist argues that reason is used to make data intelligible and that our ideas about the world come only from the world by way of sensation and reflection. For the rationalist, on the other hand, data are used to give reason its intelligibility and the meaning of the world comes to us out of our innate ideas. Churchman writes:

A strong empiricist would want to piece together the thousands of empirical studies which have been made on health, transportation, pollution, and corporations; a rationalist would argue that no "piecing together" can occur unless one posits the overall *Weltanschauung* which supplies the glue.[21]

Churchman phrases the debate as "a discussion about research strategy." Most of the past investigations of the relationship between economic institutions and social systems appear to have been either empirical or rational without much overlap. The empiricists among us had no world view or theory out of which to construct a framework into which to fit our data, and the rationalists rarely sought the data which might have made reason intelligible. One does not have to examine the literature for very long before coming across numerous examples of both approaches. If there has been a preponderance of one, it has been in an oversupply of world views and a lack of interest in data. During the last few years, one might have been able to detect a slight movement in the direction of the empirical but little evidence of an increase of an appropriate blending of the two.

William Evan, one of the discussants, expanded on the idea of other rationalities and asked an important question.

Given the fact that you do have multiple rationalities in a society, how do these different rationalities interact when they come into conflict? Obviously some of the rationalities are subordinated, become latent or inactive, relative to others.

He used as an example the conflicting demands made on the corporation by different constituencies, suggesting that each constituency presses its demands from a different base of rationality. Can a model be devised to resolve the conflicting claims upon the corporation? Would conflict theory be a useful approach? "Isn't this a tantalizing question for somebody who works in the field of business and society?"

Nobody took up the challenge, but the discussion did move to the question of what alternative rationalities actually exist, in addition to the economic and communal types mentioned by Smelser? A number of alternatives were suggested, including Daniel Bell's "sociologizing"[22] and "public household"[23] approaches, but Lee Preston suggested that there may be a lot of rational systems out there that we do not know anything about or even have a screening system or "net of research" to pick up. At this point Melvin Eisenberg warned of the dangers of getting too far away from economic rationality: "Communal rationality is what gave us the Penn-Central debacle."

Churchman interrupted to remind us of the basic difference between his "new rationalism" and Smelser's "other rationalities": "We believers in monism cannot tolerate a variety of rationalities.'' The only meaningful unit of analysis, he argues, is the world, because it enables us to make the best kinds of predictions and control decisions; this is the only rational approach to the appropriate unit. Churchman then seems to say that in the context of the world as the appropriate unit of analysis, only one rationality is possible. Smelser and Bauer disagree and on essentially the same two grounds: that is not the way it is in the real world, and it would not be a good idea if it were.

Monistic rationalism bothers Smelser because when you put the same value on everything, whatever that value is (power, dollars, or anything else), you lose a great deal of variability, miss the conflict between standards by which people actually guide their behavior, and foreclose the possibility of examining those standards that come up in different relations to one another.

> Most economically relevant decisions that are made in contemporary times are not the product of a single type of calculation; they are complicated compromises that incorporate criteria arising from the exigencies of economic rationality, social justice, environmental protection, and others. It is possible to represent some of these criteria simply as ''costs'' to be taken into account. Above and beyond that however, they constitute fundamental forces in social life, and can be more complex models of economic and social processes than we now have.

Are Smelser and Churchman really in disagreement? Bauer says that one has to suboptimize in order to live in the real world.

Kenneth Boulding entered the fray on what appears to be the Churchman side: ''In a formal sense, there is only one rationality.'' But it soon becomes clear that Boulding has simply changed the level of discussion: ''The one rationality is the decision that you *make*.'' His rationality (or weighing of alternatives) becomes a theory of bad decisions through which we learn to make better decisions, but the underlying economic, social, communal, and other rationalities remain pretty much unchanged. Boulding later revealed that he is concerned about the monisitc approach of Churchman on the ground that if anything goes wrong, everything goes wrong.

''NEW'' RATIONALISM OR ''OTHER'' RATIONALITIES

Whether one prefers Churchman's unitary ''new'' rationalism or Smelser's ''other'' rationalities, one has a vastly better conceptual tool for investigation of the relationship between business and society than has been provided by traditional assumptions about economic rationality.

Furthermore, both perceptions illuminate Smelser's second question about the most appropriate unit to identify as that within which economic activity transpires, and Churchman's query whether a "corporation" or even an industry is a meaningful component of society for purposes of study or research. After reading these two essays, the reader will probably also conclude that both the new rationalism and the "other" rationalities models will cause very different sorts of questions to be asked by researchers than has usually been the case in the past. Churchman, for example, draws sharp contrasts between the critical concepts and questions asked by a behavioral scientist or empiricist and by a rationalist.

We believe also that both the new and "other" rationalities can be used to evaluate attempts by John Rawls[24] and others to develop an acceptable alternative to utilitarianism as a basis for a rational concept of morality and the ways in which these attempts appear to be underwriting new definitions of justice, fairness, and equality. Among the principles around which public policy is oriented today is one which is being influenced increasingly by some of these changes in definition and, in some respects, is perceived to be inconsistent with economic rationality as a motivating assumption for social behavior. We refer to what has come to be known as the new equality, which abandons equality of opportunity, equality before the law, and other traditional concepts for one whose exclusive concern is equality of condition or result. How this has come about is answered in large part by a paradox: A consequence which is seen to be at odds with economic rationality was nonetheless brought about by the triumph of that very rationality. Also intimately related to this phenomenon is the principle of legitimacy, to be discussed in Part Two.

Although the market system and capitalism appear to have produced the greatest economic benefits for the greatest number and have resulted in discrepancies in distribution probably narrower than in any alternative system, inequalities in capitalist systems that would hardly attract any attention elsewhere are singled out for powerful social criticism. Tradition, the medieval belief in magical escapes from life's struggles, and the assurance of ultimate equality in heaven once legitimized even the grossest inequalities. But the market economy weakened religious sanction, destroyed traditional beliefs and replaced them with economic rationality. People ceased to do or accept anything simply because their ancestors did it or accepted it. Furthermore, inequalities were constantly being redistributed, along with everything else, in such a way that tradition no longer had an opportunity to operate and ideological support was undermined. Shaken loose from the legitimizing protection of tradition, inequality was left open to erosion by *ressentiment,*[25] the "narcissism of Small Differences,"[26] and the pressures of competitive ideologies.

Substitute systems like socialism also have lost tradition as a source of legitimacy, but they have retained the millennial quality and the potentiality that religion once provided and either concealed or discounted present inequalities in their own systems as mere transitional steps toward ultimate justice and equality. Capitalism and the market were too rational to make this promise or to be believed even if it were made. This phenomenon has been described both as the ideological weakness of capitalism and as the source of the present preoccupation with equal distributions.[27] Thus, even wars against poverty are doomed to failure because poverty has come to mean inequality or a state of mind induced by the neighbor's new car. Once a society reaches this stage, a stage which Tocqueville describes in some detail,[28] lessening inequalities and reducing the distances between the advantaged and disadvantaged does not diminish but actually increases resentment. Complete equality in wealth and income is likely only to shift resentment to unequal distributions of natural endowments such as talent, beauty, or even health.

The role played by economic rationality in this development has been large, and consequently the attempts by Smelser to integrate other rationalities into our economic calculations and by Churchman to consider the whole system before initiating basic public policy and action is a welcome effort. The integration of noneconomic rationalities into economic behavior could dilute the selfishness and calculation which are said to be at the heart of capitalism's ideological weakness and supply a better defense against the utopian appeal of socialism.[29] Furthermore, Churchman's new rationalism may provide a better mechanism for achieving understanding of the interactions among all the dimensions of society and for improving the methodology by which society decides what actions it will take and through whom.

We should not be too surprised at Smelser's conclusion that existing answers to his three core questions are unsatisfactory. Economic rationality has never been adequate to explain the social forces that impinge on economic life. We have not given the subject much attention until recently because it has not made much difference. Personal virtues appeared to be consistent with public virtues, and there seemed to be a positive correlation between the private virtues and the way in which wealth, power, and privilege were distributed in society. Environmentally destructive characteristics of the market economy were not obvious or even known. Society was content to let economic performance measure the social responsibility of business. Utility theory reigned supreme. But now society is full of social dissonance because, in spite of heretofore impeccable credentials, profit is now an embarrassing word, the market mechanism seems to guarantee environmental degradation, our economic choices in public policy seem to be limited to inflation or unemployment, and inflation is said to be a social disease, not an economic one. Nor is the doctrine of enlightened self interest seen as being enough to restore the credibility of economic rationality.

It is time we take into our calculations, as Smelser does, the fact that, at the level of institutionalization, the values of economic rationality are *always tempered* in relation to other rationalities. The perfect Economic Man never did exist, but the new incongruities between the concept of such a being and the real world are forcing us increasingly to take note of his shortcomings. We must also consider Churchman's argument that we need a new world view that provides a way of describing "component variables" of the world at various points of time. Churchman makes a persuasive case for our undertaking this search before we can hope to understand corporate behavior or assess the quality of corporate management. These then are among the major guideposts for future research in the field of business and society. In their essays, both authors suggest how the first steps should be taken.

The reader will note immediately that Smelser and Churchman treat in their essays of much more than rationality and that both of them raise many intriguing and challenging issues that have not been emphasized in these comments. The same observation can also properly be made about the other essays in this volume. The intention was not to denigrate the other issues but rather to emphasize those which gave continuity to the volume as a whole. Notwithstanding the selective character of these introductory remarks by the editors, each of the papers should be looked upon as a unit and each as a major contribution to the literature of business and society.

NOTES

1. Talcott Parsons and Neil J. Smelser, *Economy and Society* (New York: The Free Press, 1956).

2. See Smelzer's essay, p. 19. Page citations to the essays in this volume will be provided only where quick cross reference is necessary.

3. Ibid.

4. See Max Weber, *Economy and Society: An Outline of Interpretive Sociology*, eds. Guenther Roth and Claus Wittich (New York: Bedminster Press, 1968).

5. C. West Churchman, *Challenge to Reason* (New York: McGraw-Hill Book Company, 1968), p. 81.

6. Will Durant, *The Age of Faith* (New York: Simon & Schuster, 1950), pp. 74–75.

7. Irving Kristol, "When Virtue Loses All Her Loveliness," *The Public Interest,* Fall, 1970, pp. 3–15 and "On Corporate Capitalism in America," *The Public Interest,* Fall, 1975, pp. 124–141.

8. Christopher D. Stone, *Where the Law Ends* (New York: Harper & Row, 1975), particularly chap. 12.

9. Garret Hardin, "To Trouble a Star: The Cost of Intervention in Nature," *Bulletin of the Atomic Scientists,* January, 1970, p. 17.

10. Edwin O. Reischauer, *The Japanese* (Cambridge, Mass.: Belknap/Harvard University Press, 1977), pp. 154–156.

11. Daniel Bell, *The Coming of Post-Industrial Society* (New York: Basic Books, 1973), chap. 4.

12. David McClelland, *The Achieving Society* (New York: The Free Press, 1967).

13. Kenneth J. Arrow, "Capitalism, for Better or Worse," in Leonard Silk, *Capitalism: The Moving Target* (New York: Praeger Publishers, 1974), pp. 107–108.

14. Paul A. Weiss, "The Living System: Determinism Stratified," in *Beyond Reductionism,* eds. Arthur Koestler and J. R. Smythies (New York: Macmillan Co., 1969), p. 7.

15. Jacques Monod, *Chance and Necessity* (New York: Alfred A. Knopf, 1971).

16. See Churchman's essay, p. 52.

17. William Bowen, "A View of Man as an Accident," *Fortune,* December, 1971, pp. 153–154.

18. C. West Churchman, *The Design of Inquiring Systems* (New York: Basic Books, 1971), p. 71.

19. Monod, *op. cit.*

20. Erick Jantsch, *Design for Evolution* (New York: George Braziller, 1975), p. xiii.

21. See Churchman.

22. Bell, *op. cit.*

23. Daniel Bell, *The Cultural Contradictions of Capitalism* (New York: Basic Books, 1976), chap. 6.

24. John Rawls, *A Theory of Justice* (Cambridge, Mass.: Belknap/Harvard University Press, 1971).

25. Max Scheler, *Ressentiment* (New York: The Free Press, 1961).

26. Sigmund Freud, *Group Psychology and the Analysis of the Ego,* trans. J. Strachey (New York: Liveright Publication Corp., 1949), pp. 86–88.

27. Kristol, *op. cit.*

28. Alexis de Tocqueville, *Democracy in America,* trans. Henry Reeve, rev. Francis Bowen and Phillips Bradley (New York: Alfred A. Knopf, 1953), vol. 2, p. 312; see also Fred Hirsch, *Social Limits to Growth* (Cambridge, Mass.: Harvard University Press, 1976).

29. Arrow, *op. cit.*

NEIL J. SMELSER

Reexamining the Parameters of Economic Activity

When the organizers of the conference on business and society invited me to participate, they suggested in an open-ended way that I dwell on the theme of *Economy and Society* revisited. I welcomed that suggestion on several counts. First, almost two decades have passed since Talcott Parsons and I collaborated in that very exciting theroretical enterprise,[1] and that seems ample time to permit any second or further thoughts to develop and consolidate. In addition, much of my research has dealt with issues in *Economy and Society* during those two decades. And finally, some aspects of the recent history of the nation's and the world's economic life suggest that some of the assumptions that informed the arguments of that book—as well as the science of economics in general—bear critical reexamination.

I shall not summarize the arguments presented in *Economy and Society* in any systematic way in this essay; I shall only do so selectively in the course of developing new points. It would be helpful at the outset, however, to indicate what Parsons' and my mission was in that volume and how we attempted to carry it out. In a word, we attempted to demonstrate the theoretical and empirical continuities involved in the study of economic activities, on the one hand, and other classes of activities designated generally as social, on the other. We located these continuities in four contexts:

1. A *formal* context. We pointed out parallels in theoretical formulation in economics and the other social sciences—for example, parallels between supply-demand theory and various exchange theories in sociology and parallels between formulations of the notions of system and equilibrium.

2. A *systemic* context. We represented the economy as a social system, whose major classes of activity (production, investment, entrepreneurship) could be described in terms appropriate to social systems in general. Furthermore, we represented the economy as the adaptive subsystem of society, which maintains consistent relations with the other subsystems through a system of what we called "boundary-exchanges," or inputs and outputs. In

this context we generated the notion of "generalized media"—of which wealth is one among several others (power, influence, value-commitments)—that constitute the exchangeables for the several societal subsystems.

3. An *institutional* context. Focusing our analysis mainly on markets, we attempted to show that the institutions of contract, property, and occupation incorporated both economic and noneconomic ingredients into these markets and suggested that market imperfection could be approached profitably by cataloguing the variety of noneconomic constraints on market structures.

4. The context of *social change*. In particular, we attempted to show how economic growth is encouraged by a variety of noneconomic stimuli and how this growth is accompanied by—and facilitated by—typical structural changes. Among these structural changes we singled out structural differentiation, or the appearance of new and more complex roles, organizations, and social structures, in both the economic and noneconomic sectors of society.

In attempting to make my contribution most useful to the participants of the conference, I decided *not* to undertake two lines of discussion, on grounds that they would be too narrow and self-regarding. I decided not to review the reviews of *Economy and Society*—that is, to assess the critical reactions to, and intellectual impact of, that book in the years since its appearance. Also, I decided not to reassess or elaborate the technical features of the theory of action that informed its arguments.[2] Instead, I decided to identify several central themes—some explicit and some largely implicit—in *Economy and Society,* each of which concerns the relation of economic activity to its social environment. These several themes can best be identified by asking a series of questions:

1. What is the status of the assumption of *economic rationality?* What other kinds of rationalities are there, and in what social contexts are they embedded? How can we best chart the relations among the different kinds of rationalities in social life and thus improve our understanding of the social forces that impinge on economic life?

2. What is the most appropriate *unit* to identify as that within which economic activity transpires? The answer to this question varies, of course, with the type of question being asked; the unit may be household, firm, region, nation, or world. In particular, however, I wish to question the argument developed especially by Simon Kuznets that the nation-state is the most important and relevant unit for study of economic growth.

3. What are the relations of *economic growth* to the political and social structures of society? What kinds of changes in institutional and group life accompany processes of economic growth? What are the rela-

tions between economic *stagnation* and *decline* and institutional and group life? Do the latter relations simply involve a reversal of those relations accompanying growth, or do new and qualitatively different social and political problems appear under conditions of stagnation or decline?

To telegraph my conclusion, it is my impression that our existing answers to these questions are not satisfactory and are perhaps growing increasingly out of date, and that we must force new kinds of answers in the light of contemporary theoretical and empirical developments.

THE PROBLEM OF ECONOMIC RATIONALITY

Different Meanings of Economic Rationality

One of the most important postulates in traditional economic analysis is some version of economic rationality: If an individual is presented with a situation of choice in an economic setting, he will maximize or optimize his economic position; likewise, a firm will "choose the [input-output combination] which maximizes the difference between its total costs and revenues."[3] Such a postulate may be informed by different varieties of utility functions, but despite this variability it retains its character as a statement of *criteria for choice in scarcity situations* and constitutes one of the fundamental building blocks for predicting economic behavior, both for the individual and in the aggregate.

Such a postulate, while quite simple in its formulation, has been advanced in different ways, and some of these are more acceptable than others.

1. The least acceptable meaning of economic rationality is the argument that, as a matter of psychological fact, material satisfactions are the sole motivating factor in human existence and that rational choices in relation to material satisfactions dominate all other considerations.

2. If it is argued that, although economic rationality may not be the whole of human psychology, people do behave rationally when faced with economic situations, the notion becomes less objectionable. Although people in all societies, must economize, however, the number and kinds of situations in which they economize are highly variable. For example, people in a simple society might display calculation in allocating resources to produce agricultural goods but in exchanging these goods they might rely on highly traditionalized, "uneconomical" gift-giving to kinsmen and tribesmen. Regarded in this way, economic rationality itself is a dependent variable rather than a fixed postulate and may be expected to have a variety of manifestations. On the basis of his study of the behavior of African migrant laborers in the Rhodesias, William J. Barber writes:

> [The African's economic rationality]...is a rationality which can only be understood within the context of the dualistic economic structure within which he lives. If he is a wage-earner, he is well-advised—as long as the real wage obtainable from unemployment in the money economy remains at its traditional level—to keep a "foot in two camps" by moving between the money and the indigenous economies. He dare not risk a sacrifice in the output of the subsistence agricultural community which follows from his continuous absence. This situation recommends perpetuation of the migratory system—an arrangement which is both rational and economic, even though it may not appear so to the European employer or to an outside observer who expects rational economic behavior to take the same form in both the underdeveloped and Western economies.[4]

Another advantage of treating rationality as a variable rather than a principle is that the investigator may inquire into the conditions under which it is likely to develop. Udy, for example, in a comparative study of thirty-four nonindustrial societies, found his measure of "administrative rationality" to be highly correlated with variables such as the specificity of organizational roles, the independence of an organization from its social setting, and the lack of traditional ascriptive demands.[5]

3. If an economist uses the notion of economic rationality explicitly as a device to aid investigation, rather than an empirical claim, the case for it is strong. He advances no particular psychological theories but uses the notion to come to terms with the enormous motivational variability of the empirical world, and to proceed *as if* the only independent variables were measurable changes in price and income. In so treating rationality the analyst should also assume that his simplification is subject to revision or rejection if it seems unhelpful in analyzing the scientific problems he faces. In addition, he should be aware of knowledge accumulated in neighboring disciplines that throws light or doubt upon the particular version of rationality he has assumed.[6]

4. A final way of treating economic rationality is to consider it as an institutionalized value. Rationality now becomes something more than a psychological postulate; it is a standard of behavior to which people conform or from which they deviate. Thus in a business firm in a capitalist society it is not only the businessman's personal desire for profits but also the threat of negative social sanctions (for example, ridicule or loss of position) that encourages him to follow the criteria of efficiency and cost-reduction. Viewed in this way, economic rationality becomes a type of social control—exercised through the internalization of materialistic values and values of efficiency and through the institutionalization of systems of positive and negative sanctions. It becomes a typical motivational and attitudinal complex that is acquired through socialization and sustained by institutional arrangements.

In *Economy and Society* Parson and I acknowledged the third meaning of economic rationality but stressed the fourth above all.

> [From] the point of view of economic theory, economic rationality is a postulate; so far as it is empirically acceptable economic theory presumably possesses greater validity, other things equal. But from the point of view of the economy as a social system, economic rationality is not a postulate, but a primary empirical feature of the system itself.[7]

We argued that societies differ with respect to the degree to which they value economic productivity and efficiency for its own sake. We argued further that, at the level of institutionalization, the values of economic rationality are *always* tempered in relation to other values—or other rationalities, if you will; as a result, no market can be completely perfect (that is, based entirely on economic considerations), because it must take into account various political, integrative, and other considerations. We attempted, in that volume, to spell out the broad variations, in the structure of labor markets, markets for capital, consumers' goods markets— variations based on the differential degree to which these markets took into account noneconomic exigencies. In summarizing our analysis of the variability of economic rationality, we argued that

> economic rationality in its empirical sense is a function of: (1) the degree to which the relevant action is oriented to a central function in a differentiated economy as such, (2) the degree to which it is in accordance with an appropriate institutionalized and internalized value system of the economy, and (3) the degree to which the action is *integrated* within itself as a system relative to the values of economic rationality.[8]

Related Research Developments

Parsons' and my main emphasis in discussing economic rationality, then, was to stress how, in institutionalizing this as a value system in various kinds of market exchanges, other exigencies had to be taken into account. A number of developments in different social sciences have stirred interest in situations in which nonmarket mechanisms dominate— that is to say, in which principles of rational economic calculation are minimized or subordinated to some other kind of rationality and in which noneconomic sanctions control the movement of economic goods and services. Among these developments are the following:

1. One line of interest in comparative exchange was stirred by the appearance in the late 1950s of a volume edited by Polanyi, Arensberg, and Pearson.[9] Roaming through the records of Babylon, Mesopotamia, Greece, Mexico, Yucatan, and village India, they sketched a picture of the separation of trading practices from the familiar practices of free-market

exchange. In addition, they prepared a critique of the analytic power of traditional economic theory and suggested some alternatives for a better comparative economics.

Polanyi and his associates suggested that economic activities fall into three main patterns of exchange. The first, which they call *reciprocative,* is illustrated by the ritualized gift-giving among families, clans, and tribes. Another illustration is found among farmers of many civilizations who frequently pitch in to work for one another, especially at harvest times. Economic calculation, price payments, and wages are typically absent in these types of exchange. Goods or services are given because it is traditional to do so; the only principle of calculation is the loose principle that the giving and receiving of goods or services should balance out among the exchanging parties in the long run.

The second pattern is *redistributive.* This brings economic goods and services to a central source—usually governmental—and then redistributes them throughout the populace. Polanyi, Arensberg, and Pearson identified several instances of this exchange pattern in ancient Asian and African civilizations. Modern examples are organized charity and progressive taxation. Like reciprocative exchange, redistributive patterns are often characterized by an absence of economic calculation. In this case the principle of calculation seems to be one of justice or equity, that is, what each class of recipients deserves by some standard.

The third pattern of exchange, more familiar in modern Western civilization, was termed, simply, *exchange.* In this case economic goods and services are brought into a market context. Prices are not standardized on the basis of tradition but result from bargaining for economic advantage.

Sahlins extended and elaborated the model of reciprocative exchange by distinguishing among several types of reciprocity. The first is generalized reciprocity, which is putatively altruistic and for which any obligation for repayment is suppressed or left indefinite. The clearest example is food-sharing with members of a nuclear family. At most, receiving the food (say, by young children) "lays on a diffuse obligation to reciprocate when necessary to the donor and/or possibly for the recipient."[10] The second is balanced reciprocity, in which there is an expectation of repayment of an equivalent without delay, in the case of marital settlements or peace agreements. This form is more calculated, less personal than the first. The third is negative reciprocity, or "the attempt to get something for nothing with impunity, as in haggling, gambling, stealing, or plundering." Sahlins went on to argue that the best way to predict which type of reciprocation will dominate is to trace the kinship distance between parties; and he pulled together ethnographic data on patterns of giving and taking to demonstrate his central hypothesis that "[reciprocity] is inclined toward the generalized pole by close kinship, toward the negative extreme in proportion to kinship distance."[11]

In a markedly different kind of analysis, Titmuss investigated international differences in patterns of blood donation. This unusual form of gift—which is in one sense an act of generalized reciprocity in that nothing is expected in return and in another sense an anonymous, impersonal act—has survived in large part as a voluntary, unrewarded act in a few societies, such as Great Britain, but in other societies blood has become a marketable and even a profitable commodity. In the United States and the Soviet Union, for example, fully half the blood donors are paid, and in Japan almost all donors receive money for giving blood. Titmuss was unable to account for such international differences, but he speculated that the best place to look is in the "fabric of values, social, economic, and political, within which acts of giving, rewarding, compelling, or selling take place."[12]

2. Another line of interest in nonmarket transfers has been stimulated by scholars working on communist and socialist societies. These kinds of societies, characterized in ideal-typical terms, have a central authority that owns all the means of production, determines consumption through physical rationing, and assigns labor at predetermined wages. Thus characterized, the "command economy" leaves little room for market exchange.[13] In practice, of course, communist and socialist economies have not even approximated the ideal type, and many market mechanisms have developed alongside the dominant political mechanism, just as many market economies have supplemented their major economic mechanisms by a greater reliance on political and administrative controls.[14] However, while acknowledging that any given economy relies on a number of different mechanisms, Grossman nevertheless felt it appropriate to classify economies in terms of which kinds of mechanism are dominant: tradition, or "generally accepted, customary, and persistent specific patterns of relationship among economic units or agents"; market; and command.[15] This classification is not unlike that of Polanyi, Arensberg, and Pearson, though their notion of *redistributive* also contains many traditional elements. In terms of sanctions, the market economy relies mainly on economic sanctions, the command economy mainly on political sanctions, and the traditional economy on a residual group of social and political sanctions. In a quite different spirit, Galbraith, in his presidential address to the American Economic Association, complained that neoclassical and neo-Keynsian economic frameworks are incapable of analyzing the concentration of planning and power in the modern American economy, primarily because they have focused too much on market processes and have made economics "a nonpolitical subject."[16] While not implying that America is a command economy, Galbraith was nonetheless asserting that a significant amount of its economic activity transpires under the umbrella of some sort of political rationality for

which traditional assumptions about economic rationality and the market are not appropriate.

3. Still another line of interest in nonmarket transfers is found in the growing interest in the grants economy. By *grants* is meant a "one-way economic relationship whereby party A conveys an exchangeable to party B without receiving in return an exchangeable of equal market value."[17] This contrasts with the two-way exchange characteristic of market transactions, in which both parties receive economic consideration. Examples of grants are redistribution through taxation, charity donations, foundation grants, public support of children, as well as intrafamilial transfers of goods and services. The grant is defined in economic terms, and while Boulding acknowledged that a transfer from A to B "may be accompanied by certain intangible transfers from B to A in the way of prestige, status, and so on," he added that "these things are not usually classified as exchangeables."[18] This exclusion is unfortunate in a way, since so many economic grants are locked into a system of other kinds of rewards for the grantor—the politician who distributes benefits to the poor in return for votes and power, the philanthropist who secures prestige in the public eye for his good works, and the like. Despite this limitation Boulding regarded grants as having primary significance not in the economic system but rather in the "integrative structure of society"; furthermore, they are reflective of relationships of community, legitimacy, loyalty, love, and trust.[19] He suggested rather that the great increase in public grants in recent decades might be regarded as an "integrative" compensation for the decline of private transfer in financing health, education, and welfare and for the relative decline of the extended family—a private, granting agency par excellence.[20] Whatever the merits of this theoretical formulation, the focus on one-way exchanges has led economists to begin asking new kinds of questions about exchange in society, such as whether suburban communities compensate central cities for the services they provide, whether transfer payments through welfare have a substantial impact on poverty in the ghettos, and the like.[21]

Relations Among Different Rationalities

Parsons and I emphasized in *Economy and Society* that the structuring of economic relations must take into account other exigencies, and build them into market exchanges; the related lines of research I have summarized suggest that in many cases the rationality of economic calculation is subordinated to other kinds of rationality. We pay press the inquiry even further and ask whether any *other* kinds of relations obtain among the different modes of structuring economic activity. Do different rationalities come into conflict with one another, and, if so, what are the likely outcomes?

In addressing this question, I shall first move backward in time and consider Max Weber's insights regarding the relations between economic rationality and what might be called *communal rationality*—a phenomenon which has some elements of the reciprocative and redistributive modes specified by Polanyi et al. and some elements of the integrative mode which Boulding identified as a conspicuous feature of economic grants. Second, I shall examine a certain amount of empirical research on the fate of kinship structure—the prototypical institutional home of communal rationality—in periods when economic rationality and its accompanying institutional forms are on the advance. Finally, on the basis of these and other considerations, I shall suggest the lines along which our theoretical thinking and empirical analyses might proceed if we are to advance our knowledge of the relations between economic life and its social environment.

Weber's Models of Economic and Communal Rationality. In his later methodological writings[22] Weber appeared to regard his famous ideal type as a heuristic device on the basis of which explanatory models are built—that is, a device much like the hypothetical construct of economic rationality as it is used in economics. Constructing an ideal type involves stating hypothetically what course action would take if actors in a situation were motivated by a single orientation.

> For example a panic on the stock exchange can be most conveniently analyzed by attempting to determine first what the course of action would have been if it had not been influenced by irrational affects;... Similarly, in analyzing a political or military campaign it is convenient to determine in the first place what would have been a rational course, given the ends of the participants and adequate knowledge of all the circumstances.[23]

Weber regarded the laws of economic theory (including the postulate of maximization) as a representation of "the meaning appropriate to a scientificaly formulated pure type (an ideal type) of a common phenomenon."[24] Even though an ideal-type understanding is thus an explanation of behavior in some sense, Weber insisted that to generate ideal-type constructs through understanding "cannot on this account claim to be a causally valid interpretation."[25] A further procedure is necessary: "Verification of subjective interpretation by comparison with the concrete course of events is, as in the case of all hypotheses, indispensable."[26]

Weber gave great scientific importance to models based on assumptions about typical motives in typical situations. "It is," he noted, "precisely on the basis of . . . rational assumptions [about meaning] that most of the laws of sociology, including those of economics, are built up."[27] And the bulk of Weber's sociological work consists in the creation of historical models of varying levels of generality—for example, the model of bureaucracy, the model of charismatic leadership—and using these models as generalized interpretative frameworks to throw light on historical processes and developments. Weber was aware that to apply a single model to a historical situation constitutes an oversimplification, and that the proper strategy is to apply a battery of them successively to gain a firmer understanding of the diversity of historical causes operating in that situation.[28]

To create and use type models—among which would be models of economic rationality—carries knowledge to a certain level, but to carry it further models must be systematically compared among one another. This comparison involves a two-step process. First, the investigator must systematically explore the ways in which the implications of several models (that is, predicted courses of action) *reinforce* one another, are *independent* of one another, or call for *conflicting* courses of action. He must also specify—for example, in cases of conflicting courses of action— the conditions under which the forces of one historical model might prevail over the other or what kinds of compromise lines of action might emerge. What arises from this operation would be a new series of hypotheses (statements of anticipated lines of action) based on combinations of models. The second step, as in the case of the application of a single historical model, is to assess the hypotheses in the light of the best historical data.

In his historical sociology Weber made numerous comparisons and contrasts among models. His famous discussion of types of authority, for example, is in part a discussion of the way that charismatic, traditional, and rational-legal authority are oriented to issues such as how compliance with orders is secured, how financial support is maintained, and so on.[29] His comparisons, as a rule, were not as systematic as the procedures suggested in the preceding paragraph. Nevertheless, several of them are very suggestive. In particular his remarks on the relations between his ideal-type model of economic rationality and a model to be called communal rationality are helpful as a backdrop for assessing some modern research on the relations between family structure (which is a primary focus for the institutionalization of the values of communal rationality) and the economic order (which is a primary focus for the institutionalization of the values of economic rationality). Let me summarize and extend his reflections.

The themes that underscore the model of economic rationality developed by Weber are the *flexibility* of action that results from the autonomy of an enterprise and the *calculability* of action on the basis of considerations of economic utility, free from the intrusion of noneconomic considerations. Thus Weber regarded the "typical measures of rational economic action" as the systematic allocation of utilities between present and future needs, the systematic allocation of utilities based on considerations of marginal utility, and the systematic procurement and control of the means of production.[30] Rationality of markets is based on market freedom and the reduction of the criteria of kinship, status privileges, military needs, and the welfare policies in determining the distribution of resources and products.[31] Among the institutional conditions underlying maximum formal rationality of capital accounting in the productive enterprise are the following:

1. Complete appropriation of all means of production by owners and the complete absence of all formal appropriation of opportunities for profit in the market, that is, market freedom . . .

2. Complete autonomy in the selection of management by the owners, thus complete absence of formal appropriation of rights to managerial functions.

3. Complete absence of appropriation of jobs and of opportunities for earning by workers and, conversely, the absence of appropriation of workers by owners. This implies free labor, freedom of the labor market, and freedom in the selection of workers . . .

4. Complete absence of substantive regulation of consumption, production, and prices, or of other forms of regulation which limit freedom of contract or specify conditions of exchange. This may be called substantive freedom of contract . . .

5. The most complete separation possible of the enterprise and its conditions of success and failure from the household or private budgetary unit and its property interests. It is particularly important that the capital at the disposal of the enterprise should be clearly distinguished from the private wealth of the owners, and should not be subject to division or dispersion through inheritance.[32]

To the degree that such conditions are realized, the probability of a line of conduct based on economic calculation increases. It should be remarked that Weber's observations are consistent with Udy's findings that rationality of organizational behavior is associated with the independence of an organization from its social setting and the lack of traditional ascriptive demands; they are also consistent with Parson's and my observation that the institutionalization of the values of economic rationality is in part a function of the level of differentiation of economic activity from other kinds of action.

Weber did not develop a model of communal rationality as fully as that of economic rationality. Nevertheless, his writings on economic sociology are scattered with observations that suggest that this kind of orientation—of which the kinship unit provides the type illustration—contrasts on most counts with the model of economic rationality. Communal memberships rest on "various types of affectual, emotional, or traditional bases," as in the case of a religious brotherhood or an erotic relationship.[33] Members in communal units have mutual responsibility for one another's welfare. Membership in many such units, including the family, is in large part compulsory; for example, an individual cannot freely choose his parents. The principle of distribution of resources is substantive rationality, or, broadly speaking, the principle of common welfare of members. This principle "may consider the 'purely formal' rationality of calculation in money terms as of quite secondary importance or even as fundamentally inimical to their respective ultimate ends."[34]

> Haggling is excluded "between brothers," whether they be brothers in kinship, in a guild, or in a religious group. It is not usual to be calculating within a family, a group of comrades, or of disciples. At most, in cases of necessity, a rough sort of rationing is resorted to, which is a very modest beginning of calculation.[35]

In any empirical case, of course, an association based on calculation (such as a market) does develop emotional (communal) aspects, and an association based on communal values is not entirely free from considerations of expediency, calculation, and exploitation.[36] Nevertheless, in principle the criteria of calculation and the criteria of communality are opposed, and both cannot be maximized in the same situation.

As the values of economic rationality advanced and became consolidated in the Western world, therefore, communally based associations could not remain indifferent to the institutionalization of these values. The main institutional mechanism that developed to mediate potential conflict between the two principles was that of segregation or differentiation. The "sphere of private affairs" tended to become separated from the "sphere of business affairs." Furthermore, this tendency was not "fortuitous."

> It is a consequence of the fact that, from the point of view of business interest, the interest in maintaining the private wealth of the owner is often irrational, as is his interest in income receipts at any given time from the point of view of the profitability of the enterprise. Considerations relevant to the profitability of a business enterprise are also not identical with those governing the private interests of persons who are related to it as workers or as consumers. Conversely, the interests growing out of the private fortunes and income of persons or organizations having powers of control over an enterprise do not

necessarily lie in the same direction as the long-run considerations of optimizing its profitability and its market power position. This is definitely, even especially, true when a profit-making enterprise is controlled by the producers' cooperative association. The objective interests of rational management of a business enterprise and the personal interests of the individuals who control it are by no means identical and are often opposed. This fact implies the separation as a matter of principle of the budgetary unit and the enterprise, even where both, with respect to powers of control and the objects controlled, are identical.[37]

While communal principles of mutual responsibility, solidarity, and substantive rationality survive, they are separated from the productive enterprise and the market and institutionalized *within* kinship and related types of associations.

The separation is not entirely symmetrical, however; the family loses in the process. There is a "weakening of household authority." Because of the multiplication of life chances and opportunities, "the individual becomes less and less content with being bound to rigid and undifferentiated forms of life prescribed by the group."[38] Because the family also shrinks from the standpoint of size, resources, and function,

> it is becoming increasingly inopportune for an individual to join a large communistic household. An individual no longer gets protection from the household and kinship groups, but rather from political authority, which exercises compulsory jurisdiction. Furthermore, household and occupation become ecologically separated, and the household is no longer a unit of common production but of common consumption. Moreover, the individual receives his entire education increasingly from outside his home and by means which are supplied by various enterprises: schools, bookstores, concert halls, clubs, meetings, etc. He can no longer regard the household as the bearer of those cultural values in whose service he places himself.[39]

Weber was careful, however, not to press his argument concerning "the parallelism of money economy and attenuation of household authority" to its ultimate. Domestic authority and household are "relatively independent of economic conditions" and in fact "they often shape economic relationships because of their own historic structure."[40]

In these passages Weber was, in effect, undertaking the task of comparing two ideal-type models—one of economic rationality and one of communal rationality—establishing a relation of opposition or conflict between them, and generating a number of predictions of historical developments arising from these relations, especially predictions of compromise through structural separation and an accompanying defeat for communal rationality. Moreover, he qualified his analysis sufficiently to render ambiguous his ultimate judgment of the historical fate of communal rationality in the family in an environment of large-scale corporate enterprises and a money economy and thereby to foreshadow many of the confusions and contradictions that characterize research on family structure since his time.

If one includes Weber's significant qualifications on his major thesis, there are in his analysis three distinguishable assertions concerning the relationship between an institutionalized system of economic rationality and the kinship structure:

The family as an institutional system experiences a decline in significance.

The family remains "relatively independent of economic conditions."

The family "often shapes economic relationships."

A variety of empirical illustrations for each of the three assertions could no doubt be produced. But one of the less satisfying aspects of Weber's analysis is that while envisioning these different possibilities, he did little by way of specifying the conditions under which each might develop. As a result, his analysis of the relations between the institutionalization of economic rationality in the economy and the institutionalization of communal rationality in the family remains quite indeterminate.

Some Conflicting Research Results on the Relations Between Economic Activity and Communal Rationality.   Most of the comparative work on family structure and its relation to the economy has yielded a conclusion that is consistent with Weber's main emphasis: With the increasing rationalization of economic life in industrial forms, different forms of extended family have given way to simpler, more differentiated forms.[41] While investigators disagree as to whether these changes constitute a decline or positive functional adaptation of the family,[42] there is general agreement on the broad directions of structural change.

Another line of research that has developed in the past twenty-five years poses a challenge to this general agreement by suggesting that the extended family has *not* undergone a serious decline. Litwak suggested that while the demands of the modern occupational structure make for high family mobility, this has not destroyed the extended family. In fact, he asserted that "because technological improvement in communication systems have minimized the socially disruptive forces of geographical distance, and because an extended family can provide important aid to nuclear families without interfering with the occupational system," a sort of modified extended family has survived into the mid-twentieth century. Litwak attempted to buttress his assertions with studies of visiting patterns in large cities.[43] In addition, dozens of empirical studies in many industrialized societies have uncovered patterns of mutual aid (care of children, credit, assisting in the search for employment), social interaction, and other signs of vitality of the extended kin unit in industrialized societies.[44]

Add to this the numerous instances of relatively minor familial changes that actually emerge from situations that initially portend major changes. One example will suffice. In 1950, Lambiri studied a small Greek country town (population 16,500) near which a cotton factory, employing mostly women, had just been constructed. At that time standards for female comportment were strict and traditional. Women were to be "modest, compliant, and domesticate," and girls were to be "above all, chaste." Only a girl's fiance, brother, or first cousin was permitted to escort her out of doors. The factory work required that women and girls leave the town for eight hours a day, mix with others on the factory premises, and sometimes travel at night. Initially a wave of alarm spread through the community. Fears were expressed for the welfare of the family, and derogatory epithets were coined for women who worked. Yet the women, who accumulated various economic advantages in the years following the building of the factory, used their wages in traditional ways, especially to increase their dowry; and many traditional attitudes toward women remained intact.[45] Indeed, the initial alarm and anger may have themselves served as important social sanctions to pressure women to change their traditional sex-role definitions minimally, even though their occupational status was altered significantly. In any event, the "emancipation" occurred within a relatively traditional framework.

Such research suggests that communal rationality, as institutionalized in kinship units, may resist—or at least maintain a certain level of independence from—the institutionalization of values of economic rationality. Still other evidence suggests that exigencies of communal rationality actively shape economic activities and sometimes encourage economic rationality. At the broadest level economic activities are conditioned by an individual's age, sex, and kinship roles. In tribal and peasant societies economic roles are in many respects subordinate of kinship considerations. Specific economic duties are assigned to children up to a certain age, others accrue to them at adolescence, and still other activities are taken away from men when their oldest son marries.[46] In modern society such age and sex regulation persists in different forms. We exclude very young children from work, we tend to reserve certain classes of occupations for men and others for women, and we expel old persons from economic roles through retirement.

With regard to the implications for economic rationality, many studies, consistent with Weber's analysis, are based on the premise that the family's communal rationality discourages calculation on the basis of considerations of utility. Consider the following examples. Landes has argued that the peculiar structures of the French family business has kept the typical firm small and thus inhibited economic growth. Specific features of family life are the refusal to go outside the family for acquiring capital (for this would mean a loss of exclusiveness), a hesitation to separate family budgeting from business budgeting (which impedes rational bookkeeping), and recruitment into the firm on grounds other than business ability.[47] Another instance is Fox's finding that in an Indian market town, the number of small businesses was exceptionally large, but that the size of enterprise was limited by "the essentially familistic organization of business ventures and the trader's fear of larger commercial organizations because of distrust of nonfamily members."[48] An interesting twist of the same theme was uncovered by Marris and Somerset in their study of African businessmen in Kenya. Unlike their Asian-Kenyan business counterparts, they were often *unwilling* to hire relatives, because of their feelings that relatives are more demanding and insubordinate, thereby creating jealousies among other workers and otherwise interfering with the conduct of the business.[49]

Often, however, kinship proves to be an asset in economic undertakings. In tracing the growth of commercial shipping in New England, Bailyn observed that

> Kinship goes far in explaining the initiation of overseas trade in New England [during the seventeenth century] and the recruitment of the first New England merchants. Study of the family relations [especially intramarriage] in the second and third generations reveals the consolidation of these early mercantile families. And in the kinship ties secured between the established merchants and the post-Restoration commercial adventurers one may observe the final construction of the merchant group.[50]

In a recent study of ten large manufacturing family firms in Lebanon, Khalaf and Shwaryi came to conclusions that appear to be directly opposed to the French case as interpreted by Landes. Businessmen they interviewed found family members to be more competent and trustworthy as managerial colleagues as well as more loyal and committed to the firm and its purposes than outsiders—all qualities that are assets to the business. The authors observed that

> Lebanese firms have not yet reached such a size as to render the employment of outsiders in managerial positions a question of real meaning... Furthermore, they do recognize that the process of dividing responsibilities among themselves cannot continue indefinitely, and that, as the firm grows beyond a certain point, the hiring of outsiders to fill managerial positions becomes a vital and inevitable requirement.[51]

Their observations suggest that kinship, an asset at a certain stage of development, may subsequently turn into a burden.

Finally, family dynamics have often produced results that facilitate the development of a market economy. Such appeared to be the case with the Japanese rural family in relation to the formation of an urban-industrial labor force. Through primogeniture the family expelled all but eldest sons unequivocally from the land, placed them through inter-mediaries in jobs, and thus generated a steady supply of migrants to the towns. Moreover, the resulting process was sufficiently controlled and gradual that Japanese cities avoided some of the social disorganization associated with the mass migrations into European and American cities.[52] The family may also play an important and continuing allocative role in the market.

> Ties of kinship may provide a unique source of knowledge about people, and of sanctions to enforce economic contracts. The family may be your only source of credit for a business venture, for they alone how what you are worth, and how to bring pressure to bear if you fail to meet your obligations. You may choose to employ relatives for the same reasons, irrespective of the claims of kinship. All that gives the family its inalterable importance.[53]

In an exploratory interview study of 240 unemployed men in Nairobi and Lagos, Gutkind found that those men who initially come to cities to seek employment "almost invariably stay initially with close or distant relatives." A typical pattern is for a young man to stay with— and be sup-ported by—one kinsman until his welcome is exhausted, then move on to another for a limited period of time. In addition, he often relies on these kinsmen for information about available jobs, influence in seeking jobs, and so on. This particular mechanism, however, is a fragile and limited one. Gutkind found many instances of ill-will developing between guest and host and some cases of economic exploitation of relatives. Older unemployed interviewees, with a history of job-seeking, preferred relying on friends rather than relatives because of unpleasant personal situations that arose with the latter. Also, reliance on family ties alone is often not an effective means of securing employment, because of the family's limited information about control over employment opportunities.[54] The power of kinship as an integrative force in the economic setting can be even more clearly perceived when kin relations are disrupted. The disper-sion of a neighborhood during a slum clearance project in Lagos, for example, not only disrupted patterns of family interaction, such as visit-ing, but eroded the system of employment, credit, and mutual aid that was patterned on and bolstered by the network of kinship loyalties.[55]

Concluding Note

All the various lines of research on which I have touched—Parsons'
and my theoretical work in institutionalization, the work on reciprocation
and redistribution, the work on command economies and grants economy, and the theory and research on economic and communal (especially family) life—are so many different ways of discovering and pointing out that economic activity is embedded in a network of both economic
and noneconomic structures, rationalities, and sanctions.

One moral to be drawn from this fundamental fact of embeddedness
is that any pure model of economic rationality—or any other kind of
rationality for that matter—is severely limited as a *general* basis for the
understanding of economic activity. But I do not believe that this conclusion warrants abandoning such models. They have proved useful if not
necessary devices for both theory-building and empirical investigation in
economics and other social sciences. Rather, investigators should use such
models in expanded and more complicated ways, along the following
lines:

1. Systematic attention should be given to cataloguing the different
kinds of rationalities that can govern the production, distribution, and
consumption of economic goods and services—the rationalities of efficiency, social justice, social security in the broad sense, military defense,
and so on. Each kind of rationality has its own peculiar implications for
directives and priorities for economic activities, for economic growth and
stagnation, and for cumulative imbalances and injustices. Tracing out
these implications means giving higher priority to constructing formal
models of economic behavior on assumptions other than economic calculation.

2. Perhaps more importantly, systematic attention should be given to
developing models that incorporate or synthesize a number of single
models of rationality in different combinations. Most economically
relevant decisions—and the behavior that flows from them—that are
made in contemporary times are not the product of a single type of calculation; they are complicated compromises that incorporate criteria arising
from the exigencies of economic rationality, social justice, environmental
protection, and others. It is possible to represent some of these criteria—
for example, environmental protection—simply as costs to be taken into
account. Above and beyond that, however, they constitute fundamental
forces in social life and can be incorporated into more complex models of
economic and social processes more systematically than we have done so
far. In the longer run, too, it seems appropriate to construct models of
the historical relations among different systems of rationality—such as
Weber started to do—to help determine the conditions under which different principles and criteria of organizing social and economic life com-

plement one another, come into conflict, defeat one another, or are forged into compromise institutional forms. As we saw, if we regard the relations between economic and communal rationality as simply opposed to one another—as Weber tended to do—the findings that have emerged from research related to such an assumption are inconsistent and apparently contradictory. To improve that tradition of research it is necessary to do more than merely conduct more research; it must be research that is based on more complicated models combining the economic and social rationalities that constitute the institutionalized motivational determinants of behavior.

THE UNIT FOR STUDYING
ECONOMIC ACTIVITY

In *Economy and Society* Parsons and I considered the economy a subsystem of a larger social system. That larger social system was invariably identified as a society, as the title of the volume indicates. The other major subsystems of society—the polity, the integrative subsystem, and the latent pattern-maintenance and tension-management subsystem—were identified as the main environments for the economy, were held to constitute the major parametric constraints on the economy, and were represented as the major "markets" in which the economy's major outputs were exchanged for inputs of other generalized resources.[56] The implication of this formulation is that the most appropriate unit for studying the economy is the society, for therein lies its major environment and the major forces that shape it.

In quite another context and from a different methodological standpoint, Simon Kuznets developed a similar argument. His main contention is that the nation-state is the appropriate unit for the analysis of economic growth. The reason for this, he held, is that the state constitutes an important set of influences on the fortunes of economic life. The nation-state sets the "institutional conditions within which economic activities are pursued, the boundaries within which markets operate and within which human resources are relatively free to handle material capital assets and claims to them." Further, the sovereign government is "the overriding authority that resolves conflicts generated by growth and screens institutional innovations, sanctioning those believed essential and barring others."[57] In the light of these considerations, he continued, a complex and widespread process such as economic growth

can best be studied if its manifestations are grouped around units that affect its course, rather than around units that bear little perceptible relation to the process. Thus, it would obviously make little sense to study economic growth for groups of familities classified by the initial letter of their family names, for this particular classification has no obvious bearing upon the process of economic growth.[58]

Another argument for using the nation-state as the unit of study is that the data of economic activity become available through this unit. For the study of aggregative aspects of economic history, for example, the economist is virtually forced to choose the nation as the unit of analysis, because "statistics and many other types of evidence can usually be obtained only in national terms."[59] But as Kuznets has pointed out, this argument is not an independent one but rather a "reflection of the more basic arguments . . . as to the importance of nation-states in making secular decisions directly bearing upon the course of economic growth."[60] Most data refer to national units because of the fact that national units are important parts of the causal process that produces them.

The first observation to be made is that the unit to be selected for studying economic activity depends initially on the definition of the economic problem to be studied. Thus various microeconomic investigations might take the household or the firm as the classificatory focus. For purposes of argument, however, let us assume that the problem to be identified is framed in macroeconomic terms—for example, a problem dealing with level of price or output, or economic growth or stagnation. There is no doubt that Kuznet's observations have merit, and that the nation-state is still the fundamental unit in determining the institutional parameters and the boundaries for market and dealing with economic conflicts. At the same time, for many purposes of analysis this assumption may be a limited one. Many forces that affect economic data—data which are generated at the national level, to be sure—lie outside the control of the nation-state for all intents and purposes, even though the nation-state may still influence those forces in principle. The forces I have in mind are worldwide politico-economic forces. Certainly it has long been recognized that international trade, international political coercion, and the like have been important influences on the economy, but, given the trends that have characterized the economic and political relations of the world, it may be becoming more appropriate to study the world as the most salient unit or system in understanding economic processes. Rather than attempt to establish this point decisively, however, let me merely offer three observations:

1. Certainly the comparative study of the economic fate of colonies rests on the study of the *relations* between colonial power and colony, since the economic life of the colony is dominated by the political and

economic decisions of the colonial power. The example is perhaps not a fair one, since colonies are not instances of nation-states as Kuznets used the term. Nevertheless, the point still holds for former colonies that have achieved political independence. Certain patterns of economic dependence have been inherited, and the economic policies—both policies affecting domestic economic activity and policies affecting foreign trade directly— still have an overwhelming effect on economically dependent nations. Sometimes the dependency is a mutual one, as when primary-producing former colonies are almost the exclusive producers of certain resources. But, in any event, it is the relations among nations that must be taken into account to understand fluctuations in economic activity.

2. The emergence of multinational corporations in recent times further weakens the principle that nation-states are the "units that affect [the] course" of economic activity. While the extent of the effect of the multinational corporations on the world economy is a matter of dispute and not well understood, and while multinational corporations are subject in principle and sometimes in practice to regulation by individual nation-states, they are organized on a supranational basis, and their policies are tempered in large part by the world economic environment or at least that part of it in which they are involved. Certainly the impact of this new economic element confounds, at the very least, the efforts of nation-states to determine their economic policies.

3. A final phenomenon—arising at least in part from the facts of international economic dependence and the rise of the multinational corporation—concerns a feature of the emerging world economy. That feature is the apparently increasing ability of groups of national units to affect world prices and production by political decisions which may be made to "stick" for substantial periods of time and which may produce economic results that differ significantly from those that would emerge if market forces determined production, prices, and trade. In the longer run these political arrangements may be undermined by market forces—for example, economical substitutes for products may be developed to replace those that are being withheld or made costly by political constriction. Such constriction of the world market, however, may have such strong impacts on individual nations that the efforts of nations to devise policies to resist them can be only feeble at best. The most dramatic example of this is the catastrophic effects that the extraordinary increases in oil and food prices—increases stemming in part from international political decisions—had on nations such as India and Ghana that are vitally dependent on both oil and food but produce relatively little of either. While the political adaptations of the governments in the face of such crises were not negligible in their effects, the economies of those nations

faced the danger of bankruptcy despite those adaptations. The example suggests the increasing need to regard the world economy as a salient "unit ot analysis" in the study of economic activity.

ECONOMIC STAGNATION AND ITS
RELATION TO THE POLITICAL
AND SOCIAL ORDER

Structures, Groups, and Conflict
Associated with Growth

Our intellectual heritage has left us with little systematic knowledge about social and economic decline. The scholarly literature yields, on the one hand, a number of traditional historical treatments which are devoted mainly to historical detail, and, on the other, a number of grand theories of social growth and decline, which are social-philosophical and prophetic rather than scientific in character.[61] In the absence of a clear body of systematic theory and empirical findings in this area, I shall have to be quite speculative about the likely social and political implications of a long period of economic stagnation or decline.

Like most who write on social change, Parsons and I focused primarily on growth.[62] We were particularly interested in the kinds of structures that accompany and facilitate growth. Building on classical writers like Adam Smith, Herbert Spencer, and Emile Durkheim, as well as on contemporary theory and research on processes of social change, we stressed the importance of *structural differentiation* as a growth phenomenon. In essence the model stated that under conditions of dissatisfaction with economic production, when combined with a sense of opportunity and availability of facilities, a typical process of change unfolds. It begins with various short-term reactions to the dissatisfaction, which we termed "symptoms of disturbance." These gradually give way to more directed attacks on the points of dissatisfaction and the invention of new, more specialized social arrangements that are in fact more effective as organizing bases for economic production.

Parsons and I concentrated on a single example of structural differentiation—the rise of the modern, management-dominated corporation and the well-known separation of management and control. However, it is possible to generalize the model of differentiation and apply it more widely to both economy and society. That complex of changes we refer to variously as growth, development, or modernization involves, above all, the growth of more differentiated roles and social structures. The economy itself produces a proliferation of more and more highly specialized occupational roles and corporate forms. Complex educational structures appear, taking over functions previously lodged in the kinship-religious complex. As we saw, the family loses a wide range of functions as a consequence of development, and as a consequence it becomes a much more specialized institution. And it has been argued that the essence of modern religious change is in the direction of greater differentiation of religious beliefs and structures.[63]

The implications of widespread structural differentiation can be analyzed further. The appearance of more differentiated roles and structures provides a series of bases for the formation of new groups, including classes. The introduction of an industrial system, for example, leads to the formation of new groupings based on position in the industrial structure—managers, workers, professionals such as engineers—each of which develops expectations regarding its place in the society's status structure and its rights to political participation and influence. The same can be said for a complex educational structure, which develops its groups or estates of faculty, administrators, students, trustees, and so forth, all with varying degrees of consciousness and organization. While the transition from structural category (such as occupational role) to group membership is far from automatic, it is clear that differentiated social structures provide one of the most fundamental bases for group identification in developed societies.

The picture is made more complex by the fact that the development of new structures and groups is, above all, uneven. Their appearance in one sector of society sets up pressures to change in other sectors. Responsive changes in these other sectors, in turn, ramify in various directions—including feedbacks to the sector originally considered as the leader—and further multiply the pressures to change. The image of society that emerges from this "lead-lag" perspective is one of continuously generated and regenerated tensions, strains, contradictions, and pressures to change.

To illustrate the lead-lag perspective, let us suppose that the leading developmental sector is the economic one—though often empirically it is not—and the society in question rapidly introduces an industrial system and a concomitant expansion of the market system. Such a change is likely to generate pressures in many directions. For example, it may place pressure on the family and educational systems to produce a higher, or at least different, quality of skills among potential recruits to the labor force. Or, again, the development of a regional or national labor market may threaten traditional sanction systems, based on ties of kinship or locality, by which individuals previously undertook their economic performances.

To take another illustration, suppose the political sector is the leading one, and the crucial change is the introduction of a mass suffrage system—a change, incidentally, that has often closely followed political independence in many new nations. This kind of political change may raise concerns on the part of political leaders about the qualifications of the electorate and its capacity to participate responsibly in the polity, and these concerns may generate pressures to upgrade the educational system and, along with it, the political responsibility of the citizenry. Efforts to develop the educational system, however, may create further pressures to change, for one concomitant of increased education is a heightening of occupational expectations, and unless education is accompanied by a level of economic development, it will be difficult to sustain a population with a higher skill level. The society is likely to be faced with diverse groups of overeducated, underemployed, and politically dissatisfied citizens.

Carrying this perspective further, we may identify the following types of *conflict* that emerge in the course of economic and social development:

Conflicts associated with the transformation of the traditional social order. Typically these conflicts have to do with the displacement of occupational (craftsman, peasant) and other (local squire, chieftain) groups, and the resistances offered to that displacement.

Conflicts associated with the rise, legitimization, and consolidation of new groups such as capitalists, factory workers, new types of professionals.

Conflicts among various groups over various kinds of rewards and privileges. These may, in turn, take the form of: (1) status conflicts, in which members of a given status group (engineers, organized labor) strive to increase wages, social respect, political bargaining position; (2) class conflicts, in which groups organize to protest the principles on which the social rewards, especially income, are distributed. Lipset has argued that, in American history at least, status conflicts predominate in periods of prosperity and inflation, whereas class conflicts predominate in periods of unemployment and depression.[64]

Because all these kinds of conflicts are more or less continuously regenerated, the process of development evidently calls for an elaborated system of conflict management. And while the forms of conflict-management systems that have arisen in the developed and developing countries have varied greatly in structure and effectiveness, the form that predominates in the modern Western industrialized nations is some form of parliamentary democracy, with representation and compromise as the dominant modes of conflict management. Furthermore, while strategies of parliamentary governments have had a diversified history, the dominant mode of political management that has emerged since the Great Depression of the 1930s is the pursuit of policies of economic growth, full employment, moderate inflation, and seeking compromises with the major economic and social groupings of society over the relative shares of an expanding economic base.

Structures, Groups, and Conflict Associated with Stagnation or Decline

In a paper this brief and tentative, I shall neither attempt to lay out all the specific parameters of a stagnating or declining economy nor attempt to draw any formal or predictive models. Instead, I shall attempt to identify some of the probable directions of social and political change that arise under economic conditions—whether induced by the play of the market or by political control of supplies—that create a situation of high unemployment *and* serious inflation, based on higher costs and shortages of the basic materials for the economically productive sector of societies. I shall also make the debatable assumption, for purposes of analysis, that new technological advances will not be able to reverse the trend toward stagnation or decline.

In carrying out this line of speculation, one assumption in particular will inform my remarks. Growth involves *both* the increase in economic indices such as gross national product *and* the proliferation of differentiated structures, the appearance of new groups, and the development of more complex integrative structures geared to the management of conflict. Stagnation or decline involves a distinct slowing or reversal in the movement of economic indices, but it cannot be expected that the major social structures and social groups generated by growth will disappear in the same—but reverse—way they appeared. They have a certain "stickiness" because they have become the loci of the economic, political, and social interests. Regarded in this way, economic stagnation and decline leaves in its wake what might be called an *excess capacity* of social structures and politically significant groups that are resistant to change in their circumstances.

Two Likely Economic Consequences.   First, we might review which groups in society tend to suffer under circumstances of combined inflation and depression. *Inflation* typically hurts those groups whose income is based on fixed rates of pay, changes in which are usually difficult to achieve and which lag behind the general wage and price structure. I refer to such groups as pensioners, people on welfare, students on scholarships, those living off savings yielding fixed rates of interest, and so on. Such groups are the most visible victims of inflation. Groups that have strong bargaining power, such as some trade unions, also suffer, because in general wages tend to lag behind prices in the current situation; but insofar as they have bargaining power they can make up the loss more quickly than other wage sectors. Under conditions of shortages and declining economic activity, *unemployment* strikes a varied pattern of blows, depending on the precise points of constriction. Should shortages of energy continue to be a significant feature of the economic situation, unemployment would hit industries that are especially linked to and dependent upon energy sources, such as automobiles, perhaps steel, and travel and recreation. Whatever the precise pattern of unemployment and inflation, it is likely that the effect of both on the structure of income will be *regressive,* taking a greater toll on the lower economic groups in society.

Second, insofar as the cost conditions for basic industries worsen, this constitutes a worsening of the conditions of production and a diminution of the economic surplus that can be devoted to other kinds of industry and activity that are not economically productive in the immediate sense. Under conditions of energy and resource constriction, we should expect a relative squeeze on those kinds of industry and activity. It would perhaps be too hopeful to predict that societies would begin to dedicate less of their surplus to the wasteful military sector. It is more reasonable to expect that the pressure will be to cut back on education, medicine, welfare, and other social services we have come to value as integral parts of social-democratic systems. The productivity of modern nations has permitted them to devote their surpluses to gigantic military arsenals and gigantic welfare establishments. Crises of energy and resources call into question the ability of industrial nations to continue such economic luxuries.

Implications for Stratification. One of the characteristic features of stratification systems is that various kinds of visible signs come to symbolize a person's position in the stratification system—styles of dress, possession of art objects, evidence of education or cultivation, location of residence, summer residence, and so on. It is also clear that in modern history much of the symbolization of class position is closely tied to material items, and many of these are closely linked to energy: to own one's car; to own two cars; to own two sports cars; to own a boat; to own a plane; to maintain two residences between which one travels frequently for weekends or vacations.

Sticking with the energy example—because that is the one that has been driven home so vividly in the past few years—shortages and increasing costs threaten those kinds of status symbolization. Automobiles and other forms of travel will demand a greater proportion of the family income than before, and a certain proportion of families will be forced to cut back. We may observe, in fact, that in periods of economic reversal, history plays tricks on those who made it. Having taught our citizens that the signs of status are luxury and mobility, we now learn that these signs of our worth may become increasingly unavailable to us. Under such circumstances people begin not only to feel the pressure to modify their life styles but also to question the value of symbols that were once taken for granted. One read in the press in the winter of 1973-74 that Sundays without automobiles in many European countries constituted less of a hardship than was initially anticipated. Part of this may have been due to the kind of collective pleasure that people experience when they face a crisis together. But in addition people discovered that they were engaged in substitute activities that were intrinsically enjoyable to them—visiting, talking, walking with the family, and so on. Such experiences sooner or later raise the question in people's minds whether the best thing to do on Sunday or any other day is to race about the countryside in an automobile. In this way standards of symbolization of life style begin to be brought into question.

In the longer run the changed patterns of consumption—particularly the relative decline in consumption of different groups—are likely to generate serious social discontent and conflict. Citizens will endure hardships in the name of a crisis for a certain time, but this adaptation cannot be counted on in the long run. People eventually come to feel threatened, deprived, and cheated. They begin to demand things of the soceity. Every social group begins to feel that it is carrying too much of the sacrifice. Furthermore, the *pattern* of social conflict under conditions of restriction is different from that under conditions of growth. With growth the pattern is more the conflict of status groups typically associated with rising expectations. It is a kind of manic, aggressive struggle to reap a larger section of the social and economic pie, combined with a sense of expansiveness and limitlessness that gives conflict a somewhat uncontrolled character. Under conditions of static or falling expectations, however, the style of conflict differs. Groups become defensive and security-minded. They grasp what they have and resist the intrusions of others, and this gives conflict a bitter, closed character. Furthermore, they are likely to endow conflict with class overtones, raising more general questions of justice and equality and challenging the principles underlying the distribution of the valued things of life.

The changing character of economic life under conditions of resource constriction has a further implication for social justice. With the diminution of growth and productivity rates, previously disadvantaged groups find it increasingly difficult to gain parity. An example from the recent history of higher education in America will make the point. Late in the 1960s, as part of the political turmoil in American society, disadvantaged groups such as blacks, Mexican-Americans, and women became more conscious politically of the long patterns of exclusion from faculty positions in institutions of higher education. Out of this increased consciousness developed an increased political pressure to recruit from among these groups. But precisely at the moment when the promise of access was increasing, the growth rate in higher education slowed, leaving few positions open for candidates of any sort and, therefore, continuing the pattern of disadvantage intact. It is easier to realize equality of opportunity when a system is growing and new positions are being created. Sociologists like Duncan and Blau, in their research on patterns of social mobility in recent American history, found that much upward mobility is accounted for by the creation of new occupational positions in the process of relatively steady economic advance.[65] It follows that should the growth rate of the economy slow, the effect on rates of social mobility would be adverse. Add to this the fact that in periods of unemployment the unskilled, marginal laboring groups have the highest rates of unemployment—witness the examples of the American minorities, especially blacks, and the migrant workers in various European countries. One discovers once again the regressive effects associated with a slowing rate of economic growth unless active efforts—usually by national governments—are made to counter such effects.

A Possible Cultural Impact? Perhaps the most fundamental impact—although the most difficult to predict—of long-term stagnation and decline is a cultural one. Such conditions may well cause us to question a wide range of cultural values which have become almost second nature to us in the past several centuries. These values, deriving originally from what has come to be known as the Protestant Ethic but now having spread worldwide, include the following:

The valuation of *freedom* of man to exploit his natural environment.

The valuation of *work, hard work,* for its own sake.

The valuation of *mastery, achievement,* and *personal ambition* as desirable human qualities.

The valuation of *rationality,* especially scientific rationality, in the organization of economic and social life.

It seems that the headlong and mindless worship of these values constitutes a large part of the reason we now face some of our environmental imbalances and threatened shortages of resources. These values have contributed directly to the exploitation, the spoilage, and will ultimately result in the exhaustion of the environment. It is one of the ironies of history that after centuries of struggle these values have conquered the world, and at precisely the moment of victory the values themselves have proved to be archaic and outmoded, even burdensome and dysfunctional.

The cumulative impact of stagnation punctuated by crises of supply is to create a sort of cultural confusion, a cultural vacuum. We may become haunted by these questions: What have we been living for?

What is of value if these values are not? Where are we to turn if we cannot turn to these values? At the same time we are such victims of the values of the rationalistic mastery of the universe that we find it difficult to think of solutions in terms other than those suggested by them. Yet the same values, we may be made increasingly aware, will not be the appropriate ones to a situation of crisis and stagnation. To apply them blindly would be simply to worsen the situation we have created for ourselves. I am not suggesting that there is not a technological aspect to the problem of warding off a period of economic stagnation or decline. But I would suggest that the worship of the system of values that gives technology such a central role may be inappropriate in the future, and that greater emphasis will be given to more humanistic values that have fallen by the wayside as science and technology have conquered the world. And is it not only natural for values to drift in the humanistic direction? I mean here natural in the sense that it is evidently the adaptive thing to do when the scientific and technological values that have helped us survive so well into the twentieth century reach their limits as adaptive devices.

Some Possible Political Consequences.   I might conclude by speculating that the sorts of economic and social changes I have envisioned as arising from resource constriction and economic stagnation will pose a severe test for individualistic democracy as a political and legal system. This test promises to have two facets.

The first concerns the volume of conflict that societies will be called upon to accommodate. If what I have said about the impact of declining expectations is correct, there will be few groups and classes who will not be discontented and who will not express that discontent in the form of demands on the political system. And if what I have said about the regressive effects of prolonged energy and resource constriction and its effects on social justice is correct, we should expect an overload of deprivation, experienced especially by those at the lower end of the stratification system.

Two of the conditions of stable democracy are that its internal conflicts take place within a framework of general consensus about the legitimacy of the system of government, and that the level of conflict not rise above that which the mediating political processes can sustain. If either of these conditions fails to be met, the political system itself is endangered, and there arises a temptation on the part of political authorities to rely on methods more repressive than the arts of mediation and compromise to deal with internal conflict. To say this is by no means to predict that heretofore democratic societies will move in a totalitarian direction; democratic institutions have their own kind of resiliency. But they will be tempted to move in that direction, mainly because they will be confronted with conflict of a magnitude and bitterness that will contrast with the relative political quiescence of various social groups during the past quarter-century.

The second facet concerns a probable threat to institutions associated with the system of private property—institutions that permit individuals great freedom in acquiring, using, and disposing of economically valuable resources and commodities. These institutions do not require plenty. They operate like all of human life in the realm of scarcity, since most resources have never been free. But when scarcity turns to shortage, that is, when the unavailability of resources becomes a matter that affects the functioning of society as a *whole,* then the society's interest in those resources necessarily becomes a *collective* interest. Certainly this process has begun with various fuels; they inevitably will become subject to more collectivized regulation at the national level. Indeed, logic dictates that collective interest in such resources should extend to the international level. Once again I venture no predictions as to the exact pattern that the collectivization of interest in resources will take. Many options are available—nationalization, international coordination, and regulation of various sorts. But I am suggesting that the increasing role of government that accompanied the expansion and increasing complexity of the industrial democracies will continue in the same direction as these democracies suffer from constricted resources and slowing rates of growth. It is a final example of the principle that reversals in economic fortunes are not accompanied by parallel reversals in the social and political sectors. Indeed, trends in those sectors, such as the collectivization of interest in economic life, may move faster in the same direction than they moved in the advanced states of economic growth.

CONCLUSION

In this paper I have raised three questions that are directly related to issues in *Economy and Society:*

What is the status of economic rationality, particularly in relation to other institutionalized rationalities?

What are the appropriate units for the study of economic activity?

What are the social and political implications of economic stagnation and decline?

In raising and discussing them, I hope to have been both a bit negative and a bit visionary. Negative, in the sense that I have indicated some of the limitations of the traditional ways that many of us have thought about economy and society. And visionary, in the sense that I have suggested the directions we should look if we are to understand the many unsolved mysteries that characterize the relations between economy and society.

NOTES

1. Talcott Parsons and Neil J. Smelser, *Economy and Society* (Glencoe, Ill.: The Free Press, 1956).
2. Much of that has been done by Parsons himself. For his latest formulation of the fundamentals of that theory, see Talcott Parsons and Gerald Platt, with the collaboration of Neil J. Smelser, *The American University* (Cambridge, Mass.: Harvard University Press, 1973), especially chapters 2 and 3.
3. Wassily Leontief, "Mathematics in Economics," in *Essays in Economics: Theories and Theorizing* (New York: Oxford University Press, 1966), p. 23. For a recent discussion of utility function and Economic Man, see Jerome Rothenberg, "Values and Value Theory in Economics," in *The Structure of Economic Science: Essays in Methodology,* ed. Sherman Roy Krupp (Englewood Cliffs, N. J.: Prentice-Hall, 1966), p. 6.
4. William J. Barber, "Economic Rationality and Behavior Patterns in an Underdeveloped Area: A Case Study of African Economic Behavior in The Rhodesias," *Economic Development and Cultural Change,* vol. 8 (April, 1960), p. 251.
5. Stanley Udy, "Administrative Rationality, Social Setting, and Organizational Development," *American Journal of Sociology,* vol. 68 (November, 1962), pp. 299–308.
6. Thus it seems an overstatement for Black to argue that "Economic Science itself does not...inquire by what events in the realm of fact...preference schedules have come to be what they are." Duncan Black, "The Unity of Political and Economic Sciences," in *Game Theory and Related Approaches to Social Behavior,* ed. Martin Shubik (New York: John Wiley & Sons, 1964), p. 116. If accepted as a normative statement, this position would seem deliberately to encourage a posture of blindness toward knowledge in other fields that might influence the formulation of preference schedules.
7. Parsons and Smelser, *op. cit.,* p. 175.
8. *Ibid.,* p. 183.
9. Karl Polanyi, Conrad Arensberg, and Harry Pearson, *Trade and Market in the Early Empires* (Glencoe, Ill.: The Free Press, The Falcon's Wing Press, 1957).
10. Marshall Sahlins, "On the Sociology of Primitive Exchange," in *Stone Age Economics* (Chicago, Ill.: Aldine-Atherton, 1972), p. 186.
11. *Ibid.,* p. 196.
12. Richard Titmuss, *The Gift Relationship: From Human Blood to Social Policy* (New York: Pantheon Books, 1971).
13. See Oleg Zinam, "The Economics of Command Economics," in *Comparative Economic Systems,* ed. Jan. S. Prybyla (New York: Appleton-Century-Crofts, 1969), p. 16.
14. For an introductory characterization of the "mixed" character of the Soviet economy, see William N. Loucks and William G. Whitney, *Comparative Economic Systems,* 8th ed. (New York: Harper & Row, 1969), pp. 392–532.
15. Gregory Grossman, *Economic Systems,* 2nd ed. (Englewood Cliffs, N. J.: Prentice-Hall, 1974), pp. 18–20.
16. John K. Galbraith, "Power and the Useful Economist," *American Economic Review,* vol. 63 (March, 1973), pp. 1–11.
17. Kenneth Boulding, "Urbanization and the Grants Economy: An Introduction," in *Transfers in an Urbanized Economy,* eds. Kenneth E. Boulding, Martin Pfaff and Anita Pfaff (Belmont, California: Wadsworth Publishing Co., 1973), p. 1.

18. Kenneth E. Boulding, "The Grants Economy," in *Collected Papers,* ed. Fred R. Glahe (Boulder, Colo.: University of Colorado Press, 1971), p. 477.

19. *Ibid.,* p. 478.

20. Kenneth Boulding, "Urbanization and the Grants Economy," *op. cit.*

21. *Ibid.,* chap. 1-6.

22. In particular, Guenther Roth and Claus Wittich, eds., *Economy and Society: An Outline of Interpretive Sociology* (New York: Bedminster Press, 1968), vol. 1, pp. 4-22.

23. *Ibid.,* p. 6.

24. *Ibid.,* p. 9.

25. *Ibid.*

26. *Ibid.*

27. *Ibid.,* p. 19.

28. Guenther Roth, "Max Weber's Comparative Approach and Historical Typology," in *Comparative Methods in Sociology,* Ivan Vallier, ed. (Berkeley, Calif.: University of California Press, 1971), pp. 82-93.

29. Parsons and Smelser, *op. cit.,* pp. 212-254.

30. *Ibid.,* p. 71.

31. *Ibid.,* p. 83.

32. Ibid., pp. 161-162.

33. *Ibid.,* p. 41.

34. *Ibid.,* p. 86.

35. *Ibid.,* p. 107.

36. *Ibid.,* pp. 41-42.

37. *Ibid.,* p. 98.

38. *Ibid.,* p. 375.

39. *Ibid.,* p. 377.

40. *Ibid.,* p. 377.

41. See M. F. Nimkoff and Russell Middleton, "Types of Family and Types of Economy," *American Journal of Sociology,* vol. 66 (November, 1960), pp. 215-225; Rae Lesser Blumberg and Robert F. Winch, "Societal Complexity and Familial Complexity: Evidence for the Curvilinear Hypothesis," *American Journal of Sociology,* vol. 77 (March, 1972), pp. 898-920; William J. Goode, *World Revolution Family Patterns* (New York: The Free Press of Glencoe, 1963).

42. For two contrasting statements, see William F. Ogburn and Meyer Nimkoff, *Technology and the Changing Family* (Boston: Houghton-Mifflin, 1955); and Talcott Parsons et al., *Family, Socialization and Interaction Process* (Glencoe, Ill.: The Free Press, 1955), chap. 1.

43. Eugene Litwak, "Occupational Mobility and Extended Family Cohesion," and "Geographic Mobility and Extended Family Cohesion," *American Sociological Review,* vol. 25 (February, 1960, and June, 1960), pp. 9-21, 385-394.

44. These studies are summarized in Marvin B. Sussman, "The Urban Kin Network in the Formulation of Family Theory," in *Families in East and West: Socialization Process and Kinship Ties,* eds. Reuben Hill and Rene Konig (The Hague: Mouton, 1970), pp. 480-503.

45. Jane Lambiri, "The Impact of Industrial Employment on the Position of Women in a Greek Country Town," *British Journal of Sociology,* vol. 14 (September, 1963), pp. 240-247.

46. One of the best characterizations of the infusion of kin considerations into the pattern of productive activities is still Conrad Arensberg and Solon T. Kimball, *Family and Community in Ireland* (Cambridge, Mass.: Harvard University Press, 1940).

47. David Landes, "French Business and the Businessman: A Social and Cultural Analysis," in *Modern France,* E. M. Earle, ed. (Princeton, N. J.: Princeton University Press, 1951), pp. 133–146.

48. Richard G. Fox, "Family, Castes, and Commerce in a North Indian Market Town," *Economic Development and Cultural Change,* vol. 15 (April, 1967), pp. 312–313.

49. Peter Marris and Anthony Somerset, *African Businessmen: A Study of Entrepreneurship* (London: Routledge & Kegan Paul, 1971), pp. 133–146.

50. Bernard Bailyn, "Kinship and Trade in Seventeenth-Century New England," *Explorations in Entrepreneurial History,* vol. 6, no. 4 (1953-1954), pp. 197–206.

51. Samir Khalaf and Emilie Shwari, "Family Firms and Industrial Development: The Lebanese Case," *Economic Development and Cultural Change,* vol. 15 (October, 1966), pp. 59–69.

52. Ezra F. Vogel, "Kinship Structure, Migration to the City, and Modernization," in *Aspects of Social Change in Modern Japan,* R. P. Dore, ed. (Princeton, N. J.: Princeton University Press, 1967), pp. 91–111.

53. Peter Marris, "African Families in the Process of Change," in *Families in East and West,* Hill and Konig, eds. pp. 397–409.

54. Peter C. M. Gutkind, "The Energy of Despair: Social Organization of the Unemployed in Two African Cities: Lagos and Nairobi," *Civilizations,* vol. 17 (1967), pp. 202–203.

55. Peter Marris, *Family and Social Change in an African City: A Study of Rehousing in Lagos* (London: Routledge & Kegan Paul, 1961).

56. Parsons and Smelser, *op. cit.,* chap. 2.

57. Simon Kuznets, *Quantitative Economic Research: Trends and Problems* (New York: Columbia University Press, 1972), pp. 1–2. See also Kuznets, "The State as a Unit in the Study of Economic Growth," *Journal of Economic History,* vol. 11 (Winter, 1951), pp. 25–41.

58. Kuznets, *Modern Economic Growth: Rate, Structure and Spread* (New Haven, Conn.: Yale University Press, 1966), p. 17.

59. Rondo Cameron et al., *Banking in the Early Stages of Industrialization: A Study in Comparative Economic History* (New York: Oxford University Press, 1967), p. 5.

60. Kuznets, *op. cit.,* p. 17.

61. A number of these theories are summarized and criticized in Pitirim A. Sorokin, *Modern Historical and Social Philosophies* (New York: Dover Publications, 1963).

62. Parsons and Smelser, *op. cit.,* chap. 5.

63. Talcott Parsons, "Some Comments on the Pattern of Religious Organization in the United States," in *Structure and Process in Modern Societies* (Glencoe, Ill.: The Free Press, 1960), pp. 295–321.

64. S. M. Lipset, "The Sources of the Radical Right," in *The New American Right,* Daniel Bell ed. (New York: Criterion Books, 1955), pp. 166–233.

65. Peter N. Blau and Otis Dudley Duncan, *The American Occupational Structure* (New York: John Wiley & Sons, 1967).

C. WEST CHURCHMAN

The New Rationalism
and Its Implications for
Understanding Corporations

It is my purpose in this paper to examine the relevance of a growing literature on what some call the *systems approach* to human problems to the national (or international) policies governing large private corporations. The discussion is primarily based on philosophical issues, in that it draws upon the resources contained in the history of epistemology, ontology, and ethics.

I will begin by a rather brief description of some fairly recent books on the systems approach, followed by some remarks on the underlying philosophical tradition which all those works seem to espouse. This review will then form the basis of some implications concerning the role of private corporations in the systems approach. For purposes of discussion, I should point out that I have been able to find very few relevant linkages in the literature between writers on the systems approach and writers on the role of corporations, though the failure may very well be ascribed to my own rather defective information system. An example in point is a recent address by Randall Meyer (1974), president of Exxon, and Aurelio Peccei, founder of the Club of Rome, which has been supporting a number of systems approach research efforts. Although Meyer's paper refers to "national goals," he makes no mention of the process by which suitable goals are to be ascertained; and Peccei, though once a corporate executive himself, makes no mention of the role of corporations in what he calls the "humanistic revolution." But I think that there are some very important linkages between the literature on the systems approach and the literature on policies for corporations. Specifically, as I will try to show, the assumptions of the systems approach more or less directly answer corporate problems like control, centralization-decentralization, and organizational hierarchy. But also, the traditional arguments justifying private corporations and "free" markets introduce a concept which I'll call the *surrogate* client, which seems to be largely ignored in the literature of the systems approach.

RECENT CONTRIBUTIONS TO
THE SYSTEMS APPROACH

Since the Club of Rome has already been mentioned, we can begin with the work they sponsored. The background is three books by J. Forrester which appeared during the last two decades, beginning with *Industrial Dynamics* (1961), succeeded by *Urban Dynamics* (1969), and finally *World Dynamics* (1971). Some Forrester detractors, of which there seem to be many, use a simple-minded extrapolation to say that the next book will be *Universal Dynamics,* but I understand from Forrester himself that he believes the next step is a much needed *Regional Dynamics.* Forrester's basic philosophical point in *Industrial Dynamics* was that one should not study problems of the industrial corporation in pieces; such piecemeal approaches were in fact the general rule in operations research projects of the fifties, and probably still are in the seventies. There is no need to go into the details of Forresters argument here, since I will be discussing them later. Forrester also argued that the "components" of an industrial firm are linked together in a continuing feedback relation (hence the term *dynamics*). I believe the inspiration for Forrester's systems approach is to be found in mechanical engineering. In any event, once the idea of dynamic interlinkages was established, the need for the trip from industrial firm, to city, to the world seems obvious. When the founders of the Club of Rome were bemoaning the complexity of the world *problematique* (a term which can be interpreted to mean "complex of problems"), Forrester suggested to them the application of his method, which resulted in a report by Meadows et al. (1972), *The Limits to Growth,* a book which has far outsold any other on the systems approach. As the title indicates, the book attacks one sacred cow of much of corporate planning, the need to grow in order to survive. The book also attacks another planning postulate, namely, that horizons beyond five years are not feasible; with *The Limits to Growth* a couple of centuries is needed to give the proper world perspective.

Needless to say, the appearance of *The Limits to Growth* produced a plethora of criticisms, some relevant, some not. Probably most irrelevant were its "data mistakes" as such, but very relevant (for this paper) is the question of how good data can be obtained. Then there was a good deal of niggling about the modeling method (called DYNAMO by Forrester's MIT group). In the 1950s and sixties, for example, great strides were made in developing solution-methods for mathematical programming models (so that, for example, I understand there exists a linear program for one oil company which contains two million variables and thirty-five thousand constraint equations, whereas Forrester's world model contains fewer than fifty variables). I do not believe the argument is about dynamics as such, since change is not a real block in using mathematical programming. Others who have tried to improve on Forrester's model are Mesarovic (1974), also supported by the Club of Rome, and a small group at Batelle Memorial Institute under the acronym DEMATEL. Among other things, DEMATEL has tried to use experts to identify linkages between forty-seven "world problems."

There have also been a number of other approaches to viewing the world of humankind. Beer's *Platform for Change* (1975) contains his application of Ross Ashby's *Design for a Brain* (1966) to the economy of Chile (prior to the Allende debacle). Ackoff (1974), who does talk directly to corporate managers, argues that the basic attitude to planning on the part of managers is the critical problem: too many are "reactive" to crises, or at best "preactive" (tied into forecasts), rather than "interactive" (designing the future rather than waiting for it). If you wish to see how far the combination of imagination and modern scientific findings can go, see Erich Jantsch's *Self Organization and Planning in the Life of Human Systems* (1975), in which the author develops a philosophy of total evolution which goes beyond homeostasis, equilibrium states, and the like.

The works cited above are only a sample of the population of systems approaches, but they are sufficient for my purpose here. Other approaches are also based on generalizations of existing models. For example, several health planners have suggested using the epidemiological model of disease to represent the cause-effect story of all humanity's ills. Similarly, bold ecologists have dared to see the whole world as an ecosystem. Finally, there is economics, which is very difficult to spot in the growing literature of the systems approach. After all, a modern follower of Bentham would regard all the literature cited as attempts to carry out his program, a program that is surely "economics." But a great deal of what today is called economics would not be called the systems approach.

This is probably enough to say in the review of current literature on the worldwide, holistic search for the understanding of human destiny. Naturally, the cautious academic is either turned away or else frightened by all this new literature on human destiny, partly because it blatantly gives up the standards of scholarship so dear to the academic mind. See, for example, Michael's review of Jantsch's book (1975). But if you appreciate Peccei's message mentioned above, you will see that it is rapidly growing too late for deep and segmented scholarship. Indeed, the implication of his remarks is that most detailed and impeccable studies in economics, engineering, health science, and other fields are a serious waste of our research resources. At this point, the debate has become not rancorous but philosophical, or so it seems to this philosophical mind. Therefore, a short excursion into the philosophy of inquiry seems advisable.

THE PHILOSOPHICAL TRADITION OF
THE SYSTEMS APPROACH:
RATIONALISM

My own interest in the systems approach has been in its underlying philosophy, which I take to be a modern version of classical rationalism. The philosophical problems are those of *epistemology:* What is the theory of evidence to support the validity of a systems model?, *ontology:* What is the nature of the real system?, and *ethics*: What are the appropriate goals to be pursued by the social system?

I believe the underlying philosophy of the systems approach is a new rationalism, because it seems apparent that in all the books cited above the rational idea or ideal is that which gives the approach its power; the idea may be dynamic order (Forrester), homeostasis (Beer), planning (Ackoff), or evolution (Jantsch). A simplistic version may help to avoid too prolonged a discussion: for the rationalist, data are used to give reason its intelligibility, whereas for the empiricist, reason is used to make data intelligible. Or perhaps it would be helpful to cite the famous debate between Locke and Leibniz on the existence of innate ideas. The rationalist Leibniz argued that the meaning of the world for us comes out of our innate ideas, while empiricist Locke argued that our ideas come from the world via sensation and reflection. Today we might call their debate a discussion about research strategy. A strong empiricist would want to piece together the thousands of empirical studies which have been made on health, transportation, pollution, and corporations; a rationalist would argue that no piecing together can occur unless one posits the overall *Weltanschauung* which supplies the glue.

Before Kant, traditional rationalism felt it could safely assume some or all of the appropriate *Weltanschauung*. After Kant, the rationalist has to use other means than an argument from the obvious, since even the foundations of arithmetic and geometry have been questioned. Of course, there have been vestiges of traditional rationalism in pockets of inquiry, utility theory being an excellent example, which is just now having its "obvious" foundations shaken. I have discussed some modern methods of neorationalism in *The Design of Inquiring Systems* (1971), and in this paper I will extend these ideas.

Thus the new rationalist assumes a strong epistemology which says that the human intellect can grasp enough of the total picture of the world to begin to approximate answers to our basic questions; the total picture is assumed to be ontologically sound, in that it too is an approximation of reality. But the reality of the rationalist always has a value dimension which specifies the appropriate goals; *rational,* for the rationalist, includes the idea of rational goals and ideals. To be sure, this aspect of rationalism is strangely weak in most of the writings of the new rationalist today, since these tend to emphasize the human crisis, which turns out to be an ethics based on the (questionable) prescription that humans should survive. Jantsch and Ackoff are exceptions to this rule.

METHODOLOGY OF THE
NEW RATIONALISM

Since the new rationalism differs from the old (seventeenth-century) rationalism, I believe it will be worthwhile devoting some time to describing its methodology or, if you like, its research strategy. The old rationalists forged their world views from rather primitive materials. Leibniz, for example, had only a crude psychology (of perception-apperception) to use in describing how God designed the monads; Descartes could use the pineal gland to create a hypothesis about the connection between mind and matter. But today we have a great richness of images of various aspects of the world. Many of these images, as I have already mentioned, are universalizable in the sense that their way of depicting a segment of reality in principle can be used to depect all of reality. Thus many biologists who refined the concept of ecology probably never intended that the image be used except in the fairly narrow sense of a species and its habitat; but the basic concept inherent in ecology can be used (is used) to see the whole world (forever!) as a giant "ecosystem." Of course, the rationalist may create his image out of various pieces, as is often done in the general systems theory literature.

So far as I know, no one has attempted a classification of world images, though I think the time is drawing near when the new rationalist community will have to do just this. Then there will be the tricky task of finding transformation rules from one image to another, in order to ascertain whether the images are really different ("tricky" because, one recalls, so-called non-Euclidean plane geometry can be regarded as a description of a surface in three-dimensional Euclidean geometry, and vice-versa; are the two geometrical images different?).

Thus the new rationalism's methodology contains as its first step the search among the inventory of the images science has developed since Descartes for a plausible, universalizable image. As I have already indicated, there are a remarkable number of these—ecology, epidemiology, homeostatic theory, programming being just a few. The next methodological step is to pose certain crucial questions about a candidate image. First, can one discern more or less clear criteria of better and worse states of the world within the logic of the image? These criteria may take the form of stability-survival conditions, so that one state of the world is worse than another if it is less stable. Or there may be a concept of equity of the living forms in the system which provides the basis for the better-worse judgment. Or the image may contain an explicit hierarchy based, say, on lower and higher forms of life. And so on. I might note that one famous world image, the materialist, presumably fails this test. In the atomic world of Democritus or the particle world of today's physics, there seems to be no place for a "better-worse" relation (is it better to be matter or antimatter?). Thus the materialist image of the world is universalizable because it is almost obvious that one can see all things as complex manifestations of the behavior of matter, but such a world view is not acceptable to the new rationalism because it lacks a value comparison.

Second, the image must provide a way of describing component variables of the world at various points of time. These are individuated aspects of the world which can be changed from one condition into another and which are such that one can determine how a given change influences the better-worse condition of the whole world. For example, one image might enable us to describe industrial production as a component variable. To qualify, the image would also have to tell us what happens to the quality of the world (say, in the next two hundred years) if industrial production is increased 10 percent in the period 1976-85; if survival is the relevant gauge of value, then the answer of the image might be that turning the industrial production knob up 10 percent will increase the probability of the destruction of the human species by .05. Note the strong ontological assumption underlying this methodological step: the component variables can be changed by humans, and such changes *cause* changes in the value of various states of the world. Freedom and causality therefore are essential ingredients in the image. In order to make the predictions we also need to have environmental variables which are not under our control but which also influence the outcome values (for example, weather, earthquakes, ice-cap melting).

There is, of course, the question of who the decision makers are and who they should be. As I will try to show, this question is one of central importance to the new rationalism but has been largely ignored, perhaps because the new rationalists, like the old, take the answer to be rather obvious. Spinoza's *Ethics,* for example, has a message for each of us, namely, that our appropriate role is understanding God's world. Each of us, therefore, is a decision maker. Similarly, in Kant's "Kingdom of Ends," it is each Will which is motivated by the moral law. But such universal decision making clearly will not work for most of the images of the new rationalism. Forrester, I believe, pointed out that the average citizen cannot understand society, since society "by its very nature" is a nonlinear feedback system. If society is such a system, then who is to run it? The answer seems obvious: people who do understand nonlinear feedback systems. Indeed, in some of the writings of the members of the Club of Rome, there is the implication that the decision makers of the world should move out and let the enlightened rule. I hope it is clear enough without my having to emphasize it that most managers of corporations must be deemed totally incompetent by many new rationalists, simply because they do not—or cannot—understand the whole-world imagery.

But the truth is that there is a serious hiatus in the methodology of the new rationalism with respect to the image of decision making. I believe that many rationalists would prefer to find a single unit of power in society which could be persuaded to move the component variables in appropriate ways, as Plato hoped to find in Dion in Syracuse and Stafford Beer in Allende in Chile. But this hope is both too simple and too dangerous; dangerous because it puts the rationalist on the side of totalitarianism.

I will be returning to the question of the decision makers later, but right now I should complete the methodology. Naturally, an image by itself is empty, even if universalizable. Hence some procedure for collecting data for the image is required. Here we run into a very peculiar aspect of the methodology. It would be very nice if we could transform the image into a model with parameters and if we could then go out into the world and measure the parameters. An example of this approach is to be found in Galileo's *Dialogues,* where by reasoning alone he had deduced that the distance traveled by an unmolested falling body is proportional to the square of the time of fall. He then devised an experiment which both tested his reasoning and (for a given inclined plane) measured the proportionality factor. But the methodology of the new rationalism is not that easy. Consider, for example, the cost of operating a component of the system, which is usually a critical parameter. How is such a cost to be measured? Not by the dollars actually used but rather by the opportunity foregone of doing something else. This is the same rational point that the image builders make from the beginning: You cannot understand how a given activity works unless you understand how all the other activities work. To estimate the cost of this workshop, we would have to estimate how each of us could have used his time in the best alternative "lost opportunity."

Of course, now the methodology appears paradoxically circular: To understand the world we need a universal image, and to give content to the image we need data, but to get the data we need the image. The paradox is really not a deadly one, however, as the history of experimental science has shown. What is done in practice is to use historical data, even though it may be in error, or use some good intuitive judgment to modify the data. Then we build content into the model, which itself is partly in error. With the model, we can begin making some new estimates, and thus by continuing to modify the model, hope to approximate reality closer and closer. There are all kinds of questions to be raised about such a methodology, but they need not concern us here.

It should be clear from the above that there is no such thing as a test of a universal image; there is no question that a linear program believer can "put to nature" to test whether society can "in fact" be represented by a linear program simply because all our experience can be molded into such a universal image. But there is a process of confirmation of the images, as each rationalist becomes more and more impressed by the way his image "sweeps in" aspects of social reality. I find that the various image builders are becoming more confident each year that their image is the right perspective.

Such a remark with its somewhat cynical overtones brings me to the final step of the new rationalist methodology, namely, the individual rationalist himself. He surely cannot escape putting himself into his own image, especially because he must be awfully important for the world if he can image universally how things should work; after all, redesigning the future (Ackoff, 1974) or providing the world with a platform for change (Beer, 1975) are hardly minor matters. It is to be expected, therefore, that the image builder will include in his image an explanation of how he came to be, and why he came to be, and why he believes he is right, or on the right track. If one does expect such a thing, he will be disappointed. The new rationalists are remarkably shy about telling us about themselves.

With this introduction to rationalist methodology, I would now like to turn to the "linkage" I mentioned earlier and ask how the literature of the new rationalism relates to our understanding of the modern, private corporation. There are several implications of the literature I would like to pursue: the significance of empirical studies of corporations, the significance of corporations themselves, and the managing of corporations. In this discussion I will be talking from the point of view of the rationalist as I interpret him.

THE EMPIRICAL STUDIES
OF CORPORATIONS

It must be fairly obvious to the universal image builder that a large part of the literature describing specific corporate behavior is probably irrelevant or only marginally interesting. For example, in the late 1950s Leavitt and Whisler (1958) considered the possible influence of the coming computer age on centralization and decentralization in corporations, predicting a trend toward centralization. Other behavioral science writers followed suit, and a small literature emerged on the subject. But the question of the systems approach would not be "will managers tend to centralize?" but rather "will the potential speed-up in feedback enable the managers better to control the enterprise, and will better control be worth the price?" The fact that the predicted centralization did not occur, at least as strongly as some predicted, cannot be interpreted without some image of how the whole corporate system works.

I cite this example mainly to illustrate why two rather extensive literatures—of behavioral science and the new rationalism—fail to interact and not to place any blames. Clearly there is a problem here from the point of view of both parties: the rationalist might wonder why the behavioral literature is so weak and irrelevant, while the behavioral literature might wonder how the behavior of the systems people ever happened.

One should realize the sweeping criticism that emanates (by implication) from the new rationalism of a great part of social science research. For example, the guidance that is given to many doctoral candidates to seek specific projects where they can "carve out" a manageable piece to work on is foolish advice to a mind bent on understanding the world and people's place in it. Furthermore, nothing stands as a contribution to knowledge unless it can be linked to the universal image.

But the real difference between the rationalist and behavioral-empiricist literature can be captured by the distinction between manager and management. In the rationalist's imagery, the critical concept is management, not manager. He sees management as the process of turning the appropriate knobs of the component variables, and he usually does not include in the image the characteristics of some individual manager.

The distinction between management and manager has wholesale implications for the study of corporations. First of all, to the rationalist there is the sensible question whether the corporation, or even a collection of corporations, such as an industry, is a meaningful component of society. To recall, a component is a variable in the image which can be changed by the decision maker and the influence of the change on the better-worse relationship can be estimated. It seems very likely that a corporation defined as a collection of individuals (managers, stockholders, employers) and their owned resources will not be viewed as a component of the social system, because there is no way in which this collection can be seen to satisfy the necessary conditions. Perhaps something broader, like "industrial production," is needed, which component would include a great deal of government activity as well as private. But the situation at the present time is fuzzy; in Beer's brain-model he does regard the individual plant as a component.

However, even if we do regard the corporation (and related activities like consumers and government) as a sensible component, the questions the rationalist addresses about such an entity are quite different from those of the behavioral scientist. Consider, again, centralization versus decentralization. To a rationalist, whose basic ontology is monism, the question as to whether society should be managed centrally or decentrally is trivial: centralization in principle is always required. But this obvious answer does not necessarily imply a centralized manager or group of managers; it implies centralized management.

Indeed, when the logic is spelled out, one sees that all management functions are so interrelated that there is no hierarchy in the rationalist image. Consider, for example, the very mundane task of inventory management. In order that this management function well, it needs to have certain types of information, for example, demand, holding costs, shortage costs, reorder costs, and the like. But each of these types of information is generated by other sectors of the system: by the demand subsystem, the financial subsystem, and so on. Now if one of these subsystems is behaving badly (in terms of the overall better-worse relation), then inventory management needs to know this, because, for example, it is irrational to control inventory against a "bad" demand. This point is often missed by the rationalist himself, so that many operations research texts tell the students to estimate probability distributions of demand from past data without warning them to look and see whether past demand has been approximately rational (and in my experience it often has not). It is also irrational to control inventory by using a cost-of-capital based on a "bad" financial policy. Hence, "good" inventory management requires judgment about corporate financial policy—and labor policy, and marketing policy, and so on.

One can see that for the rationalist it is always the case of the tail wagging the dog; every management function runs the show. This is even true in Beer's Chilean cybernetic system, where signals of trouble go "up" a hierarchical control system and some go up to the "conscious" level of Allende and company; but Allende himself is controlled by the people who people the "lowest" level.

Note that I have said nothing about the individual manager who appears on the organization chart as the production manager or inventory manager. To a rationalist, such labeling may appear to be irrelevant, because the critical question for him is not who is called what, but how management ought to function.

THE QUALITY OF CORPORATE
MANAGEMENT

Thus far I have mentioned only the rationalist's attitude toward be-havioral studies of the firm. If we turn to the corporation itself, I think it is fairly obvious that the rationalist would judge the quality of corporate management today to be low. First of all, because he is himself the grand planner, he would argue that there is virtually no good corporate planning at the present time. I should hasten to point out that he would probably not blame corporate managers for this situation, because blaming on the whole is not a very efficacious activity in systems design. He would see that the so-called management information system of most corporations is terribly inadequate, simply because the information needed to perform the various functions does not flow from the considerations already illus-trated in the case of inventory management.

But what does our rationalist intend to do about it? If one reads the literature supported by the Club of Rome, the answer seems to be that we need to create a mood of world crisis in the minds of corporate managers, so that they will veer from the disaster-ridden goals they now pursue to goals which will avert the impending disasters. But if one asks how such a mood is to be created, the response is not clear. One suggestion is to expand the Club regionally, so that important corporate managers can learn the results of the Club's and other research efforts which increase understanding of the world system. But why should this method work, even approximately? Indeed, there seem to be good reasons why it will not, and some of these are to be found in the discarded literature of the behavioral scientists.

I have now come back to the hiatus in rationalist imagery which I mentioned earlier: namely, the image of the decision maker or what might be called the anatomy of decision making.

THE SURROGATE CLIENT

I am going to try to develop a model of social decision making, partly based on experience and reading, partly on some of my own dab-bling in behavioral science, in an attempt to understand the process of implementation. Like most models, it is not new, since it borrows from fairly well-known material.

Society, too, has tried to identify components of the social system, usually based on tradition and a very gradual change. These components are areas of society like medicine, law, education, and industrial production-distribution. To become a qualified decision maker in these areas, one has to acquire certain specialized skills and meet certain standards. But also, in order that someone function well in his area of decision making, he must himself be rewarded appropriately. There is no question that society—and especially future generations—is the right "client" of the system, but in order to operate the system we seem to need surrogate clients who are directly served by society in order that they may serve the real client.

All this is fairly obvious, I hope. Examples abound. The surrogate client of a hospital is the doctor, the surrogate client of a university is the faculty, the surrogate client of the law is the lawyer. And, I believe, the surrogate client of a corporation is the manager. Now I am back to the individual manager and not the function of management. In this analysis, I am sweeping all examples of surrogate clients into one class. To be sure, the defense of each type differs. Corporate managers defend their right to be decision makers on the basis that the free market creates better products through competition, while educators defend their right on the ground that an intellectual base is required. But all surrogate clients are the same in the sense that each benefits from society in order to make appropriate decisions in his area.

The model I have in mind says that this design of decision making produces segments of society which harden, in the sense that they become less and less competent to respond to change and less and less competent to be a true surrogate client, that is, represent the interests of the real client. There are several possible explanations for this phenomenon, each of which has its historical tradition. One explanation can be found in egoistic hedonism and simply says that greed begins to dominate in each sector, an explanation I find dull and rather ugly (and I take ugliness to be one sensible criterion of rejection of a theory). My own hypothesis is that each sector tries to reflect the whole world in its own way of perceiving reality. Thus the academic believes he and his colleagues understand how the world works, economically, politically, aesthetically, whatever; and he is reinforced in this belief by his colleagues who believe likewise. But there is also the tendency to reflect the whole world in such a way that large change in the academic sector is seen to be inadvisable. In other words, we tend to design our image of social reality so as to conclude that our sector is stable and satisfactory. Hence there is no need to change, except slowly and cautiously, because the academic view of reality is solid. Similarly, corporate managers "understand the world"; they understand what government, labor, consumers are trying to do and react accordingly. Large changes in corporate structure are seen to be socially undesirable. The analogy is in Leibniz's *Monadology,* where he depicts each monad reflecting all other monads, although imperfectly. But in this version of the monadology there is the added idea of a monad's reflection of all other monads so as to minimize its will to change itself. This may be the reason why a number of scholars, disillusioned by the large model building of the new rationalists, turned to the philosophy of "muddling through," sometimes called *incrementalism* (Lindblom and Braybrooke, 1963), since incremental planning fits the mood of the managers.

The above is, of course, an oversimplified version of the model of social decision making, because within each sector there is a continuing struggle for domination based on some criterion of quality like excellence in the academic world or net earnings in the corporate world. But for my own purposes here the simplified version will do.

THE NEW RATIONALISM REVISITED

Now an interesting comparison arises. I earlier described the new rationalist as one who believes he grasps reality *in toto*. But if in other sectors of society decision makers also believe they understand reality, what is rationalism's basis for claiming it is right and the rest are wrong?

There are some obvious answers to this question, all of which I believe are wrong. The first is that the rationalists see the ("real") need for change while other decision makers do not. But the rationalists do not see the need to change themselves or their particular way of constructing world images. It is all the other sectors that need changing, not they. But this state of affairs is probably true of most sectors. I have several times been told by corporate managers that they do not like academics, and many academics are equally frank on the subject of corporate managers. Few of us like doctors and lawyers any more, and so it goes. Each sector would probably like to change other sectors quite drastically.

A second obvious answer is that the rationalist is right, at least in his doomsday predictions. But as I have argued above, he is surely not right—or at least not informed—about how social change should take place, and according to his own philosophy a "right" prediction is inseparable from a "right" implementation.

A third obvious answer is that the rationalist is rational and decision makers in corporations are not, or at least are not except in a very limited sense. This seems to be the answer that many rationalists accept, but it too will not do. First of all, I have been hinting that there are some severe gaps in the rationalist's own thinking because he leaves out himself and the process of decision making in his images of the whole world. In some sense, the rationalist may not be rational. But more to the point, he would find it difficult today to argue that *rational* means acting on a comprehensive and integrated model; such a claim, I said, could reasonably be made by seventeenth-century rationalist, but not by a twentieth-century one. It would be extremely difficult to show that the way in which an astute corporate manager understands the world is irrational; descriptors like "shortsighted," "piecemeal," "conceptually weak," often used by the rationalist as ammunition against the managers, reflect more the life style of the rationalist rather than any reality. Most rationalists are what Carl Jung (1959) calls "thinking types," who tend towards quantity, consistency (in the narrow sense of formal logic), coherence, and the like as their conceptual value base. But intuitive and feeling types understand the world quite differently but still rationally. (Jung himself may have slipped here, since he says that thinking and feeling are rational functions, while intuition and sensation are nonrational; I would say that in today's world of depth psychology, all functions are rational if they operate in a healthy manner.)

MORALITY AND FUTURE GENERATIONS

Now, there is a glimmer of a clue as to why the rationalist may be right in his claim that he is comprehensive, because his comprehensiveness includes future generations. At this point, I need to explain my own bias. It is that the source of all our moral values as human beings is to be found in our expectations concerning the values of future generations. Some moral prescriptions, therefore, are simply our version of what a future human being would ask us to do if he or she were here to ask it. "Thou shalt not irreversibly destroy a species," is just such a moral request. From the moral point of view, we are the caretakers of the world of our progeny.

I have no intention of defending this version of morality here, but I need it in order to complete my argument. It amounts to saying that our generation is morally obligated not to make decisions which may seriously harm the quality of life of future generations, or, on the positive side, we are to enjoy the moral elation of creating a world in which our progeny's quality of life is far greater than ours.

I come back to the new rationalists and I see that indeed they have a deep concern for future generations. This concern, I think, should be the business they are in, and *not* model building. The various criticisms of the Meadow's world modeling usually missed the mark; the question is whether concern for the next two hundred years makes sense and whether some form of modeling will help in this concern. There are other ways besides modeling of addressing the question of what we should do with respect to the future: the Sierra Club, Delphi technique, and astrology are examples.

And it is probably true that other sectors of society tend to ignore the moral issues of future generations, despite the lip service they pay to it. I know enough about the way in which we are managing our nuclear energy production to believe that we are immorally ignoring the potentially dangerous events which might disastrously alter the lives (if they are alive!) of future people. If one believes the Club of Rome we are on the way to a world of giant starvation.

So in the end, I find myself siding with the rationalists, though remaining skeptical about the truth of any of their imagery. I would rather like to regard the imagery as a set of stories about the future, just as we have stories about the past. The imagery, in fact, might be regarded as high-class science fiction. But its impact should be to awaken our moral sensibilities.

INSTITUTIONALIZING FUTURE CONCERN

When I wrote the first draft of this paper, I suggested a possible solution to the problem of how we get society to change and, specifically, how we introduce a powerful concern for the future. The suggestions were based on the idea that we probably cannot change the institutions of our society and especially what I called the "sectors." But we might introduce a new institution whose task is to evaluate major decisions in terms of the consequences for future generations or to suggest decisions which are deemed to make future life have a higher quality. At the corporate level this suggestion calls for a managerial function, not long-range planning but something like moral responsibility, that is, an examination of the corporation's influence on future lives. At the national level the suggestion calls for a new branch of government which would examine all legislative, executive, and judicial decisions in terms of their moral import. I even went so far as to suggest that the representatives of this branch are only tentatively elected; their final election would take place after their constituencies were born and old enough to vote.

The trouble was that I could not see how to design power into either the corporate or the federal example. To allow the "moralists" veto would soon corrupt them morally. To make them into "advisors" would transform them into advertisements ("The XYZ Corporation worries about your kids' kids!"). I suspect that my trouble was that I wanted to institutionalize morality just as some people want to legalize it, but it cannot (should not) be done.

My conclusion is that the rationalists do not know enough about social decision making to be able to prescribe how change for the better of future generations should take place. Perhaps the knowledge already exists in some suitable form in a body of literature of which I am unaware. The only relevant literature I have found is on "incrementalism," mentioned above, and "change agents." (Bennis, 1968). The advocates of the incrementalist model of social decision making believe that organizations can only be changed in small steps and that the strategy of the planner is to find where the change potential exists and push in that direction. But this literature contains no world image which suggests why a specific change, no matter how small, will make matters better. Indeed, a great deal of the change-agent literature seems blithely to assume that he is always working for the better. But the rationalist knows that an apparent improvement (for example, a cure for cancer) will have all kinds of reverberations throughout the social system which need to be examined before implementation can take place.

My conclusion is therefore a question: how can we begin to understand the nature of social decision making so that a rationalist would know his appropriate role in this process? Note that I am *not* saying "so that the rationalist can implement his recommendations," because such a strong role may not be appropriate given the uncertainties and philosophical criticisms of the new rationalism.

THE INDIVIDUAL

This last comment inspires one further criticism and one possible answer to my question. The theme harks back to an earlier discussion about managers and management. There I said that most new rationalists are concerned about management, not managers; now I will say that they think in terms of class logic and not individual logic. There is another literature that also tries to understand humans and their world, which is based on the meaningfulness of the individual and not the classes to which he belongs. Part of the literature is in phenomenology (Husserl, Heidegger, Sartre). But the part which impresses me is in such writers as Jung (1959) and Hillman, *The Myth of Analysis* (1973). Jung argues that unless the decision maker has developed himself, that is, gone through the process of individuation, he is in no position to make social decisions. In other words, he might say that the explanation for the failure of decision making (and the "hardening" of societal sectors) is to be found in the underdeveloped psyches of individual decision makers. Hillman believes he can see the influence of the archetype in decision making; for example, for a while we were dominated by the archetype of growth but now by the archetypes "ecos" and stability. Hillman also suggests that the rationalist's "better-worse" relationship may be a "myth."

I see no way to reconcile the Jungians and those I have called new rationalists, nor do I want to. I believe we simply distort the world picture by attempting to reconcile the ideas of society and the feeling of uniqueness that each individual has. In any event, I believe that the image of nature which depth psychology holds cannot be adjusted so as to become integrated with the global images I have discussed.

REFERENCES

1. Ackoff, R. L. *Redesigning the Future.* London: John Wiley & Sons, 1974.
2. Ashby, Ross. *Design for a Brain.* New York: Barnes & Noble, 1966.
3. Beer, Stafford. *Platform for Change.* London: John Wiley & Sons, 1975.
4. Bennis, Warren G. and Slater, Philip E. *The Temporary Society.* New York: Harper & Row, 1968.
5. Boulding, K. E. *The Image.* Ann Arbor: University of Michigan Press, 1956.
6. Churchman, C. W. *Design of Inquiring Systems.* New York: Basic Books, 1971.
7. ——— and Ackoff, R. L. *Psychologistics.* Philadelphia: University of Pennsylvania, 1946.
8. Forrester, J. *Industrial Dynamics.* Cambridge, Mass.: M.I.T. Press, 1961.
9. ———. *Urban Dynamics.* Cambridge, Mass.: M.I.T. Press, 1969.
10. ———. *World Dynamics.* Cambridge, Mass.: M.I.T. Press, 1971.
11. Hillman, James. *The Myth of Analysis.* Evanston, Ill.: Northwestern University Press, 1972.
12. Jantsch, E. *Self Organization and Planning in the Life of Human Systems.* New York: George Braziller, 1975.
13. Jung, C. G. *Psychological Types.* New York: Pantheon Books, 1959.
14. ———. *Two Essays on Analytical Psychology.* New York: Pantheon Books, Bollingen Series XX, 1953.
15. Leavitt, J. J. and Whisler, T. L. "Management in the 1980's." *Harvard Business Review,* November-December, 1958, p. 48.
16. Lindblom, C. E. and Braybrooke, D. A. *Strategy of Decision Policy Evaluation As a Social Process.* Glencoe, Ill. and New York: The Free Press, 1963.
17. Mesarovic, M. *Mankind at the Turning Point.* New York: E. P. Dutton, 1974.
18. Meadows, D. H. et al. *Limits to Growth.* New York: University Books, 1972.
19. Meyer, R. "The Role of Big Business in Achieving National Goals." President's Lecture Series, The Florida State University, 1974.
20. Michael, D. "Review of Jantsch" (1975). *Futures,* December, 1974, pp. 518–522.
21. Peccei, A. "The Humanistic Revolution." *Successo* (international ed.), January, 1975, pp. 155–162.
22. Singer, E. A. *On the Contented Life.* New York: Henry Holt and Co., 1936.

PART 2

Legitimacy

Where rationality is a way of perceiving and analyzing one's surroundings, both material and abstract, legitimacy is measured by the degree of congruence between what people, by whatever process, come to want to do or actually do, on the one hand, and social values, on the other.[1] In a society where a rational thought system prevails and is, thus, one of the moral values, whether the things people want or do is rational plays a role in legitimacy. Institutions, organizations, social ideas, ideologies, distribution of social values such as power and wealth, economic systems, and most other products of human life are subject to the dynamics of legitimacy. A growing literature explores the domain of legitimacy and wanders over much of the sociological and political spectrum.[2] Kenneth Boulding, as do many of the other commentators, concentrates his attention on the business institution and on legitimacy as one of its "survival functions." Although Boulding uses the term *business institution* to describe the locus of his concern, his primary target seems to be the corporation, or even more specifically, the large corporation.

Boulding's paper raises the questions of what the survival functions of the business institution and the factors in the total environment are that have a bearing on the probability of survival either of individual units or of the system as a whole. He classifies the survival functions as market and nonmarket environments and predicts for the next few decades that the survival of the business institution will depend much more on its nonmarket than on its market environment and that, among the crucial characteristics of the nonmarket environment, survival will depend to a much greater extent on the ability to retain legitimacy than on any other factor, including the internal dynamics of the market environment itself.

The connection between legitimacy and organization survival has long been noted by sociologists, political theorists, and other observers, but legitimacy has been examined empirically only on very infrequent occasions. The empirical work that has been and is being done, however, is beginning to develop several conceptual frameworks within which new and more important empirical explorations can be carried out. John Dowling and Jeffrey Pfeffer recently suggested a conceptual framework in which organizational legitimacy is defined as the "congruence between the values associated with the organization and the values of its environment."[3] Talcott Parsons' framework, predictably, is oriented more toward the congruence between organizational action and the values and goals of the overall social system.[4] Shirley Terreberry encourages the assessment of legitimacy through the existence of resource or informational transactions between organizations.[5] Both the normative and the structural characteristics of legitimacy are emphasized by David Apter, who also argues that the empirical study of legitimacy is crucial to the study of politics.[6] There are, of course, many other approaches.

What Boulding adds to the conceptual level of the discussion is the enumeration and recommended study of each of the "component characteristics of the business institution to see where their legitimacy may be threatened." Among the threatened legitimacies outlined by Boulding are the market as a social institution, exchange, profits, private property, capitalism, and international business.

A CRISIS OF LEGITIMACY?

The so-called crisis of legitimacy in America and, especially, in the corporate system, is by now familiar to all who have interest in the relationship between business and society. "America is undergoing a crisis of legitimacy," wrote Theodore Levitt in 1973.[7] Equally familiar are the more common explanations for this crisis. Size and concentration of power in the large corporation play important roles, as do the separation of ownership and control (in the historical meaning of these terms), the meaninglessness of "ownership" in the corporate sector, the perceived absence of easily recognized and accepted forms of responsibility and accountability of managers (and the resulting inconsistency with the democratic values of society), the belief that the personal virtues of frugality and hard work are no longer correlated with the way in which power, privilege, and property are distributed in society at large and, increasingly of late, the belief that corporate promises of performance have failed. The arguments in support of the legitimacy of corporate and managerial power are also well known and range from social responsibility to social Darwinism. The Protestant Ethic has its own legitimacy problems these days, and concepts of private property and ownership do not ring very true when applied to the large corporation. A technocratic ethic, based on performance, has become popular in some sectors and has been closely associated with social responsibility, with managerial capitalist ideology, and with the professionization of management.[8] While crisis may at present be too strong a term to use in this context, certain issues of legitimacy clearly exist and could rather quickly become critical. Boulding's emphasis on the areas of threatened legitimacy is therefore particularly important.

If we ended our discussion here and moved on immediately to Boulding's paper, we would have missed the flavor of what the subject of legitimacy is really about. Boulding said as much in his oral comments on his own paper. What *is* the subject of legitimacy about? It is really about all social institutions (from family to corporations to governments) and their relationships to the larger society. In other words, it is of basic importance to all discussions of society and its institutions. Kenneth Boulding said during his oral presentation that he was a pluralist and, as such, did not really believe that there was any one thing on which everything else hangs, whether it be economics, sociology, political science, or whatever, but

> *if there is one thing on which everything else hangs, it is the dynamics of legitimacy.* If you lose legitimacy, you have lost everything. You are an absolutely dead duck, no matter how much threat you have. The whole Vietnam episode is an example of how utterly helpless even the richest and most powerful nation in the world is, in the absence of legitimacy.[9]

Yet it is not just the importance of the dynamics of legitimacy that must be emphasized, it is also the complexity. During the discussion of the Boulding paper, Mayer Zald commented that "legitimacy is the toughest concept in political science, one of the great unanalyzed concepts," and went on to describe the source of at least some of the complexity as being in the intimate relation between legitimacy, on the one hand, and power and authority, on the other, and particularly in the symbolic and convoluted landscape that lies between the wielder and wieldee of power and between the grantor and grantee of legitimacy. Berle has said that "whenever there is a question of power there is a question of legitimacy."[10]

Boulding also describes the dynamics of legitimacy as "terribly puzzling" and points out another reason why that is so. "Legitimacy derives from two separate and contradictory sources, and that is very troublesome." The two contradictory sources identified by Boulding are the "positive payoff" and the "negative payoff" sources, or, in Skinnerian terms, positive and negative reinforcement. The largesse, support, approval (for example, buying output) or adulation of society provide legitimacy for an institution and remove it when they are taken away. If this were all there was to it, you could reduce legitimacy to utility theory, says Boulding, and the whole thing would be easy. There is a negative payoff, however, that also creates legitimacy, the "sacrifice trap," as

Boulding calls it. "If you suffer from anything, you will get trapped in it, because your identity becomes bound up with it."

> The blood of the masses is the seed of the Church; the blood of the soldiers is the seed of the State; the tears of the children are the seed of the family; the agonies of the students are the seed of the alumni association.

One can also add to these layers of complexity the observation that there is internal legitimacy within the institution and external legitimacy that affects institutions from without. Not even the individual escapes the interplay of the dynamics of legitimacy; Max Weber speaks of the "legitimacy or deservedness of one's [own] happiness."[11] Little wonder that the "concept of legitimacy has been strangely neglected in American political science,"[12] and elsewhere.

This volume is not the proper place to undertake the development of a new and integrated theory of legitimacy. One of our major goals for the workshop/conference and for this volume, however, has been to identify areas of potentially valuable research. Certainly no more fertile plot could be ploughed in the whole range of relationships between economic institutions and social systems than that which we know as legitimacy. Not only is it an important side of the triangle that is the symbol of this volume, but it is also a key to the understanding of all manner of social phenomena and "provides a linkage between the organizational and societal levels of analysis."[13]

A CONCEPTUAL OUTLINE OF LEGITIMACY

Beyond pointing out some of the avenues of promising future research, what this brief introduction to the Boulding paper can best do in order to increase understanding of the important and exceedingly complex social concept of legitimacy is to outline briefly one of the useful conceptualizations of legitimacy and then to pursue that conceptualization through a few levels of analysis. It would not be untoward if we selected as our illustrative concept a slightly modified version of Parsons' approach: organizations are legitimate to the extent that their activities are congruent with the goals and values of the social system within which they function.[14] Legitimacy, then, is a condition that occurs with the congruence of organizational activities with social norms. As noted earlier, legitimacy is a major factor in organizational survival. Parsons observed many years ago that, as a consequence, organizations will habitually and naturally take steps to ensure their legitimacy. "Legitimation is the process whereby an organization justifies to a peer or superordinate system its right to exist . . ."[15]

While legitimacy is a condition, legitimation is a *process* or a *dynamic*. Changes in social norms, goals, and values necessarily bring about changes in the ways in which organizations seek to legitimate their activities, and, it should be noted, organizational efforts at legitimation also have an impact on social norms. There is a powerful competitive element at work also in this process of legitimation, as each organization seeks to improve its own legitimacy or seeks to protect itself from threats to its legitimacy. Though not usually so denominated, no small part of modern corporate strategy is concerned with matters involving legitimacy.[16] Market mechanisms play a major role in the competitive aspects of legitimation and in the changes in organizational activities and social goals and values which result.

An organization may seek legitimacy in one or more of several alternative ways. An organization may adapt its activities and its methods of operation to conform to what it perceives to be the prevailing standards of legitimacy. Door-to-door salesmen, for example, may vanish in some industries as that marketing method becomes identified in the public mind with shoddy merchandise or "suede shoes" sales techniques. Second, the organization may seek to change the public norms and values to conform to its own activities through advertising and other means,[17] as Avon apparently did successfully with the door-to-door marketing of cosmetics; but this approach is much less common because it is much more difficult. Third, an organization may seek, instead of or in addition to the other means of establishing its legitimacy, to identify itself with other organizations, persons, values, or symbols that have a powerful legitimate base in society. Endorsements and membership on boards of directors by distinguished citizens are common examples of this means.

One must be aware that while the analysis above may appear to be quite suitable for a single organization or firm, it requires considerable modification to make it appropriate for an institution consisting of many separate organizations or of all organizations of a particular type. What might be said meaningfully about a single large corporation, for example, might be a bit fuzzy if applied to the corporate system or to all large corporations. The basic principles are still appropriate, but the absence of a single decision-making or motivational locus considerably complicates the picture. Unfortunately, the institution most often cited in the United States today as being in a crisis of legitimacy is not General Motors, Lockheed, or even the automotive or aerospace industries but "American business," or the "system of large corporations," or "corporate capitalism."

In this institution there is no single set of goals, norms, values, and activities but instead a vast interactive, but only very loosely organized, complex of individuals, organizations, industries, and associations carrying on a tremendous variety of activities under many different methods of operation and possessing an almost infinite variety of goals and values, many of which are contradictory. Each organization or unit within the complex is busy seeking its own legitimacy by whatever means seem most suitable to its needs, while only rarely outside the groves of academe is anyone concerned with the legitimacy of the whole.

Some of the issues raised in Part One in connection with the tension between monism and reductionism are pertinent here. Perhaps it is possible to see and understand the problem more clearly now and to appreciate the interplay between reducing the target to manageable size and the need for a world view that encompasses and gives meaning to the whole. It is much easier to conceptualize the dynamics of legitimacy in the context of a single focal organization than it is to build a workable model of legitimacy for a whole business, corporate, or economic system. One should not despair, however, and for several reasons. Although the ways of legitimation are not as clear as with the individual organization, the concept of legitimacy within the broader system and many of the issues surrounding it are not obscure. Legitimation is still the process whereby an institution justifies to the society its right to exist, and that right is still based upon the congruence of activities and social values. Furthermore, we do learn something about legitimacy in the aggregate by studying and understanding the dynamics of legitimacy in the individual organization; some agglomeration does take place, and more will occur as our tools improve. We are, after all, just getting started. A word more about this problem after we consider the potential for empirical research.

POSSIBLE RESEARCH APPROACHES

There is no one approach to empirical research on institutional legitimacy and the process of legitimation that appears to be more promising than others. Different disciplinary fields have used a variety of approaches, most with some degree of success. Sociologists and organization behaviorists have suggested a focus on legitimacy as a constraint on organizational behavior.[18] If one hypothesizes that legitimacy is a constraint on behavior, then one would expect to find that organizations whose activities are out of phase with social norms and values will tend to bring those activities into conformity. This approach is essentially the same as the empirical side of the type of discussion of social responsibility that emphasizes corporate response to changing social expectations. Changing social values with regard to minority employment and nondiscrimination in economic intercourse began to have their impact upon organizational behavior long before the coercive role of the law was brought into play. Whether this occurred under the label of seeking legitimacy or of social responsibility is not at this point of major importance. Mayer Zald and Patricia Denton have called attention to the way in which the drift away from religious values in society ultimately resulted in the secularizing of such originally religious organizations as the YMCA.[19]

Dowling and Pfeffer further hypothesize that these adaptations will be more quickly and readily perceived in organizations whose activities are more visible than others and in those which are more dependent on political and social support.[20] Several studies already seem to bear this out and also to confirm the hypothesis that size increases the problems of legitimacy and produces more legitimizing behavior.[21] These authors also forecast optimistically that "measures of the congruence between organizational and societal values can be computed" and another avenue of empirical research can be opened up.[22]

Political theorists (for example, David E. Apter) have tended to model legitimacy using principles of legitimacy as components, and these models have been used to study political systems, modernizing societies, and politics generally. Apter's interesting study of modernization is built, to a large extent, upon a model of legitimacy using both moral and structural dimensions.[23] He draws attention to the correlation between certain prevailing principles of legitimacy (as, for example, liberty and Marxian potentiality) and certain forms of government.[24] Apter also conceptualizes legitimacy as a constraint (although he calls it a "condition") on the behavior of governments.

> If it is correct that both types of legitimacy [moral and structural] provide the limits within which governments must operate, then the effort to reinforce them, or at least prevent their decline, represents the ultimate political objective.[25]

Experience in some modernizing societies appears to support Apter's hypothesis.

Robert Dahl and Charles Lindblom (a political scientist and an economist), in their *Politics, Economics and Welfare,* identify legitimacy as an important factor in the effectiveness of the social mechanisms through which groups of individuals seek to attain their goals.[26] They devote one section of the book to the issues surrounding the legitimacy of managerial power and control. Without going into the substance of their argument, it can still be pointed out that they relied heavily on empirical evidence, including survey, opinion, and interview data, and commented in their preface that "most of our propositions are meant to be testable by a logical use of empirical evidence."[27] These authors view legitimacy, not as a constraint on organizational behavior, but as a positive and necessary element in the efficient functioning of social institutions. In their own words, "legitimacy facilitates the operation of organizations . . ."[28] Among the many interesting propositions set forth by them and begging for empirical testing are: (1) The main motivation behind the quest for some form of worker participation may be striving for control relationships that will legitimize the role of management.[29] (2) Codetermination is an effort to convey legitimacy to discretionary decisions that cannot be adequately influenced through the price system.[30] (3) The only workable solution for the long run is the professionalization of management, minority worker representation on the board of directors, and majority representation secured either by direct government appointment or by giving the government the power to veto directorships.[31] (4) What workers might get from codetermination to some extent they can already achieve, and are achieving, by collective bargaining.[32]

LEGITIMACY AND LEGALITY

Legitimacy is not coextensive with, nor is it defined by, legality. Law may be intended to confer legitimacy and may actually do so, but law does not necessarily confer legitimacy, and legitimacy does not always imply legality. Even a constitutional amendment did not legitimize Prohibition. In a democracy the law is likely to be more or less consistent with social values, goals, and norms, but not perfectly so. Witness much of the law in the realms of domestic relations and sexual practices. There are a number of reasons why we do not find an easy way out of our dilemma by equating or defining legitimacy in terms of legality. Generally speaking, the law confirms changes in social values and norms but does not create them. Thus the law is always somewhat out of phase with social change and always hurrying to catch up. Even when the law plays its teaching and shaping role in society (a role some legal philosophers deny exists), it is never in exact coincidence with social values, except, perhaps, for some short, indeterminate time. Sometimes it never even gets close, as with Prohibition. Much organizational behavior is wholly outside legal enactments or may operate at a level where the law does not penetrate, but is still confirmed as legitimate by social values. An example might be the practice, considered to be legitimate in most circles until quite recently, of chief executive officers' naming their own successors. Dahl and Lindblom underscore the complexity of legitimacy dynamics in this connection by pointing out that power or control may be legitimate to the wielder but illegitimate to a subordinate or legitimate to one subordinate and illegitimate to another.[33] Law normally does not encompass these variations. Two or more inconsistent social values may exist at the same time, and each may confer legitimacy on some kinds of organizational behavior. Activity which society legitimizes in the private sphere may not be legitimate in the public, or vice versa, while the law tends to be more consistent. On the other hand, Philip Selznick writes that "legitimacy carries the lively seed of legality."[34]

All this suggests that empirical research on legitimacy is much needed and is feasible, both on the level of the individual organization and on various levels of aggregation. One can hope that Boulding's paper and what has been said here will help to stimulate the kind of empirical exploration that will improve our understanding of the important social phenomenon of legitimacy and enhance our ability to deal with the growing problems in the relationship between economic institutions and social systems. Even social norms and values are capable of identification and examination, in a number of different ways, and are discernible in the writings and communications of a society at a given point in time.[35] Comparisons between these norms and values and the norms, values, and activities of constituent subsystems of the society such as the economic sector can reveal valuable information about legitimacy and its dynamics.

Whether the present status of the corporate system with regard to legitimacy is most accurately described as a crisis, a tension, or simply an issue is, perhaps, not important. The system of large corporations is not going to evaporate on Monday morning because society has withdrawn its approval. Experience has taught us that the sudden and dramatic demolition of social organizations and institutions is not likely to occur solely because their legitimacy has declined, disappeared, or been questioned. By whatever criteria they are legitimized, large enterprises are the essential structural mechanisms for the conduct of economic activity irrespective of social system or dominant ideology. Rather, the erosion takes place slowly and often almost imperceptibly, and if the organization or institution is aware of what is happening, it begins to resort to the legitimizing techniques discussed above, an effort which may or may not be successful. Where, however, the issue of legitimacy is related to, or simply contemporaneous with, a social crisis of broad proportions, the survival of the organization or institution may, even in the short run, be very much in doubt. It is said, for example, that the status of the large corporation reached this critical phase during the Great Depression, when several perceived weaknesses in legitimacy (many of them the same as are perceived today) were joined by a severe social crisis, the onset of which was attributed, at least in part, to the very organization whose legitimacy had been weakened and to the very factors which had contributed to the decline of legitimacy. Indeed, many of the legal developments of that era such as the establishment of a national collective bargaining system, the regulation of national securities markets, and reform of the banking system were, in part, efforts to rebuild the legitimacy of key sectors of the American economy.

We would like to raise a few last issues before passing you on to the Boulding essay. It probably has occurred to you, as it did to the participants in the workshop/conference, that the familiar concept of trust plays an important role in the broader concept of legitimacy. You may recall that in his paper Smelser suggested that when communal rationality becomes institutionalized, it provides trust and tolerance and thus builds a bridge to legitimacy. One might even be tempted to say that they were the same thing, but they are not. Boulding used the two terms almost interchangeably in some of his comments during the Conference.

> This is the absolutely essential element in any social organization: trust. It is the feeling of being betrayed that destroys legitimacy. If you trust somebody and they let you down, it is very hard to build back up again. You can get away with almost anything else, but the most dangerous thing, from the point of view of legitimacy, is simply telling lies; that is all it is, an ethic of veracity.

Several members of the conference took Boulding to task for what he also agreed was an overstatement, but almost everybody endorsed the view that trust is a vital component of legitimacy. One person suggested that to define legitimacy as the condition of being trusted by society was not really very far off the mark.

Legitimacy does seem to possess other components, as we have seen, and it might even be argued that some organizations or institutions, while not fully trusted, are nonetheless seen as legitimate. The CIA, perhaps? Furthermore, there is another dimension of legitimacy, to which Arthur Stinchcombe has called our attention, that is not much affected by confidence and trust. Where legitimacy is usually perceived as the appropriateness which the society or the people give to institutions, it may also be looked at as the support and approval that superior institutions give to inferior institutions or that people with monopolies of force at higher levels give to those at lower levels.[36] As Mayer Zald commented at the workshop/conference, the legitimacy of an institution may depend on "whether agglomerations of power will back it up."

Earl Cheit remarked on another aspect of the dynamics of legitimacy that seems not to be related primarily to trust. Large segments of the society, said Cheit, question the appropriateness of large organizations because they are thought to be out of control or such that society cannot get its hands on the levers of control. This view is closely related to the belief that large corporations are not accountable, that there is no place in the organizational structure of the large corporation where society can grasp the levers. To put it another way, how does one elicit a moral response from General Motors with respect to the size, efficiency, or safety of its products, or how does Tom Joad in *Grapes of Wrath* get a moral response from the bank that has ordered a bulldozer driver to knock down his cabin?

IDEOLOGY AND LEGITIMACY

A treatise needs to be written on legitimacy, and this is not it, but two final points should be made. First, one should note the relationship between legitimacy and ideology. Even if we use a considerably simplified conception of ideology, like "the link between action and fundamental belief,"[37] we must open up the list of social elements with which organizational behavior must be congruent in order to possess legitimacy to include ideology, as well as "norms, values, and goals," Congruence with prevailing ideology would seem to be as important as any other element in creating legitimacy. A special problem of the crisis of corporate legitimacy in the United States is that there is not any widely accepted alternative institution or ideology to legitimize it. We may not be entirely happy with the corporate mechanism as it exists, but a clearly preferable alternative has not surfaced. There are not very many people who believe that nationalization or socialization is a better solution, and what else is there?[38] We may be in a position where the legitimacy of the dominant economic institution is in doubt but where there is no readily apparent substitute institution or even an ideology that might suggest or legitimize one. Not very much is known or hypothesized about the social processes that might accommodate that dilemma.

Boulding raises but does not dispose of a basic philosophical issue which has unsettled mankind for generations.

> There seems to be a certain unstable equilibrium of legitimacy between those whose pull is towards freedom and those whose pull is toward justice...What we look for here indeed is a somewhat uneasy balance between the public and the private, between freedom and justice.

We are not going to dispose of it either, but we do call attention once more to the overwhelming importance of discussing the compelling issues of business only in connection with the great philosophical issues of our time. One cannot appropriately deal with legitimacy (or rationality or responsibility) without taking into account some basic social dilemmas, including the association that some segments of society see between freedom and anarchy and justice and tyranny. Boulding pursues the point further in his book, *The Organizational Revolution.*

The last issue to be raised here questions whether legitimacy is an all or nothing concept. Can an institution be a little bit illegitimate? The members of the workshop/conference did not do much with this puzzler. Certainly some aspects of an institution's activities can be legitimate while other aspects are illegitimate, or partially so, but the main problem here, it seems to us, is a conceptual and semantic one. Is illegitimacy correctly perceived as being the absence of legitimacy, as dark is perceived as the absence of light? Is the same message conveyed by *illegitimate* as by *lacks legitimacy*? Or are legitimacy and illegitimacy not necessarily on the same continuum, as black and white in one sense are not? In part this is just a semantic game. Our interest is in whether an organization or institution possesses legitimacy, not in whether it is illegitimate. Certainly one can speak of "strong or weak bases of legitimacy" in society, "threats to legitimacy" or the "decline of legitimacy" without having to invoke the concept of illegitimacy. Perhaps, further exploration of this issue should be left for another time and place. It is enough that attention is called to a potential semantic or conceptual trap.

We come now to Kenneth Boulding's paper, "The Legitimacy of the Business Institution." It does not contain all that Boulding has had to say on the subject. The reader should, if a wider exposure to Boulding's views on legitimacy is desired, look at some òf the references provided in the paper itself or in the bibliography provided by the editors. The paper is certainly not the last word on legitimacy. It is not even Boulding's last word. As he remarked at the workshop/conference, he could rewrite it somewhat differently every month for a year and still not entirely crystal-lize his thoughts on the topic. A cut must be taken somewhere, however, and this paper represents that cut. This introduction gives some rather substantial clues as to issues that are not settled (which is most of them) and to some of the major areas of potentially rewarding research. Bould-ing's paper should do the rest of what is necessary to fill in the legitimacy leg of the "rationality, legitimacy, responsibility" triangle, and to bridge the gap to the next topic: responsibility. "The issue of legitimacy in economic organizations is closely involved with good corporate citizen-ship or responsible professional management."[39]

NOTES

1. Alvin W. Gouldner, *The Coming Crisis of Western Sociology* (New York: Basic Books, 1970), p. 424.
2. See Bibliography.
3. John Dowling and Jeffrey Pfeffer, "Organizational Legitimacy: Social Values and Organizational Behavior," *Pacific Sociological Review,* vol. 18, No. 1 (January, 1975), pp. 122-136.

4. Talcott Parsons, *Structure and Process in Modern Societies,* (Glencoe, Ill.: Free Press, 1960), p. 175.

5. Shirley Terreberry, "The Evolution of Organizational Environments," *Administrative Science Quarterly,* vol. 12 (March, 1968), pp. 590–613, at 608.

6. David E. Apter, *The Politics of Modernization* (Chicago: University of Chicago Press, 1965), esp. chap. 1.

7. Theodore Levitt, *The Third Sector* (New York: AMACOM, 1973), p. 2.

8. See, for example, Gerald F. Cavanaugh, *American Business Values in Transition* (Englewood Cliffs, N. J.: Prentice-Hall, 1976), pp. 177–187; and Earl F. Cheit, "The New Place of Business," in *The Business Establishment* (New York: John Wiley & Sons, 1964), pp. 175-176.

9. From the transcript of the workshop/conference discussion.

10. A. A. Berle, Jr., *Economic Power and the Free Society* (New York: The Fund for the Republic, 1957), p. 16.

11. Max Weber, *The Sociology of Religion,* trans. Ephraim Fischof (Boston: Beacon Press, 1964), p. 107.

12. Robert A. Dahl and Charles E. Lindblom, *Politics, Economics and Welfare* (New York: Harper & Brothers, 1953), p. 114 fn.

13. Dowling and Pfeffer, op. cit., p. 131.

14. See note 4.

15. J. W. Maurer, *Readings in Organization Theory: Open-System Approaches* (New York: Random House, 1971), p. 361.

16. See, for example, H. Igor Ansoff, "Managing Strategic Surprise by Response to Weak Signals," *California Management Review,* Winter, 1975, pp. 21–33.

17. For examples in the use of the political process, see Edwin M. Epstein, *The Corporation in American Politics* (Englewood Cliffs, N. J.: Prentice Hall, Inc., 1969).

18. Dowling and Pfeffer, op. cit., p. 131.

19. Mayer Zald and Patricia Denton, "From Evangelism to General Service: The Transformation of the YMCA," *Administrative Science Quarterly,* vol. 8 (September, 1964), pp. 214-234.

20. Dowling and Pfeffer, op. cit., p. 133.

21. *Ibid.*

22. *Ibid.,* p. 134. Charles Perrow is not as sanguine; see note 38 infra, p. 100.

23. Apter, op. cit., chap. 1.

24. *Ibid.*

25. *Ibid.,* p. 237.

26. Apter, op. cit., fn. 11.

27. *Ibid.,* p. xxi.

28. *Ibid.,* p. 115.

29. *Ibid.,* p. 480.

30. *Ibid.,* p. 483.

31. *Ibid.*

32. *Ibid.*

33. *Ibid.,* p. 115.

34. Philip Selznick, *Law, Society and Industrial Justice* (New York: Russell Sage Foundation, 1969), p. 30.

35. Dowling and Pfeffer, op. cit., pp. 124–125.

36. Arthur L. Stinchcombe, *Constructing Social Theories* (New York: Harcourt, Brace & World, 1968), pp. 162-163.

37. Apter, op. cit., p. 314.

38. See comments by Boulding on the legitimacy of socialism.
39. Charles Perrow, *Organizational Analysis: A Sociological View* (Belmont, Calif.: Wadsworth Publishing Co., 1970), p. 100.

KENNETH E. BOULDING

The Legitimacy of the Business Institution

Human society has been compared to a great pond. In a pond within a certain geographical framework enclosed by the shores and the bottom there coexists a great variety of populations of living, and indeed, of nonliving species of all kinds. Beginning with water molecules, dissolved salts, oxygen, carbon dioxide, going on to viruses, bacteria, one-celled organisims, plants, amphibians, fish, and so on. A pond often exhibits at least a temporary equilibrium in which the size of each population may take place through migration, as when the water in the pond captures a molecule from the atmosphere or when an animal migrates into the pond, or by disassociation, or synthesis, as when methane forms from rotting vegetation, or in the case of living organisms, by birth. Departures from the population take place through chemical reactions, through out-migration, or through deaths. If the entrances into and the departures from any given population at any given period are equal, then the size of the population is constant. The entrances and departures depend on the size of all the other populations. This gives us a set of equations which may be capable of an equilibrium solution. If, for all populations, entrances and departures are equal so that all the populations are constant over time, we have an ecological equilibrium. Ecological equilibria are always temporary because irreversible changes are constantly taking place. In a strict sense equilibrium is unknown in the real world, though temporary equilibria are quite meaningful. If, for instance, we take 25 percent of a certain variety of fish out of a pond, it will not be very long before the population is back to where it was before, assuming that the equilibrium itself has not been disturbed by this operation.

Human society, likewise, exhibits these ecological equilibria of social species. Just as a pond contains populations of various kinds of living species as well as chemical species, so human society consists of populations of corner groceries, gas stations, automobile manufacturers, counties, states, Seventh Day Baptists churches, families, Rotary Clubs, units of the League of Women Voters, and so on. Each of these populations consists of a number of identifiable elements or individuals, each of which conforms to a common definition. Each population is subject to additions through entrance with the formation of new individuals of the species and is subject to subtractions or departures as these individuals disintegrate and disappear. We can identify married couples, for instance, as a social species, of which a representative is born every time there is a marriage and dies every time one of the partners dies or the marriage is dissolved. If there are more marriages than dissolutions in any period, the number of married couples will be increased by precisely that excess; if there are more dissolutions than marriages, their number will decline.

The addition to and subtraction from any population of a social species likewise depends on its total environment, that is, on all other populations. Ecological equilibria are perhaps less common in social systems than they are in biological systems, but something approximating them is by no means unknown, at least within a certain range of variation. There are times when certain species exhibit population growth over considerable periods. If we look at automobiles, for instance, we find that additions exceeded subtractions over a period of seventy or eighty years, and the population of automobiles, therefore, has been almost continuously increasing. It will not increase indefinitely, however, and there must come a time at which the population of automobiles will stabilize and the number of new automobiles produced each year will approximately equal the number that are scrapped. We see the same phenomenon in nation-states. We have had a very large increase in the population of nation-states in the last thirty years. This increase, again, will not go on indefinitely. Sometimes species decline to extinction or virtual extinction like sedan chairs, Albigensians, or alchemists. Sometimes they decline to a low-level equilibrium. Equilibrium here, however, always represents a temporary tendency, never an absolute.

What, one may ask, has all this got to do with business? Business firms may be identified as one social species, or perhaps it would be more accurate to say a genus of social species, and their survival depends very much on the dynamics of the interaction of the populations of all other social species. The business firm, moreover, is not a universal species: it exists in some social systems and not in others, just as fish exist in some ponds but not in others. There is a little problem here of the definition of the species, as there is indeed in the case of many social species. Biological populations are fairly sharply marked off from each other, at least by the capacity for interbreeding. The social ecosystem is multisexual: the automobile, for instance, is produced by the interaction of several hundred different social species and there are often no simple rules and definitions to separate one population from another. Individual organizations frequently exist which are hard to classify. Is, for instance, the Tennessee Valley Authority or AMTRAK or COMSAT a "business," or is it something else? The general field is by no means homogeneous, however, and there are well-defined clusters of individuals which can be defined as a species or population, even if the definition sometimes has to be a little arbitrary. Businesses form such a cluster.

We can define a business for the moment as any organization that is characterized by the following distinctive features which gradually narrow down the field:

1. It is a social organization, that is, a structure of fairly well-defined roles, occupied by persons, with communications between them, which exhibits inputs and outputs of persons, communications, and artifacts of commodities.

2. It obtains its inputs and disposes of its outputs primarily by exchange. In a very large proportion of cases one of the objects exchanged is money, that is, it buys its inputs and it sells its outputs. This distinguishes it from organizations like governments, which rely on one-way transfers—for instance, in taxes—to obtain inputs of money, or philanthopic foundations, which rely on one-way transfers in grants for their outflow of money. The business, then, is an institution which exists primarily in a market environment. It also has internal transformation and production operations by which its inputs are transformed, either in time and place or through chemical and physical rearrangements. A manufacturer transforms raw materials and labor into a product, wholesalers and retailers transport commodities through time and space, and so on.

3. Businesses are private, in the sense that the capital stock with which they operate is for the most part privately owned. There are some difficult cases here like Lockheed and the defense-related businesses, but every definition is a boundary with considerable areas of no-man's-land in it.

4. Businesses make profits, which may be defined as the difference between the money value of outputs and the money value of inputs, the first being "revenue" and the second "cost." The survival of a business is very closely related to its ability to maintain an adequate level of profits. If it makes losses, that is, negative profits, for very long, its net worth will disappear and it may be forced into bankruptcy or be absorbed by another business. Government institutions, because of their ability to obtain grants through taxation, are not so much subject to this requirement.

5. Businesses interact with capital markets in the sense that they may borrow, sell stocks, and so on. They have balance sheets showing their assets, liabilities, and net worth.

Anything which conforms to these five characteristics has a fair chance to be recognized as a business.

Within the general genus of business organizations a considerable number of species may be distinguished according to various different criteria. There is, for instance, the distinction between corporations and unincorporated business. A subspecies of the corporations is the cooperative, in which the residual ownership rests with the members who are either providers of input to the business in the case of producers' cooperatives, or takers of output in the case of consumers' cooperatives. This is a small but not insignificant population. In the case of the regular corporation the net worth is owned by the stockholders and in unincorporated businesses by individuals or partners. Unincorporated businesses, and indeed some corporations, shade off into the professions—lawyers, and the like—the operations of which would be businesses from the point of the above definition but for some purposes are regarded as sociologically distinct. There are also what the Conference Board calls "intersects,"[1] that is, organizations which are partly private and partly public, partly in the market environment and partly in a "grants environment," so that it is hard to tell whether they are businesses or government organizations. In socialist countries the trusts exhibit many of the characteristics of businesses in that they buy and sell labor and commodities and exist in a mostly market environment. They differ, however, in the fact that they receive their capital from the state and do not participate in a capital market to any great extent and are not so dependent on a profit for their survival.

Having defined business as a social species, the next question is: what are its survival functions? That is, what are the factors in the total environment which are relevant to the probability of survival either of an individual business or of business as a social species? An important principle is that survival depends both on the market and on the non-market environments. A business which makes losses for a sufficient period of time, that is, which is purchasing inputs and selling outputs in markets where the value of the outputs does not exceed the value of the inputs, is on the road to disappearance. At any one time, of course, some businesses will be making losses and will be on the road to "death"; others will be making profits and will be growing.

Profits above a certain level have a tendency to promote growth in the size of the business, partly because they may not all be distributed to the owners and hence may lead to a continuing increase in net worth, or because a profitable business is in a favorable position in the capital market and can easily sell bonds, obtain bank loans, or issue more stock. There are limits, however, on the growth of any particular business, depending on the nature of its internal production function and the nature of its environment. For every type of organization we can postulate an optimum size and, if it grows beyond this, a business will become less profitable. If the growth is very rapid so that there is a large "overshoot," the results could even be catastrophic. What the optimum size is, of course, varies enormously from industry to industry—it is relatively small in agriculture and very large in automobile manufacturing.

A failure of profits in the individual business is unlikely to threaten the survival of the business institution, that is, the whole species of businesses, as long as the total amount of profits is adequate. Some businesses may then be making losses and disappearing, but others will be making profits and growing and others will be created, so that although there will be a turnover as in any population, there is no reason to fear that the species will decline to extinction. If, however, the total of profits disappears as it did in 1932 and 1933 in the United States, when the aggregate of corporate profits was negative, then very large numbers, indeed a majority of firms, will be making losses and the whole business institution will be threatened. This, however, is a very rare situation. In the last thirty years, for instance, the proportion of national income going to profits has been relatively stable. Nevertheless, one has to reckon with the possibility of conditions like those of 1932 and 1933.

Economists are still in considerable disagreement about the determinants of total profits. There is agreement that price deflation (as in 1929–1932) has a marked effect in creating a shift out of profits into other forms of income, especially interest, simply because profits are made by buying something at one time and selling it (or something into which it has been transformed) at a later time. If in the interval all prices have fallen, the chances of making a profit are much less and the total of profits will be diminished. Figure 1, showing the distribution of income in the United States by distributive shares in the last forty-four years, is very instructive in this regard. It will be seen that in the Great Depression profits were squeezed out by the rise in interest and in wages or labor income, but that since then they have been remarkably stable. It is a little surprising that the long inflation has not produced a larger proportion of national income going into profits.

As we look forward into the next few decades, the survival of the business institution would seem to depend much more on its nonmarket environment than on its market environment. Even though one cannot be absolutely certain, the skills of managing the economy are so much greater today than they were in 1929 that it seems a little improbable that we would have a repetition of the catastrophic experience of the Great Depression. A sharp decline in gross private domestic investment, of course, would raise very severe problems both for full employment and for the maintenance of profits, but in the light of the very large investments which seem likely to be necessary in the development of alternative sources of energy to fossil fuels, it seems that decline in domestic investment is unlikely. It may be indeed that we will need to increase the

FIGURE 1. National income by type of income, U.S.A., 1929-1973.

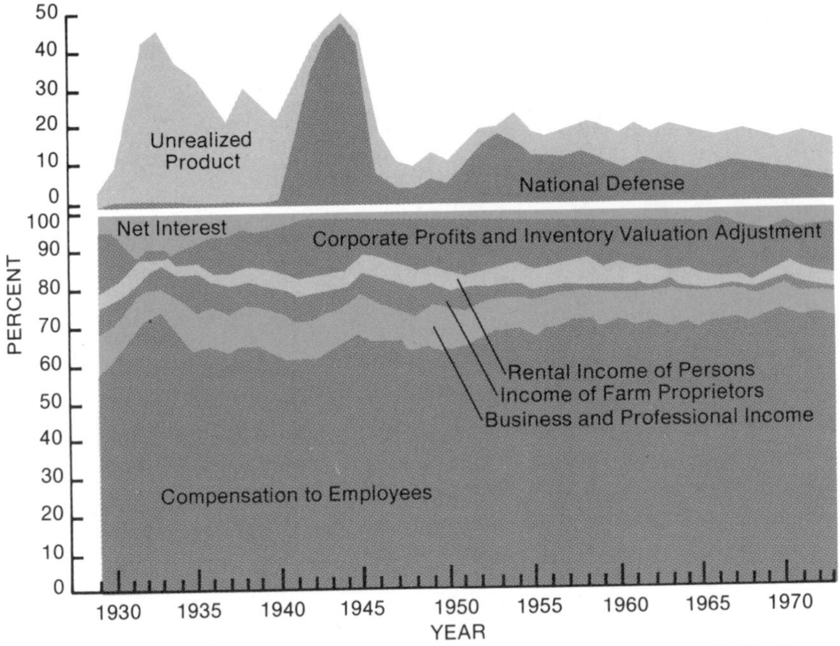

Source: *Economic Report of the President,* February 1974 (Washington, D.C.: Government Printing Office, 1974).

proportion of national income going into domestic investment to offset the declining availability of fuels and materials. If this is the case, then, if we are to prevent a disorganizing inflation, it may well be that we will have to encourage personal saving to a far greater extent than we have done in the past or else substitute public saving of some kind for it. Assuming, therefore, that the market economy will continue to function, though probably with less spectacular success than it has in the last thirty years, the survival of the business institution will depend much more on its ability to retain legitimacy, which is one of the most crucial characteristics of its nonmarket environment, than it will upon any internal dynamics of the market environment itself.

The nonmarket environment of business consists of a number of sectors. There is the legal environment, that is, the laws, regulations, and possible sanctions under which it operates. There is the political environment, which constantly creates new laws and new sanctions, and also is a very powerful part of the "grants economy" in providing taxes, subsidies, and so on. Then there is what might be called the cultural environment, which consists of the values and attitudes of the general population as well as those of business leaders, and the set of customs, manners, modes of behavior, and so on that cluster around these values. The cultural, political, and legal environments all interact. Cultural changes can have a profound effect on political action and on the legal structure: witness the abolition of slavery, Prohibition, antitrust legislation, and so on. The political and legal structure also feeds back on the culture as we see it in such things as antidiscrimination legislation, affirmative action, and so on, which sometimes produces the values which support it but sometimes, as in the case of Prohibition, has quite the reverse impact. These interactions are extremely difficult to predict. The law sometimes lags behind the culture, sometimes runs ahead of it, and sometimes backfires, and it is very hard to say which pattern in any particular case will happen.

I have distinguished two principal nonmarket organizers of society in addition to exchange which I have called the "threat system" and the "integrative system."[2] The threat system involves sanctions, such as the penalties of the law (most of us pay the amount of taxes we do only because we would get into more trouble than it would be worth if we did not). The integrative system relates to such matters as perceptions of status, identity, legitimacy, loyalty, community, and so on. In an exchange relationship a person's behavior is affected primarily by his or her perception of the terms of trade, that is, what will be got per unit of what is given. In the threat system behavior is likewise determined by what might be called the negative terms of trade: How many bads will I suffer if I do not conform to the threatener's request? In the integrative system, on the other hand, behavior is determined by perceptions of identity, community, and legitimacy, that is, of "what I am and what you are."

I have argued that in the long run the integrative system tends to dominate the other two even though the interrelations among them are complex. Exchange power and threat power sometimes create integrative power and sometimes do not. A loss of legitimacy is particularly destructive to any institution, and in social systems legitimacy is perhaps the major element in the survival function. Both threat power and exchange power (wealth) are effective only if they are widely regarded as legitimate. In a certain sense power is always exercised by the frequently implicit and tacit consent of those over whom it is exercised, and if this integrative power is lost the other forms of power simply disintegrate. The war in Vietnam is a superb example of this, where the United States with enormous threat power and exchange power was quite helpless in the face of its fundamental illegitimacy. Legitimacy, furthermore, can sometimes disintegrate very quickly, so that it is often very precarious to project the legitimacies of today into tomorrow.

It is worth looking at all the various component characteristics of the business institution to see where their legitimacy may be threatened. I am not sure that the legitimacy of the different parts are additive; it may be that there is a certain threshold of illegitimacy for any one component beyond which the whole system becomes illegitimate, but that is a very difficult question of fact.

We should look first, then, at the legitimacy of social organizations themselves, particularly of large organizations. Insofar as they increase human efficiency and have positive payoffs organizations tend to be legitimate. On the other hand, there are sources of delegitimation in the feeling of alienation which individuals may suffer when they find themselves caught in the hierarchical machinery of large organizations. Hierarchy, of course, has peculiar pathologies of its own. It is these which give rise to diseconomies of scale and the existence of an optimum size of any particular form of organization. Even when the organization is efficient in terms of simple accounting and in the transformation of money values from inputs into outputs, there may be important costs of revenues which do not get into the accounting system or which are not part of the agenda of the decision makers. Under these circumstances legitimacy may be eroded by the presence of these unmeasurable features.

This is probably why paternalism is rarely stable in business and why there has been a very noticeable shift from informal reciprocal arrangements into collective bargaining and formal industrial jurisprudence in the shape of grievance procedure and the like. The significance of collective bargaining is probably not so much that it is collective but that it is bargaining. It is collective simply because this is the only way to economize bargaining. It would be almost intolerably costly to write an individual contract for every employee, yet without contracts the employer-employee relationship is subject to inevitable failures in mutual communication and to slow erosion of legitimacy. Collective bargaining itself, incidentally, has its own pathologies, particularly when the bargaining relates to terms of trade—for instance, to wages—for here the complexity of the system is such that the bargain is really a fraud in the sense that the parties to the bargain are not present. Increases in money wages rarely result in any transfer from profits to wages, so that they tend to be paid by the general public. The results of this, however, are very far from apparent and it may take a while yet before this perception begins to erode the legitimacy of collective bargaining as we now know it.

The problem of the legitimacy of organization as such, especially large-scale organization, is not peculiar to businesses. It applies to any organization and it may be offset by the legitimacy of other elements in the institution. The Protestant Reformation represented in some degree alienation from the "big church." Nationalist and separatist movements represent alienation from the "big state." Oddly enough, alienation from "big business" does not seem very effective, otherwise we would have expected the breakup feature of the antitrust laws to continue far beyond 1911. There is a little puzzle here that would be well worth investigating.

The legitimacy or otherwise of exchange and of the market as a social institution is a problem which has been much neglected by economists but which nevertheless is extremely important. Exchange, at least in a formal contractual sense, is a relatively late development in human societies. Early societies tend to be integrative, familistic, operating with grants or informal reciprocity internally and through threats in relation with external societies. The phenomenon of "silent trade" recorded by Herodotus is at least a symbol of the difficulty in legitimating trade with the enemy. There has in human history been a movement from "status to contract," as Sir Henry Maine observed, but this has been by no means an easy or swift transition. In Europe trade was given a pretty low status by the medieval Church, and the capital markets, as reflected in the attitude to usury, an even lower status. Both poets and the aristocracy have tended to despise the "money grubbing" aspects of commercial life. Even Adam Smith, who was supposed to be the prophet of capitalism, took a dim view of merchants and manufacturers and tended to idealize farmers and country gentlemen.[3]

Karl Marx had a positive hatred of exchange as an institution, which pervades all his work. He had the typical intellectual aristocratic attitude toward those who conduct the ordinary business of life. His hatred of exchange as such, and the calculatingness that it seems to involve, probably accounts as much for his hatred of capitalism, which he saw very clearly as a system in which exchange is the dominant human relationship, as do his views on exploitation and on the sole creativity of labor. Schumpeter in his great book on *Capialism, Socialism and Democracy* makes the same point; although Schumpeter was essentially favorable to capitalism as a creator of variety, freedom, and development, he did not think it had much chance of surviving because it could not sustain the integrative structure necessary for a society based on exchange. He thought that capitalism could survive only as long as the integrative structure derived from earlier societies persisted, but that capitalism with its rationality and dynamism undermined these feudal survivals and so laid the seeds of its own destruction. Veblen idealized engineers, largely because they see exchange considerations just as a limitation on their technical abilities, and he despised the businessman who imposed these limitations in the interest of profit.[4] Whereas Adam Smith at least saw exchange as a producer of the division of labor, and hence of riches and widespread enjoyment of the conveniences of life, Veblen essentially saw it as a technological constricter preventing the engineers from building all the beautiful roads, bridges, and machines that they would like to.

This integrative weakness of exchange may have a number of psychological sources. The act of exchange itself is abstract and involves little beyond common courtesy in terms of human relationships. It can even be mechanized, as from a vending machine. Complex and intimate human relationships have almost universally been regarded as unsuited to exchange, witness the low status given in almost every society to prostitution, in spite of its almost universal popularity. Exchange, furthermore, is a constant, undramatic reminder of the reality of scarcity as it is expressed through the price system. Exchange as expressed through the price structure is a rationing device, indeed a very superior one, which can take care of individual differences far better than any system of authoritative allocation. Nevertheless, it is seen constantly as a limitation and, for those who haven't learned economics, often as a rather arbitrary limitation. I remember a history teacher of mine in high school saying: "Can't we all just go take what we want from the shops without all this fuss of paying for it?" in blissful ignorance of economics!

If there are forces making for the delegitimation of exchange, there are perhaps even stronger forces making for the delegitimation of profits. Even labor income may be suspect in the enthusiasms of high ethics—"To give and not to count the cost, to labor and ask for no reward," a classic statement by Saint Ignatius Loyola of the ethic of spontaneous love. If even labor income is suspect, then how much more is profit, which is derived not from human activity as such but from the mere passive ownership of capital. I recall a story told me by my grandfather about how as a young man he got into an argument with a local squire in rural Devonshire and asked him what he had done to deserve the income from his broad acres, whereupon the squire drew himself up and said: "My ancestors fought for it," whereupon my grandfather squared off and said: "I'll fight you for it now." Needless to say the offer was not taken up. Even Adam Smith makes slightly sardonic remarks about people who love to reap where they have not sowed.

The trouble is that the case against profit is a simple one and the case for it is a complex one, so that it is not surprising that there is a constant erosion of the legitimacy of profit in the form of Marxist and generally left-wing criticism. Furthermore, the traditional defense of profits by economists is not perhaps the best that could be made. This traditional defense, which dates at least from Nassau Senior,[5] is that profit is the reward of abstinence, waiting, or lacking, to use different words that economists have given the function, which is necessary in society if capital is to be accumulated. Accumulation always means producing more than is consumed, and why should anybody do this, it is argued, unless there is a reward for this peculiar kind of function or activity?

It is argued, furthermore, that the rate of profit, or the closely related rate of interest, which is the rate of growth of the value of capital in the absence of any withdrawals or consumption of it, is a necessary parameter in the making of rational decisions involving processes of production of different time spans. The argument that there is a social function which might be called "waiting," and that this should be accompanied by a rate of time discounting so that present values are less than future values, is a very cogent one. Nevertheless, by itself it is not a sufficient defense of private capital and capitalism simply because alternative social institutions in government might be devised to perform the same functions. In the socialist countries the state through its tax system and allocation system performs the function of waiting, indeed often does too much of it and unnecessarily sacrifices the present generation for the future. There is also no reason why socialist states cannot include a rate of profit or interest or time discounting in their evaluations of the present value of various projects.

The real case for profit is perhaps that this is the price that we have to pay for decentralized decision making, for the only alternatives to a profit system would seem to be the highly centralized decision making of the centrally planned economy. The case for decentralized as against centralized decision making is essentially an ecological one; all decision-making processes have a certain probability of bad decisions and even catastrophic decisions. When decision making is centralized, if anything goes wrong then everything goes wrong; if it is decentralized, a catastrophic decision here or there will only affect part of the system. There is also a general argument that centralized planning inevitably involves a very large scale of organization and that this will exhibit strong diseconomies of hierarchy and lack of communication.

The case for decentralized decision making is a very strong one and it is surprising that it is not more used. Closely connected with the problem of the legitimacy of profit is the legitimacy of private ownership, or private property, which is a necessary concomitant to private profit. These are indeed part of a single system of organization. Nevertheless, they may have their own sources of legitimacy or illegitimacy. There is a curious tension here between privateness and publicness reflected in the fact that both of these are desired and have legitimacy of their own, and yet in a certain sense they are opposites. Private property gives liberty to the owner over the claims of the community. It defines an area of both freedom and responsibility within which the property owner is sovereign. It makes every person a king of his own possessions. It furthermore allocates responsibility in a way that public property rarely does. There is indeed a magic in property, especially small property and personal property, which leads to its conservation and improvement. Public property is always liable to the "tragedy of the commons," in which the pursuit of private interest will lead to public property being overused and even destroyed. The contrast even in socialist countries between carefully tended private property and the neglected and weed-grown collective fields is a mute testimony to this principle.

Nevertheless, pure individualism is not enough. There are public goods which cannot be allocated to private property. There must, therefore, be a community and a public institution to provide for these. There seems to be a certain unstable equilibrium of legitimacy between those whose pull is towards freedom and those whose pull is towards justice. I recall a debate I had with Reinhold Niebuhr about this many years ago, in which I pointed out that the issue between us was that he was afraid of freedom, seeing always behind it the specter of anarchy, whereas I was afraid of justice, seeing always behind it the specter of tyranny.[6] What we look for is a somewhat uneasy balance between the public and the private, between freedom and justice. It is not surprising if sometimes this balance swings against privateness.

I would not go all the way with Schumpeter in supposing that capitalism is doomed by its very success. The experience of the twentieth century with socialism in the form of centrally planned economies, with their dull, rather tyrannical societies, certainly suggests that the alternative to the business institution, at least in the present stage of world history, is disagreeable enough that the erosion of the legitimacy of the business institution, which we have seen in the twentieth century, might be halted and even reversed. There is no socialism except what we must call socialist nationalism, as we cannot after Hitler called it national socialism, that is, centrally planned economies based on the absorption of all property short of minor personal property into the hands of a national state and the consequent running of the economy as a single firm. The socialist state indeed is a one-firm state. If General Motors absorbed the whole American economy, we would have something very much like a centrally planned economy. Even the Department of Defense within the American economy is a centrally planned economy, a socialist quasi-state, larger than any socialist state but the two largest.

The legitimacy of socialism, therefore, is much more closely bound up with the legitimacy of the national state than is the legitimacy of capitalism. The legitimacy of the national state, however, though it seems almost unassailable at the moment, may be less secure than it seems. It is derived partly from the fact that the national state is an expression of community and a provider of public goods, but also it is derived from what I have called the "sacrifice trap," in which the national state imposes enormous sacrifices on its citizens.[7] If these get to be too large, its whole legitimacy could collapse almost over night. Under these circumstances, capitalist society would be much less vulnerable to a sudden collapse of legitimacy than would socialist societies.

Nevertheless, the continued legitimacy of the business institution is by no means absolutely certain. Perhaps it depends more than anything on two factors: First, on the ability of the market-oriented societies to develop a mixture of institutions both public and private that permits the benefits of decentralization, together with the advantages of a well-functioning relative price system, in the allocation of resources, but which also provides for the provision of public goods; and, second, on the development of a sense of community, especially a sense of world community which is now so necessary, even to the point of regarding the distribution of income itself as in part a public good to be provided through the public grants economy.

I began with the metaphor of society as a great pond, deliberately choosing a somewhat neutral illustration. The opponents of capitalism describe it as a jungle. Perhaps what we are all really looking for is a garden. A garden is still an ecosystem, its individual life processes are highly decentralized, and the gardener does not interfere with the processes by which a seed becomes a plant. Nevertheless, there is a gardener and as a result ⋅of his or her activity the mix of different populations in the ecosystem is "distorted" in favor of human values. I recall once walking in the incredible luxuriance and chaos of a Brazilian jungle with Lionel Robbins and remarking as we looked around that this proved anarchy was possible, whereupon Robbins came back quickly with the remark that it did not prove that it was desirable! A pure, raw, unregulated capitalism could indeed be an anarchic jungle. However, provided there is an adequate sense of community and public institutions to express it, it can be a garden, far more responsive to the values of those who live there than one would find in a rigidly planned collective farm of the socialist state.

APPENDIX: THE LEGITIMACY OF INTERNATIONAL BUSINESS

The legitimacy of international business presents some rather special problems. They cannot be discussed fully here but should be mentioned. The rise of the international business corporation is one of the more striking social changes of the past one hundred years, even more of the past fifty years, and the whole question of the role and legitimacy of these corporations in the world economy is under considerable discussion.[8] International corporations have been very successful in creating economic organizations around the world. They certainly seem richer and more powerful than most of the small national states and may be the forerunners of a world economic order. Nevertheless, they are under severe attack and their legitimacy is by no means unquestioned. They are also highly vulnerable simply because they do not operate under any system of world government. If one thinks of the articles of incorporation as a kind of legitimating constitution, the corporation does not really derive much legitimacy from the State of Delaware or from Luxembourg, or wherever they may be incorporated. They are engaged in constant negotiations with the large number of national states within which they operate, and they are constantly vulnerable to expropriations or to denial of the right to operate. I have suggested that the international corporations should press for United Nations charters, for small and weak as the United Nations is, it is the one symbol of world legitimacy, and if some price had to be paid for this in the shape of United Nations regulation it might be well worth it. Oddly enough, the relations between the international corporations and the socialist countries seem to be constantly improving. The really vulnerable area is the poor countries and the tropics in which they operate and which sometimes they tend to dominate simply by mere size and competence. What will happen to the multinational corporations over the next fifty years I would hardly venture to prophesy. One thing is certain—they should not take their legitimacy for granted, for legitimacy that is taken for granted is often suddenly and surprisingly withdrawn.

NOTES

1. Kenneth E. Boulding, "Intersects: The Peculiar Organizations," in *Challenge to Leadership: Managing in a Changing World* (New York: Free Press, for The Conference Board, 1973), pp. 179-201.

2. Kenneth E. Boulding, "The Relations of Economic, Political and Social Systems," *Social and Economic Studies,* vol. 11, No. 4 (December, 1962), pp. 351-362.

3. "The mean rapacity, the monopolizing spirit of merchants and manufacturers, who neither are, nor ought to be, the rulers of mankind, though it cannot perhaps be corrected, may very easily be prevented from disturbing the tranquility of anybody but themselves." *The Wealth of Nations* (New York: Modern Library, 1937), p. 460.

"Country gentlemen and farmers are, to their great honour, of all people the least subject to the wretched spirit of monopoly." *The Wealth of Nations,* (New York: Modern Library, 1937), p. 428.

4. Thorstein Veblen, *The Engineers and the Price System* (New York: Viking Press, 1933).

5. Nassau Senior, *An Outline of the Science of Political Economy* (London: G. Allen & Unwin, 1938).

6. Kenneth E. Boulding, *The Organizational Revolution: A Study in the Ethics of Economic Organization* (New York: Harper & Brothers, 1953), p. 254.

7. Kenneth E. Boulding, *The Economy of Love and Fear: A Preface to Grants Economics* (Belmont, Calif.: Wadsworth Publishing Co., 1973).

8. See especially Richard J. Barnet and Ronald E. Muller, *Global Reach: The Power of the Multinational Corporation* (New York: Simon & Schuster, 1974).

PART 3

Responsibility

Responsibility, the third and final side of the equilateral triangle symbolic of the search for new directions in business and society, must be viewed in the perspective of the other two sides: rationality and legitimacy. For responsibility constitutes a logical link between these two concepts, complementing each and also contributing its own unique dimension to complete and to provide coherence to the business-society relationship. On the one hand, responsibility in a democratic society is integral to the very notion of legitimacy: in order for social institutions to be legitimate they must be responsible to persons or collective interests that are outside of them and affected by them. On the other hand, fundamental to determining the rationality of the behavior of social actors, be they individuals or organizations, is the compatibility between the ends or goals of the actor and the means by which the actor seeks to obtain its objectives. Responsibility is an essential factor in determining both means and ends. Put another way, intrinsic to the idea of rationality, of weighing and selecting among alternatives, is the notion of responsibility. In order for rational decision making to occur, decision makers must take into account the implication of their decisions and be prepared to have their decisions evaluated in accordance with criteria external to themselves. In the context of analyzing the relationship between business and society, responsibility is then both a perspective intimately linked with legitimacy and a process closely associated with rationality.

Few topics have stimulated greater debate and less agreement among analysts of business institutions in the United States than that of the responsibilities of these organizations and their managers to other sectors of American society. Indeed, it is not exaggerating when we suggest that in the United States, in a manner which is virtually unique among Western industrial societies, the subject of social responsibility has been the conceptual sun around which much of the philosophical discussion concerning the business and society relationship has revolved for almost a century.[1]

Although what has been designated the "gospel of social responsibility," the ideological emphasis within the business community itself upon objectives and obligations beyond the narrow, profit-maximizing goals posited for the firm by microeconomic theory, can be traced to the late 1950s and early 1960s, a deeper, more fundamental conception of business responsibility dates back to the late nineteenth century when the American industrial economy was assuming its modern form.[2] In the first volume of the *American Journal of Sociology* published in 1895, Albion W. Small, one of the leading figures in early American sociology, threw down a symbolic gauntlet to the Age of Enterprise when he wrote that "not merely public office but private business is a public trust."[3] Few of his contemporaries, particularly among businesspeople, were prepared to accept such an all-encompassing and challenging notion of business responsibility. Bred as they were on the doctrines of laissez-faire capitalism, that curious admixture of classical economics, neo-Calvinism, social Darwinism, Lockian political philosophy, and a large component of antistatism, most were not going to adapt easily or quickly to the new concepts of business and society.[4] However, Small was reflecting the deep-seated concern that the emergence of large corporations had stimulated in certain parts of the American public. This concern included both a fear of the rapidly spreading economic, political, and social power of large industrial organizations and a felt need either to render them formally accountable to the public or to evolve new concepts of responsibility based on a redefinition of the relationship between these organizations and other sectors of society.[5]

RESPONSIBILITY AND THE LEGAL PROCESS

The legal process has served as the primary means by which the public has sought to impose standards of responsibility and to render business accountable for its actions. During the past ninety years, but particularly since the 1930s, federal and state legislation and judicial decisions have dramatically redefined the obligations of business to employees, competitors, customers, minority groups and women, the physical environment, various levels of government, and the general public. Few observers would contend that this legal deluge has resolved all the areas of potential conflict between business and society or made business truly accountable or responsive to the public. Today there is widespread recognition (ironically, most fully developed among lawyers) that the legal process, while essential, cannot be a sufficient condition either in defining the societal role of business institutions or in making them truly accountable to the public. Professor Christopher Stone's recent book, *Where the Law Ends,* provides compelling documentation of the inherent inadequacies of legal mechanisms to deal adequately with the complex and dynamic relationships between business organizations and other facets of our social system.[6] Hence legal accountability, while useful, cannot be relied on as the only method for determining the responsibilities of business firms. Law serves to define the lowest common denominator of responsible business behavior, that for which our society has defined clear standards of accountability. The limitations of the legal system have, if anything, increased concern in the United States over the question of social responsibility. For this and other reasons, one finds greater attention paid to the issue of responsibility in this country than in any other Western industrial society.

The most important reason goes back to the question of legitimacy. The issue of responsibility is inevitably raised in a democratic society whenever institutions acquire substantial power. In such a society it is essential that institutions which wield power be legitimized in order that the existence and exercise of such power is deemed appropriate or rightful by those outside the institution. As Professor James Willard Hurst noted in his now classic study of *The Legitimacy of the Business Corporation:*

> That legitimacy means responsibility—that an institution with power must be accountable to some judgment other than that of the power-holder—expresses the prime emphasis that culture puts on the individual as the ultimate measure of institutions.[7]

In American society power and responsibility are reciprocally correlated concepts. The existence of the former inevitably raises issues concerning the character of the latter. Similarly, freedom and responsibility are inextricably linked values in a democracy, and the extent of freedom, the absence of public constraint on an institution, is related to the responsible use of power.[8]

A second reason for the long-standing concern with the social responsibility of business in the United States has to do with the strong ideological preference which has existed in this country for private rather than public (state) action. This preference has meant that business organizations perform many essential economic functions that in other countries are usually performed by state entities. Basic transportation, communications, military production, and the extraction and processing of raw materials are examples. Thus there has arisen a great dependency relationship between business and American society.

Third, unlike those European countries where many societal leadership functions have been preempted by traditional nonbusiness elites, including a titled, landed artistocracy and an established church, and business is a relatively new arrival on the social scene, in the United States such traditional elite structures did not exist, and business elites have held important leadership roles in our national scene from the very beginning. While never entirely accurate, Calvin Coolidge's dictum, "The business of America is business," reflects the much greater societal role played by business in the United States than abroad. Over the years we have given business institutions and their leaders more scope and taken them far more seriously than they have been taken elsewhere and, in return, have expected more of them. When these expectations have not been met, there has often existed a sense of relative deprivation, or even of betrayal, and a feeling that business has somehow let the public down.[9]

Finally, there has been rather wide acceptance in this country for several decades of an idea propagated by the business community that business management is not simply an occupation but a profession. An important component of this concept of professionalism is that of a responsibility to the public which ultimately transcends that owed to an organization or to a client. The idea has developed that professional managers have an obligation to examine fully the implications of their actions for those persons or groups affected by them and to be cognizant of the impact of their decisions upon the more amorphous "public interest."

THE SEARCH FOR PARAMETERS OF RESPONSIBILITY

While the concept of business social responsibility has received general acceptance during the past two decades, a precise set of parameters for the concept has not. Nobody is now arguing that business should act irresponsibly or in ways that are either illegal or in flagrant disregard of contemporary communal standards of behavior. Even Milton Friedman, who has been one of the most articulate spokesmen of the "minimalist" position, acknowledges the obligations of the firm "to stay within the rules of the game, which is to say, [to engage] in open and free competition without deception or fraud" as it acts upon its one and only social responsibility—"to use its resources and engage in activities designed to increase its profits."[10] However, beyond that minimum, there is no agreement regarding what it is that constitutes socially responsible behavior. Actually, one of the salutary developments of the 1970s has been the recognition by students of American business that it is not feasible to develop a single, comprehensive, universally and eternally applicable definition that delineates the societal role of the business firm. Even the use of such commonly accepted criteria of business responsibility as performing the economic function in a manner as economically efficient as possible, in accordance with the law, while conforming company interests to the national interest, is subject to exceptions and qualifications. Consider the following examples: (1) Microeconomic efficiency may dictate the widespread substitution of machinery for human labor, thereby enhancing the productivity of the firm but causing unemployment in the process. (2) Obeying the law may require the firm to engage in governmentally mandated racial discrimination, such as is the case in South Africa or Rhodesia. (3) Conforming company interests to national interests may involve a business firm in providing materials for an unpopular war or serving as an instrumentality of United States foreign policy in support of a military dictatorship.

Concepts of the social role in American business are dynamic and have evolved in step with this country's stage of economic development and changing social values. In the same way, the responsibilities of single business firms must be defined situationally or contextually in each individual case. More specifically, the social role of an individual firm is a function of such factors as

1. Its economic task
2. Its competitive position
3. Its specific relationship to a given social problem
4. The urgency of the problem
5. The availability within the firm of human, financial, and technological resources to address the problem
6. Available alternatives to action by the firm
7. The likely consequences to the firm and to other social interests of its activity or failure to act in a given situation
8. The comparative weights of competing societal pressures and priorities

For example, the specific responsibilities of a regional bank differ substantially both in degree and in kind from those of an integrated multinational oil producer. Moreover, the social obligations of a single company will change over time. Such a situational or contextual perspective of business responsibility is for the individual firm a necessary refinement of the more sweeping and hence less operational ideas of responsibility that prevailed in the past. Yet another caveat is necessary. The basic questions about the social responsibility of business at both the micro and macro levels relate to the ongoing day-to-day operations of business. Like charity, social responsibility begins at home. It is inherent in the *economic* role that enterprise plays in American society. Thus it is issues relating to the *products* and *processes* of a business rather than the nature and extent of its philanthropic contributions that constitute the cutting edge of the social role of the firm. In essence, socially responsible business behavior involves a course of action in which the business community, the industry, the firm, and the manager anticipate and accept the total consequences of their decisions.[11]

At the outset of this discussion, we suggested that responsibility logically links together legitimacy and rationality. We explored how, in a democratic society, making power and its exercise both responsible and accountable is essential to the achievement of legitimacy and is an important component in maintaining the pluralistic character of American society. Turning now to rationality, a strong argument can be made that decision making in a climate of responsibility represents the ultimate in rational decision making. Rationality here has two aspects: First, there must be a decision process whereby the decision maker assesses all available information in determining corporate action and thus makes better decisions. Second, there is a perspective that views the long-run well being of business as being related to the maintenance of a pluralist social and political system in the United States. The development of a concept of business responsibility which conforms to the prevailing social norms concerning appropriate business activity, thereby permits key sectors of the business community to retain greater autonomy, thus contributing to the maintenance of social pluralism generally. From a managerial perspective, an expanded concept of social responsibility is rational because it avoids imposing additional legal accountability which may infringe on the autonomy of the business sector. There have been many examples in the last century of government intervention in situations where business behavior has not been compatible with societal norms. Frequently, these governmentally imposed standards of behavior, which constrain managerial autonomy and discretion, are more onerous to society than the problems to be alleviated or the standards that might have emerged had business regulated itself and monitored its own activities. The intervention also results in further concentration of power in government which, in turn, erodes the pluralism of power and decision making, undesirable developments in a democratic society.

RESPONSIBILITY AND THE AVOIDANCE
OF SOCIAL DISSONANCE

A broadened perspective of social responsibility is rational also because it avoids social dissonance, which may have cost and profit implications for the firm and, in virtually all instances, make the manager's life more difficult, as well as place unneeded and avoidable strain on the organization. Business firms that have been obliged in the past to deal with disgruntled shareholders, customers, environmental groups, and ethnic minorities, can bear witness to the difficulties involved.

Rational behavior for the business community revolves around the question of whether business will always be caught in a reactive and defensive posture in which its zone of action becomes very limited or whether business will order its decisions, structures, and relations to its environment in a manner which meets changing societal expectations and, at the same time, maintains the flexibility of the business institution. The answer to this question will go a long way toward determining the character and quality of America's political economy. Responsible behavior will contribute thusly both to the legitimacy of our business institutions and to the rationality of their interactions with other sectors of society. The Bowen, Letwin, and Brooks papers should be viewed in this context.

In his retrospective essay, "Social Responsibilities of the Businessman —Twenty Years Later," Howard R. Bowen traces the historical development of the concept of business social responsibility and places it in the context of the various means by which society has sought to exercise control over business enterprise: competition, public regulation, countervailing organizations, and self-regulation. For Bowen, whose *Social Responsibilities of the Businessman,*[12] published in 1953, was one of the earliest examinations of the social responsibility concept, social responsibility means *self-regulation in the social interest* voluntarily adopted by the corporation without the pressure of competition or public intervention. In his contribution to the current volume, he divides the years following the Second World War into two distinct periods so far as public and business attitudes toward corporate social responsibility are concerned. The first period, which occurred shortly after the conclusion of World War II, quickly waned during the 1950s when the public's confidence in business was at a high point and interest in social responsibility was subsidiary to such concerns as economic growth, prosperity, and the advantages of free-enterprise over communism. During the decade following the mid-1960s, however, much of this public confidence in business was replaced by widespread skepticism about the compatibility of business behavior with basic American values, and interest in social responsibility was resuscitated. While expressing some doubt concerning the degree to which various types of business performance have become more socially responsible in the period following the publication of his earlier book, Bowen retains his belief that the doctrine of social responsibility has had utility in the "harnessing of business activity to the social interest." He offers a "theory of the firm" in which socially responsible policies and action are essentially those intended by the firm to "augment its intangible assets" or to "reduce intangible liabilities" so that the firm, by pursuing enlightened self-interest, betters its position vis à vis the society by adhering to community standards concerning acceptable corporate behavior. Bowen concludes by saying that "voluntary social responsibility," while necessary, can never alone be a sufficient condition for constraining business power and that public control, on terms established by the public and not the corporation, is necessary if the economy is to be accountable to the American citizenry.

William Letwin's provocative essay, "Social Responsibility of Business in an Insurance State," subjects the social responsibility concept to the scrutiny of an American-born and -trained political-economist whose longtime scholarly and teaching career at the London School of Economics and Political Science has afforded him an invaluable comparative perspective of the operations of large-scale business organizations in both Britain and the United States. At the outset of his paper, Letwin points out the inherently "cloudy" and, from his perspective, inadvertently "deceptive," character of the notion of the social responsibility of business. For him only individuals, "conscious . . . moral beings," can have responsibilities, but not *business,* which is an activity, nor *business firms* nor the *business sector,* which are abstract organizational and institutional constructs aggregating human activity. Hence for Letwin the social responsibility of business has meaning only in the context of "all the human beings who are connected with the activity of business." Furthermore, the word *responsibility* can be applied in several different contexts, including moral duty, legal duty, and simple factual causation. While moral and legal responsibility may overlap, in no society are they identical. He also points out that *society* itself is an abstraction dealing with "a set of relationships" among persons living in a particular country. Thus Letwin redefines the social responsibility of business as raising the question of what obligations of a moral, legal, or combined moral-legal character the persons who are engaged in business activity have toward other persons living in the same country.

Letwin lays considerable stress on what he perceives to have been a general tendency in the domain of legal responsibility: the emergence of "the Insurance State." In other words, he sees that the legal process has acted to spread the unfortunate consequences of risk from the individual to society (that is, all individuals). Letwin illustrates his thesis with a number of examples: the substitution of strict liability in tort for the older principle of caveat emptor as the basis for allocating risk in the defective-product situation; the spread of unemployment compensation and other job-protection mechanisms, with the state becoming the de facto employer of last resort; and public control of pollution. The consequence of these and other "compulsory insurance" schemes, suggests Letwin, is to spread the risk and the cost from the few to the many. The modern state devotes increasing amounts of time and financial resources to providing these and other forms of insurance. This development, according to Letwin, has brought about the "Insurance State." Letwin goes on to express a number of reservations regarding these events, advancing a proposition that is most troublesome in the context of our focus on responsibility: the emergence of the Insurance State has had the effect of expanding "the legal responsibilities of its subjects with the ironical result of making them act *less* responsibly."

Turning from legal to moral duties, Letwin points out that the moral responsibilities of the business executive are not of a single piece but are of diverse types, varying with the many different kinds of behavior in which he engages and his proximity to those affected by his actions. Hence the determination of moral responsibility is inherently a much more complex and perplexing issue than the assignment of legal responsibility. Letwin concludes his analysis by posing the question of why the doctrine of social responsibility, which is essentially a very old issue relating to the ethical and legal responsibilities of all participants in a community's economic life toward each other, has recently generated such intense interest. In Letwin's view, it is not the growth of the business-oriented society which is the central phenomenon but rather the acceptance by society of the view that the ethics of business are not, and should not be "separate and distinct from ethics at large." Letwin goes even further to say that the moral quandaries and responsibilities of business have a persistent quality that makes it likely that they will be with us even when we proceed beyond the current socioeconomic stage he calls the Insurance State.

TECHNOLOGY ASSESSMENT AND RESPONSIBILITY

In contrast to Letwin's more generalized and enduring concerns about the social responsibility of business, Harvey Brooks' essay, "Scope of Business Responsibility in the Assessment of Technology," focuses on specific and very contemporary issues: the changing role and responsibilities of industry with regard to the social assessment of technology and the implications of these changes for industry's future place in technological innovation. In Brooks' view, of all the issues falling under the rubric of "business and society," this is probably the most important and the most likely to have profound impact on the institutional evolution of business and its relationships with the public and the political system. In the past, technological innovation has functioned on the assumption of *laissez-innover,* with the market operating as the final judge of technological priorities in research and development. In one sense, technology assessment (TA) is a normal and traditional activity of business, but in its modern usage TA deals with "those aspects of a proposed technology which cannot be subjected readily to the tests of market acceptability or economic efficiency." The secondary and unintended consequences of the application of technology, including the externalities and the social costs and benefits, are often difficult to reduce to a common economic measure.

The fundamental issue raised by TA is the "responsibility of the corporation, and indeed the individual technologists who work for it, for the remote and perhaps unintended consequences of their activities.'' The changing attitude toward technology is a consequence of changing public attitudes and expectations, of changes in the nature of technology itself, and of a growth in our scientific knowledge which should enable us to deal more confidently with hitherto unforeseeable consequences of technological application. Brooks cites the automobile, DDT, polyvinyl chloride, and freon as examples of products the impacts of which have recently become capable of being reassessed only because of new social expectations, or new techniques made possible by recent scientific discoveries, or both. He describes the irony in the fact that some environmental legislation puts ''much greater faith in the capabilities of technology to solve problems under sufficient pressure than the technologists themselves would believe.'' Recent federal legislation and the substitution of strict liability for the older principles of negligence and warranty as the standard by which products and technologies are judged have, in essence, required industry, almost irrespective of cost, to avoid all risks which can be made avoidable technologically. Industry's response to these changes, suggests Brooks, has been primarily defensive.

Brooks identifies three historical responses by industry to changing public expectations concerning its products and processes. First is industry's primarily *active-defensive* response pattern to public regulation, which denies the need for regulation and questions the facts or the analysis on which regulation is premised. Second is the more recent *passive-responsive* mode under which industry is prepared to live by the rules established by political authority without either anticipating them or trying to do better than the legally prescribed standards. Third is the *active-anticipatory* response in which industry strives to mitigate social costs and even to induce the public imposition of the most stringent technologically feasible standards. After posing the question of how business can improve on these responses, Brooks suggests that they be replaced by a response in which an industry or a firm seeks to anticipate new regulations and constraints on particular technologies that it uses but does not engage in active political involvements in the enactment of legislation or in the advocacy of particular regulations or standards.

Brooks then deals with the thorny issue of motivating individual managers to take into account the social cost consequences of their decisions. He proposes, within limits which will not stifle managerial initiative and innovation, the imposition of direct liability on corporate executives responsible for certain types of corporate action and the legal protection of responsible or legitimate ''whistle-blowers'' who disclose to the public or public authorities corporate activities that are deleterious to society. Brooks then notes that the technology-assessment process must not become so cumbersome and restrictive that it stifles technological innovation. If used properly, assessment mechanisms have not only the capacity to protect the public from harm, but also the ability to affect the innovation process itself, including the direction of the innovation. He concludes by relating the question of TA to the socialization-of-risk theme emphasized by Letwin. Brooks says that if the public insists on increasing protection from unforeseen risks to its own health and safety, it may become necessary to invent new forms of insurance which will help firms and individuals to protect themselves against the risks of unforeseen scientific developments that suddenly change the social assessment of an activity in which a high investment has already been made. We see here yet another manifestation of the Insurance State.

RESPONSIBILITY AND THE BUSINESS-SOCIETY RELATIONSHIP

In the discussion of the three papers, as well as at other points in the workshop/conference, the participants focused upon a variety of issues concerning the concept of responsibility as it pertains to the relationship of business and society. Among the more important of these issues were:

1. What is meant by *social responsibility*? By what criteria can we determine the social responsibilities of business? Can there be any agreement on a definition of the term? Is the term inherently meaningful? Does it refer to ends (policies) or to means (process) or both? Can the concept apply to organizations as well as to individuals?

2. How new is the concept of social responsibility? Is its character static or dynamic? Which aspects of the social responsibility discussion extend back over the past century or even longer, and which are uniquely contemporary?

3. What is the relationship of social responsibility to the activities of business and to the normal economic tasks and profit-making goals of the firm, as opposed to its "voluntary" undertakings?

4. Assuming that general agreement can be found concerning the meaning of social responsibility, how does one implement socially responsible practices in a firm, an industry, or the business community at large? What positive reinforcements are available to motivate socially responsible behavior? To what extent is motivation provided by intraorganizational influences and to what extent by factors external to the enterprise?

5. Are evaluative mechanisms available to assess or measure whether a business organization is behaving in a socially responsible manner? Is there access to theoretical concepts and methodological tools for making such assessments?

6. Has the development of the business and society field over the past two decades played a role in the contemporary interest in, and concern for, the question of social responsibility?

7. Why has there been greater attention paid to the issue of social responsibility in the United States than in other Western industrial nations?

Any student of the American business environment will realize immediately that these seven issues did not originate in the workshop/conference but have been high on the agenda of all thorough discussions of the social responsibilities of business enterprise for many years. Although for analytical convenience we have identified seven distinct groups of issues, they do to some extent overlap and blend one into the other. Let us, however, look briefly at each of these seven subissues in the context of the discussions sparked by the papers.

Not surprisingly, the question of the meaning of the term *social responsibility* generated considerable comment. Very early in the workshop, Frederick Sturdivant suggested that a managerial decision-making perspective, denominated *social responsiveness,* which seeks to enable business institutions to respond to changing societal expectations, is a more useful approach to determining the social role of business than is focusing upon ill-defined normative notions of responsibility. Harvey Brooks expanded on this theme by suggesting that social responsiveness is "part of the process of maximizing long-run profits." In other words, he suggested that essential to the ability of the business enterprise or of any organization (whether a hospital, a university, a governmental agency, or a labor union) to function effectively within its environment is its capability to accommodate to dynamic expectations. While the Sturdivant-Brooks view appeared to receive general approval, the mainline discussion focused on the issue of business responsibility rather than responsiveness.

Although there were no supporters of the view associated with Milton Friedman, that the doctrine of social responsibility of business is a fundamentally subversive concept and that the sole responsibility of business is to maximize its profits, Fletcher Byrom effectively advanced the position that the basic responsibility of business in a private system is to charge prices that allow it to earn those profits which will enable the firm to perform its economic function efficiently and which will assure the continuation of the enterprise. Most of the participants found Byrom's formulation acceptable as a statement of a minimum level of responsibility, but there was little agreement beyond that point. Milton Moskowitz, for one, suggested that a fundamental aspect of the social responsibility issue is that "the private pool of investment capital in this country is limited to a very tiny, tiny, minority." Keith Davis perhaps best summarized the consensus of the discussants when he broadened Howard Bowen's concept of responsibility as "self-regulation" by suggesting a responsible businessman is one who makes choices that have more favorable consequences than other available choices have. In other words, when he makes a choice, seeking more favorable social consequences, he has acted responsibly.

Implicit in the Davis formulation is the idea, articulated by S. Prakash Sethi, George Steiner, and others, that the essential issues of social responsibility are an inextricable part of the ongoing, day-to-day operations of the business firm and of the normal decision-making process relating to these operations. With a British perspective, Barbara Shenfield suggested that "balancing the interests of various claimants upon the corporation was basic to the British understanding of social responsibility." Melvin Eisenberg offered a useful distinction between those voluntary aspects of business behavior, such as the conferring of business largesse through corporate donations, and those arising as a consequence of the routine daily activities of the firm.

RESPONSIBILITY: INDIVIDUAL OR ORGANIZATIONAL?

A key topic of debate concerned the issue of whether the concept of business responsibility pertained only to the activities of individual managers or was also relevant in evaluating the performance of the business organization. This issue was raised by the contention in Letwin's paper that only individuals can have responsibilities, a view supported vigorously by Earle Birdzell, Joseph McGuire, and Byrom. It was staunchly opposed by Lee Preston, who argued that

if we understand that in a world of organizations, there are organizations that are actors that go on as the people in them change, we know that there is such a thing as organizational responsibility and perhaps even organizational personality and perhaps even organizational morality.

The "newness" of social responsibility similarly engendered vigorous debate. While it was noted at the outset of the conference that in the ancient Greek city-states "there were concerns for social responsibility which sounded amazingly modern in character," and while Bowen traced the antecedents of contemporary concerns with the social responsibility of business to the social gospel movement of late nineteenth-century America, there was unanimous agreement that there was actually something new and different in the post-World War II concern with social responsibility. Among the new elements said to be important in generating this concern were, as Phillip Blumberg pointed out, pressures from sources both internal and external to the corporation. Included among these were what has been termed by David Vogel the "publicization of the corporation" (the transformation of a company into a public institution which reflects public concern),[13] increasing dissatisfaction with particular aspects of corporate behavior and corporate power, and the growth in public awareness that the legal process cannot regulate all aspects of corporate behavior or satisfy all dimensions of public dissatisfaction with the operations of institutions in the society. Bowen combined concern with the social responsibilities of business with the legitimacy issue, noting that in a sense the amount of interest in social responsibility is a measure of the extent to which corporate enterprise is highly regarded, viewed as legitimate, in the society.

A common area of agreement among the participants was the idea that, while the legal process and the marketplace both play invaluable roles in channeling and constraining business behavior, neither mode of social control is sufficient, either individually or jointly, or to determine the responsibilities of business. Indeed, it was the law school dean, Blumberg, who stressed the importance of nonlegal, nonmarket external pressures in inducing socially responsible behavior. He pointed out that, to the degree that corporate responsibility reflects involuntary pressure, the manager can be relied upon to contribute to social solutions. In many areas these other external pressures, in conjunction with the law and the market, will determine the behavior of business organizations. Striking a somewhat different note than Bowen, Blumberg sees a limited role for altruism in determining a zone of discretionary behavior between the floor imposed by either law or the climate of social opinion and the ceiling imposed by the pressures of the competitive marketplace.

One's views regarding the extent to which business behavior can be channeled by these distinctive modes of social control, as well as views of the modes which should be employed at a particular time, are dependent upon one's perceptions concerning the nature and extent of business power in our society, an area about which there was substantial disagreement among the participants.

William Frederick made a useful point regarding the analogy between the role of technological assessment as an effort by society to reassert its dominance over technology and social responsibility as a more generalized societal attempt to get business leaders to make some appraisals of the social effects of their decisions. This approach was congenial to a number of the discussants who considered it most useful to students of social responsibility as a decision-making process whereby managers take into account all of the reasonably foreseeable consequences of their decisions.

The notion of process inevitably evoked comments concerning the relatively crude state of the art of evaluating the social performance of business. Raymond Bauer emphasized the difficulties in making evaluations in both the specialized instance of technology assessment and the more generalized case of the measurement of the social performance of business organizations. Key among the problems is the determination of which values and whose are to determine the nature of the measuring criteria used.

The Letwin thesis concerning the emergence of an "insurance state," a concept which Wayne Broehl later expanded to "the insurance world," sparked considerable disagreement concerning which institutions in society should serve as the primary structural mechanisms for risk distribution. As George L. Bach said, the real problems are "Who really does pay? How do the burdens get shuffled through the economic and social process?" Regarding product liability and the fellow-servant role, as lawyers Eisenberg and Blumberg stressed in the words of the latter,

> What law is attempting to determine is: who is in the best position to bear the loss in the short run and to pass it along to society as a whole in the long run...and...who is in the best position to protect himself against liability of this sort? At least part of the issue generated by concern about the social responsibility of business is that of locating risk within the society: who is to be considered responsible, especially legally, if the undesired occurs? Should it fall upon individuals, categories of individuals, the organization, or the state?

In essence, it is the questions of who pays when a loss occurs, of whether the ultimate payer is to be taxed directly or indirectly, and of whether imposing such a tax will stimulate behavior which is socially desirable as a matter of public policy.

Kenneth Boulding provided a colorful framework for the question of how far the concept of social responsibility should be carried. Business, he said, is and ought to be regarded, in its societal obligations, as being more akin to the plodding but dependable donkey than to a horse. The one is a reliable beast of burden that performs quite well its prosaic economic tasks, while the other, a great white charger, bounds across the social heavens like Pegasus carrying whatever size and type of load society thrusts upon it. The moral here is that we should ask business to do only what it is trained and equipped to do and what it does well, rather than impose upon it all societal tasks under the sun. Like most analogies, however, this one is limited. While most observers of four-legged beasts can agree on the differences between donkeys and horses, reasonable people may differ markedly in what they consider to be appropriate roles and burdens for these two animals. So it is with the concept of social responsibility and the many tenable views of what it is and how much of its burden should be carried by business.

One final caveat is necessary before the reader moves on to the Bowen, Letwin, and Brook essays. The uncertainty surrounding the concept of social responsibility and its own rapidly changing character are reflective of and reflected by developments which have been taking place in the entire business and society field. There is an increasing effort to define the terms of reference and to replace philosophically, and even ideologically, predicted meanings with concepts that are more nearly the product of logically powerful analysis and also, where possible, rigorous empirical research. To the extent that scholars in the field continue to develop more sophisticated ways of exploring questions of business responsibility, this increased sophistication will undoubtedly have a favorable impact on business behavior and on the field of learning known as business and society. The issue of the social responsibility of business enterprises and of their managers will remain one of the major areas of inquiry in the realms of research and teaching and a significant dimension of business decisions and behavior.

NOTES

1. Reasons for the particularly American interest in the social responsibility of business are suggested in Edwin M. Epstein, "The Social Role of Business Enterprise in Britain: An American Perspective: Part I," *The [British] Journal of Management Studies,* vol. 13, No. 3 (October, 1976), pp. 213–233, and "The Social Role of Business Enterprise in Britain: An American Perspective: Part II," *The [British] Journal of Management Studies,* vol. 14, No. 3 (October, 1977), pp. 281–316.

2. See Morrell Heald, *The Social Responsibility of Business: Company and Community, 1900–1960* (Cleveland, Ohio: Case Western Reserve University Press, 1970) and Earl F. Cheit, "The New Place of Business: The Gospel of Social Responsibility," *The Business Establishment,* ed. Earl F. Cheit (New York: John Wiley & Sons, 1964), pp. 152–192.

3. Albion W. Small, "Private Business is a Public Trust," *The American Journal of Sociology,* vol. 1, No. 3 (November, 1895), p. 282.

4. See Max Lerner, "The Triumph of Laissez-Faire," in *Paths of American Thought,* eds. Arthur M. Schlesinger, Jr., and Morton White (Boston: Houghton-Mifflin Company, 1963), pp. 147–166.

5. Richard Hofstadter, *The Age of Reform* (New York: Vintage Books, Random House, 1955), pp. 215–271.

6. Christopher D. Stone, *Where The Law Ends: The Social Control of Corporate Behavior* (New York: Harper & Row, 1975).

7. James Willard Hurst, *The Legitimacy of the Business Corporation in the Law of the United States, 1780–1970* (Charlottesville, Va.: The University of Virginia Press, 1970), p. 58.

8. Carl L. Becker, *Freedom and Responsibility in the American Way of Life* (New York: Vintage Books, Random House, 1945).

9. See, e.g., "America's Growing Antibusiness Mood," *Business Week,* 17 June, 1972, p. 100. The reaction of American business leaders to public dissatisfaction with business performance is examined in Leonard Silk and David Vogel, *Ethics and Profits: The Crisis of Confidence in American Business* (New York: Simon & Schuster, 1976).

10. Milton Friedman, *Capitalism and Freedom* (Chicago: University of Chicago Press, 1962), p. 133 and Milton Friedman, "The Social Responsibility of Business Is to Increase Its Profits," *New York Times Magazine,* 13 September, 1970, pp. 122–126.

11. Illustrative of the newer, more managerial perspective of social responsibility are the essays compiled in Archie B. Carroll, ed., *Managing Corporate Social Responsibility* (Boston: Little, Brown & Company, 1977).

12. New York: Harper and Brothers, 1953.

13. David Vogel, "The Corporation as Government: Challenges and Dilemmas," *Polity,* vol. 7, No. 1 (Fall, 1975), p. 34.

HOWARD R. BOWEN

Social Responsibility of the Businessman—Twenty Years Later

The concept of corporate social responsibility has a long history. Indeed, it is about as ancient as humanity's thinking about ethics, which goes back to the dawn of civilization. Among the most pressing ethical issues of all ages have been those arising from human relationships between producers and consumers, buyers and sellers, masters and servants, lenders and borrowers, landlords and tenants, and princes and merchants. The literature of philosophy and practical affairs of all eras is full of references to what we call corporate social responsibility. Such ideas are found in Aristotle and Plato, in the Bible, in the writings of the medieval theologians and the practices of the guilds, in Adam Smith and other works of the Enlightenment, in various papal encyclicals of the nineteenth and twentieth centuries, in the literature of the American muckraking period at the turn of the present century, in numerous opinions of the Supreme Court, in many statements of American business leaders, and in the writings of many contemporary philosophers, economists, and churchmen.

The modern literature on corporate responsibility is vast and impressive. Nevertheless, the subject remains peripheral to the mainstream of economic thought and at the same time controversial. The controversy arises because the question of corporate responsibility is closely akin to the perennial (in some ways insoluble) question: How should private enterprise be controlled or regulated in the public interest?

Society has usually relied on some combination of four controls over private enterprise: (1) competition; (2) public regulation; (3) countervailing organizations such as labor unions, cooperatives, and consumer groups; and (4) self-regulation. Self-regulation may be organized through guilds, trade associations, or professional organizations, or it may occur independently within single enterprises. Self-regulation may be motivated by ethical sentiments directed toward the social interest, by the desire to forestall outside controls, or by the hope of exercising monopoly or monopsony power, or by the intention of gaining other advantages for the enterprise. When we speak of corporate social responsibility, we are talking about self-regulation in the social interest. We are talking about how the corporation can enlarge its service to society through policies voluntarily adopted without the pressure of competition or public intervention.[1]

THREE HISTORIC EPISODES

In reviewing modern business history in America, one can detect three waves of keen interest in corporate social responsibility among businessmen and three corresponding waves of interest among intellectuals. Each of the three episodes was in response to severe attacks on corporate business. Indeed, the extent of discussion of social responsibility has been inversely related to the degree of public confidence in corporate enterprise.

The first wave of interest occurred just before World War I. It was a product of the era that produced the social gospel movement, the muckrakers, and the Sherman and Clayton acts and other social legislation. It is perhaps epitomized in the words of Walter Rauschenbusch, the great architect of social gospel, who once wrote:

> Business life is the unregenerate section of our social order. If by some magic it could be plucked out of our total social life in all its raw selfishness, and isolated on an island, unmitigated by any other factors of our life, that island would immediately become the object of a great foreign mission crusade for all Christendom.[2]

This pre-World War I period produced Andrew Carnegie's concept of the "gospel of wealth,"[3] Justice Louis D. Brandeis's great book, *Business—a Profession,*[4] and the early writings of J. M. Clark[5] which later emerged as his *Social Control of Business.*[6]

The second wave of interest in the concept of social responsibility occurred immediately after World War II. During the Great Depression, big business and the capitalistic system had come under severe criticism. During the war, the superb performance of business in producing for the military effort and the prominent position of leading businessmen in the federal government had tended to rehabilitate the prestige of the business community. Immediately after the war business leaders took advantage of the situation by going on the offensive in support of the capitalistic system. An early move was to establish the Committee for Economic Development (CED) which consisted of the more "liberal and enlightened" members of the business community. And the doctrine of social responsibility was preached often and widely by the most prominent businessmen of the time—for example, Frank W. Abrams, Chester I. Barnard, Ralph E. Flanders, Marion B. Folsom, Clarence A. Francis, Eric A. Johnston,

Fred Lazarus, Jr., Thomas B. McCabe, Frank W. Pierce, Clarence B. Randall, Beardsley Ruml, and Robert E. Wood.[7] My book, *Social Responsibilities of the Businessman*, was a product of this period. My purpose was to explore the concept of social responsibility as expounded by so many business leaders of the time and to provide a critical evaluation of the concept.

With the consistent prosperity and economic growth of the 1950s and 1960s, big business and the capitalistic system gained in public acceptance and political security, and the discussion of social responsibility waned. Recent events and issues, however, have brought the matter to the fore again, and that is why this symposium has been organized.[8]

Big business and the capitalistic system are again under question and again the idea of social responsibility is being widely examined. The extent to which big business has lost the confidence of the American people, both relatively and absolutely, is reflected in the following data showing the percentage of persons in the United States reporting "a great deal of confidence" in major social institutions.

TABLE 1   Confidence of the American Public in Major Social Institutions: Percentage Reporting "A Great Deal of Confidence"

	1966	1972	1973	1974
Medicine	72%	48%	57%	50%
Higher educational institutions	61	33	44	40
U.S. Supreme Court	51	28	33	40
The military	62	35	40	33
Organized religion	41	30	36	32
Televised news	25	17	41	31
Executive branch, U.S. Government	41	27	19	28
Press	29	18	30	25
Major companies	55	27	29	21
Congress	42	21	29	18
Organized labor	22	15	20	18

Source: Louis Harris and Associates, Inc. Reported in *Chronicle of Higher Education*, 14 October, 1974.

SPECIFIC AREAS OF SOCIAL RESPONSIBILITY

A discussion of corporate social responsibility is somewhat sterile and abstract unless it relates to the substantive areas of policy and conduct to which the responsibility applies. In my book I tried to identify the important issues and areas of concern. In doing so, I reviewed the writings of moralists, religious leaders, social critics, economists, and students of social welfare. I found that the following substantive areas were of widespread, though not necessarily universal, interest:

1. A general attitude or disposition on the part of businessmen to view business leadership as a stewardship based on the motive of serving society.
2. Respect for the dignity and worth of all human beings.
   (a) A spirit of compassion in all personal dealings and relationships.
   (b) Equal opportunity to all for personal development and advancement.
   (c) Avoidance of discrimination based on race, sex, religion, political view, national origin, social status, or physical appearance.
3. Economic efficiency, productivity, and growth as a way of ameliorating poverty and drudgery and as a way of meeting the needs of society.
4. Sound labor relations.
   (a) Acknowledgement of the right of labor to organize and acceptance of the duty to bargain in good faith.
   (b) Strengthening of the sense of vocation among workers and of meaning from work.
   (c) Arranging work and compensation in ways that would protect the integrity of the family.
   (d) Wholesome, safe, and healthful working conditions, reasonable hours, and reasonable provision for the physical and cultural needs of workers.
   (e) Equitable allocation of compensation among cash, amenities of the workplace, working conditions, hours, security, and other conditions or benefits.
   (f) Fairness in the incidence of unemployment when layoffs are unavoidable.
5. Desirable conditions of work for executives and other white-collar employees.
   (a) Avoidance of special privileges relating to working conditions, security, benefits, and status symbols.
   (b) Minimizing undesirable effects of business life on incentives, personality, and family life.
6. Honesty and law observance with special concern for subtleties and for indirect or remote effects of policies and decisions.
7. Recognition of externalities (including environmental impacts).
   (a) Social costs.
   (b) Social benefits.
8. Truthfulness, restraint, and good taste in advertising, selling, propaganda, and mass communications.
9. Avoidance of undue power and influence.
   (a) In relations with federal, state, and local government.

    (b)   In relations with foreign governments.

    (c)   In relations with civic, charitable, educational, and religious organizations.

10.   Consideration, fairness, and integrity in relations with

    (a)   Customers

    (b)   Suppliers.

    (c)   Public officials.

11.   Fair competition and renunciation of monopoly profits even when obtainable.

12.   Economic stabilization.

    (a)   Cyclical.

    (b)   Seasonal.

13.   Concern for future generations with respect to

    (a)   Investment and depreciation of capital.

    (b)   Discovery and depletion of national resources.

    (c)   Discovery of knowledge and technology.

14.   Active efforts to bring about less inequality in the distribution of income.

    (a)   Tempering market influences to take account of justice and human needs.

    (b)   Proper definition of revenue, costs, and profits.

    (c)   Equitable disposition of profits.

In addition to all these subjects of common concern, Protestant thinkers of the time placed great emphasis on participation of workers and consumers in business policy.[9] Catholic social thought of the time was even more explicit on this point. Catholic leaders advocated the adoption of industry councils at the level of plants, industries, regions, the total national economy, and even the world economy. These councils would include managers, workers, and the public. They would provide participation of all interested parties in broad policy making and would bring a social point of view to the climate within which business decisions are made.[10]

The above list of topics represents a kind of amalgamation of the objectives under review by the diverse individuals and groups who were pushing the social responsibility idea in the years following World War II. Obviously, it was a big agenda. Perhaps no one, not even the most dedicated moralist or the most incorrigible optimist, actually thought businessmen would embrace the entire list. Certainly businessmen themselves had no such ambitious program. Moreover, the items on the list were not sharply differentiated as to priorities. It would be hard to single out a few items commanding special attention. The attitude was that there are many areas of business responsibility and that the business community should undergo a conversion in basic attitude which would change business behavior over a wide range of fields.

In any event, by 1953 the steam behind efforts to reform capitalism was largely spent. The nation was in no mood to condemn the capitalistic system; attitudes were widely favorable to corporate enterprise. This was due partly to the fact that American business was known to have played a decisive role in World War II and partly to the fact that the nation did not lapse back into the postwar depression that had been widely predicted and feared. Confidence in American business, which had been undermined during the Great Depression, was largely restored. By 1953, the nation was more concerned with the Korean War, the Cold War, McCarthyism—all anticommunist in orientation—than in reforming capitalism. And the social responsibility movement quietly dwindled away. Even the issues relating to labor organization and collective bargaining, which had been so controversial before and immediately after World War II, were becoming less intense as collective bargaining became widely accepted and as the law and practice of labor relations were stabilized. America was well on its way to an era of prosperity in which economic growth was the principal goal, the capitalist ideology was firmly entrenched, and confidence in corporate business was perhaps at an all-time high.

Today, the mood of the country is quite different. Confidence in all our institutions has been shaken, but the relative position of corporate business has been greatly eroded. Today, economic efficiency, productivity, and growth—the staples of corporate enterprise—are valued less highly than they were twenty-five years ago.

Most of the issues I identified in 1953 are still present, but some of them have become critical and intensely controversial. Among these issues are: discrimination among persons; vocation and meaning in work; honesty and law observance; externalities especially as related to the environment; advertising, selling, and mass communications; corporate influence on government; corporate impact on international affairs; provision for future generations including especially use of natural resources; and distribution of income. These are the issues to which the concept of social responsibility, if it is to be significant today, must be related. It is obvious, however, that the nation is in no mood to turn these issues over to the mercies of corporate social responsibility. Few believe that all or most corporations will voluntarily achieve satisfactory standards of nondiscrimination among persons; or that they will do all that is necessary to restore the environment; or that they will use adequate restraint in their selling, advertising, packaging, and labeling activities; or that they will offer products that are serviceable in meeting the needs of consumers; or that they will refrain from exerting undue influence on government; or that they will adequately consider future generations in the exploitation of natural resources, and so on. In view of recent revelations about the influence of corporate business on government, confidence in the ability of democratic government to restrain business is shaky, and cynicism is rampant. It is in this atmosphere that the concept of social responsibility is again being advanced.

PROGRESS SINCE 1953

In my book, I was very cautious in my claims about the extent of useful results obtainable through voluntary assumption of social responsibility by business. My observations and experiences over the past twenty-five years have heightened my skepticism. I have detected few gains in the quality of business stewardship over that time. Corporations have increased their participation in community affairs and their financial support of activities in health, education, and welfare. However, they have scarcely been wildly generous in the amounts of their charitable contributions—perhaps for good reason, since such costs would be passed on to consumers in higher prices. Moreover, the charitable giving has been regarded almost universally as an adjunct of public relations. Corporations have also accepted and adjusted to collective bargaining with labor unions. In doing so, however, they have routinely raised prices to compensate for higher labor costs, and it is easy for the onlooker to suspect a kind of subconscious but effective collusion between organized labor and corporate enterprise, or to suspect a game in which concessions are made to labor which are immediately withdrawn by raising the prices of what workers buy. Considerable progress has also occurred in the past twenty-five years in working conditions and fringe benefits. Also, many corporations have caught the spirit of affirmative action, and progress has been made in ameliorating discriminatory practices. Many corporations have also improved their practices with respect to public reporting of their activities.

On the other hand, considerable ground has probably been lost in corporate relations with government, in honesty and law observance, in the degree of hucksterism reflected in the quality of goods, and in methods of merchandising.

In judging trends in the performance of business, however, caution is necessary. The standards by which one judges tend to rise over time, and improvements in business practice may thus be overlooked. If one compares business practice in 1875 with that in 1975, no one would doubt that enormous improvements have taken place. But over a short period of twenty years or so, it is easy for favorable changes to be unrecognized because of rising standards.

Despite my skepticism about progress since 1953, I continue to believe that corporate social responsibility has a role in the harnessing of business activity to the social interest. I also believe that absence of a sense of social responsibility greatly complicates the task of controlling business through governmental regulation. As Professor James W. McKie has said, "... government in a country like the United States cannot regulate effectively without at least some cooperation from the regulated."[11] Even the most ardent advocate of laissez-faire recognizes that the free enterprise system requires that the "rules of the game" be followed. These rules at the very minimum include "open and free competition, without deception or fraud."[12] One can scarcely avoid adding to these rules such elemental standards as observance of law both in letter and spirit, restraint in the exercise of influence on government, and general human decency and regard for human welfare in relations with workers, consumers, suppliers, and all other persons affected by business.[13] These elemental conditions do not exist as fully as they ought to; yet they do exist in considerable measure, and it is only because they do that a system of private enterprise is tolerable.

A THEORY OF THE FIRM

I should now like to turn away from reflections on the past twenty-five years, and place the concept of social responsibility in perspective as part of a general theory of the firm.[14]

The business firm may be defined as a unified and consciously cooperative social system engaged in the production of goods and services for a market and organized for the pursuit of common goals of which one is profit. It is distinguished from the larger economy by the fact that it is consciously *administered,* whereas the economy is coordinated by exchange transactions guided by prices in a market. As D. H. Robertson once described firms, they are "lumps of butter in a pail of buttermilk." The concept of the firm could easily be extended to include nonprofit private organizations such as colleges and hospitals, mutual and cooperative organizations, governmental corporations, local authorities, and even governmental bureaus. All of these have much in common.

The firm is more than the sum of the individuals of which it is composed. It is an entity which persists through time and has a life of its own. It acquires a personality—traditions, customs, rules, values, attitudes, tendencies, loyalties, and behavior patterns. These personality traits evolve—usually slowly—through adjustment to new conditions. It is no fiction that ascribes to the corporation the legal status of *person.*. The firm is seldom, if ever, actuated by a single value or goal. Among the goals are survival, profit, growth of net worth or employment, prestige, power, innovation, doing a good job (Veblen's "workmanship"), peace and quiet, and so on. These general categories may obscure a wealth of detail. For example, there are values in producing certain types of products, in aesthetic design, in location in certain areas, in research and advanced technology, in handsome offices, in selling at low prices (or driving a hard bargain), in having one's stock listed on the big board (or in keeping ownership in a closed group), in establishing a family dynasty, in leadership in community activities, and so forth. All of these values together constitute a complex system in which the firm is attempting to achieve a maximum position. The firm is like a consumer with limited income choosing from a multitude of goods.

In seeking the chosen goals, the firm is confronted at any moment with certain given conditions. One of these conditions is its assets and liabilities as defined by ordinary accounting conventions and recorded in the balance sheet. The other conditions facing the firm are a set of intangible human relationships with labor, suppliers of capital, suppliers of goods and services, the world of knowledge and technology, including the firm's own research and development department and the staff in whom its current technology resides, the multitude of relationships within the firm which we call *organization,* the customers who buy the firm's products, and finally those who impose various constraints on the firm.

These intangible human relationahips partake of the nature of assets or liabilities. Whether, for a given firm, each one should be classed as an asset or a liability would depend on whether it is on balance positive or negative. For example, strong worker loyalty would be classed an asset, but bitter worker hostility would be classed as a liability.

These intangibles, mostly human relationships, may be formally classified as follows.

1. Supply functions.
    (a) For labor—reflecting the firm's ability to retain and recruit labor at various rates of compensation.
    (b) For capital—reflecting its ability to obtain capital at various rates of interest or with various dividend policies.
    (c) For purchased goods and services—reflecting its ability to acquire raw materials and other goods and services at various prices or costs.
2. Technology.
    (a) Technical knowledge, trade secrets, and patent rights.
    (b) Organization of the firm as a going concern including division of labor and definition of roles, communication system, rules, customs, and traditions.

3. Demand functions—reflecting its ability to sell specified amounts of its products at various prices.
4. Constraints.
   (a) Competition.
   (b) Public regulations.
   (c) Stockholder demands.
   (d) Socially accepted norms and standards of behavior.
   (e) Conscience or sense of responsibility within management.

These intangibles are among the most important conditions facing the firm at any given time—though the policies and actions of the firm are determined by its perceptions and expectations about these conditions (with appropriate probabilities attached), not by the conditions themselves which are never fully known.

Many of the policies and actions of the firm are directed toward bettering its position with respect to these intangibles. It tries to encourage worker loyalty and reduce worker hostility, to build up the reputation of the company as a good place to work, to strengthen its credit standing, to enhance its reputation as a sound company in which to invest, to follow dividend policies that will attract investors, to be of good repute among suppliers, to achieve supplier loyalty, to foster general company loyalty, to earn a reputation for good products, to develop well-known brands, to achieve significant product differentiation, to gain a reputation for fairness in competition, to curry the good will of legislators and public regulatory agencies, and others.

These intangibles are clearly very significant determinants of the overall position of the firm.

If a company is successful in bettering its position as related to these intangibles the company is in effect augmenting its true net assets, even though such intangibles seldom appear on a balance sheet. Their importance is suggested by this hypothetical question: Suppose a large and successful corporation were to be forced to divest itself of *either* its physical assets *or* its intangible assets, which would it choose? The decision would almost surely be to retain the know-how, patents, organization, worker loyalty, and public good will in preference to the physical assets. With the intangibles, it could soon replace the physical assets, but with the physical assets alone, it would be a long and costly process to recreate a successful company. The importance of the intangibles is also illustrated on a national scale by the quick recovery of Japan and Germany after the physical devastation of World War II.

In short, these intangibles are a key to a great deal of business behavior. Undoubtedly that ineffable quality called *business judgment,* which businessmen value so highly, is in large part the capacity to assign correct values to the intangibles in business decisions, and success in business is heavily dependent on the ability to acquire intangible assets.

The intangible assets and liabilities of corporations are probably becoming more important relative to the items recognized in traditional balance sheets. This increasing importance is due to the rising significance of technology, to the wide dispersion of markets and the resulting value of trademarks, dealerships, sources of supply, and other channels of communication and distribution, and to the increasing importance of government, not only as regulator of the economy, but also as a customer. Conventional accounting, therefore, may be relevant to an even smaller proportion of the decisions and actions of business enterprises. Indeed, it is surprising that accountants have not responded by devising techniques that would reflect in standard accounting records the many important intangibles. Security analysts and acquisition scouts for conglomerate corporations, however, have learned to appraise expertly the intangible assets and liabilities.[15]

Returning now to the concept of social responsibility, the bulk of those corporate policies and actions that are said to derive from a sense of social responsibility are actually intended to increase intangible assets or decrease intangible liabilities. They are designed, for example, to attract labor to the company, to raise the productivity of the labor force, to strengthen worker loyalty and thus to cut down on labor turnover to forestall collective bargaining or to soften labor demands, to reduce the compensation necessary to attract labor of given quality, and so on. In these ways the value of the labor force is increased or the liabilities with respect to labor compensation are decreased. Similarly, some policies and actions, ostensibly in the social interest, are designed to cultivate potential customers or suppliers and thus to increase the asset value of established market relationships by shifting demand and supply functions. Other policies and actions—seemingly related to social responsibility—are intended, for example, to reduce the dividend rates necessary to attract equity capital, to reduce interest rates, to forestall public regulation, or to create a general atmosphere of public good will which will be helpful for all of these purposes.

COMMUNITY STANDARDS

Some of the policies and actions designed to augment intangible assets or to reduce intangible liabilities, may well be in the social interest. That they may be motivated by the desire to better the position of the firm does not necessarily render them socially undesirable. Indeed, the behavior of firms in their own interest is strongly influenced by the standards of the community concerning working conditions, fringe benefits, quality of products, pollution, exploitation of natural resources, price policies, and so on. The firm acquires intangible assets (or extinguishes intangible liabilities) by complying with these standards or even exceeding them.

The standards may be unspoken and uncodified, but they exist. There are standards of living which define minimal propriety and decency for a family. Just as family standards of living rise over time, so also do corporate standards of living. The behavior of corporations is much influenced by these standards. Meeting or exceeding them confers benefits on the corporations and adds to intangible assets or removes intangible liabilities; falling short of the standards reduces assets and creates liabilities. The corporation will meet those social responsibilities which the community imposes upon it but not much more. I expressed this idea in 1953 as follows:

> The fact that businessmen are interested in those responsibilities which are affected with the long-run private interest as well as the public interest should be cause for neither surprise nor regret. Rather, it should be a source of profound satisfaction that the private and the social interest are found to be coincident over significant areas, because action in the social interest is doubtless more reliable when it is reinforced by the private interest. The fact that businessmen consider certain actions which are in the social interest to be also in the long-run self-interest is due not to a sudden conversion of businessmen, but rather to a change in the climate of public opinion within which they are operating. It is self-interest in a new setting. The things that are expected of businessmen today—and which they, therefore, regard as their responsibilities—are based upon a shift in public attitudes regarding business and its role in our society. This implies that, under the pressure of public opinion, businessmen can be persuaded to accept new duties and obligations which today they do not accept simply because the public does not expect them to be accepted. The means of achieving higher morality in business behavior is to create public attitudes which enlarge the moral responsibilities of business. Once this is done, business, with its new and broadened concern for public approval, will respond. [16]

In a sense, the onus of corporate social responsibility rests upon the community, not on the corporation. In the last analysis it is the community which defines the standards which the corporation is expected to meet. However, the socially accepted norms and standards of corporate behavior are by no means independently determined by the community. They are influenced by the corporation. Just as the corporation often regulates the regulatory agencies to which it is subject, so it often influences the standards for corporate conduct which the community imposes. A recent news report provides a graphic illustration:

General Motors Corporation has sent letters to more than a million of its stockholders, dealers, and suppliers praising President Ford's energy program and urging them to write their congressmen and senators in support of the President's call for a five-year postponement of tighter air pollution standards for automobiles.[17]

The costs of meeting community standards are, of course, shifted to consumers in the form of higher prices. There is no evidence that on the whole the costs involved in meeting social responsibilities or living up to community standards have resulted in lower profits for corporations. What happens is that the nation systematically realizes its growth in productivity partly in the form of additional product and partly in the form of higher standards with respect to working conditions, product quality, pollution abatement, and the like. In the process of economic growth, there is a constant tension within the community over the degree to which the rising productivity should be devoted to additional product and the degree to which it should be invested in the intangibles. In general, business has been on the side of growth in product and has resisted investment in the intangibles. But whenever community pressure becomes insistent, business goes along.

In the past when economic growth has been relatively steady, the incorporation of rising community standards into business practice has been quite easy. Should the rate of growth slacken, the rise of community standards might be slower and corporations might show less alacrity in meeting these standards.

CONCLUSION

The final question is whether corporate enterprise ever responds to its social responsibilities as a matter of principle even when it is not in the corporate interest to do so. Of course it does. Businessmen even when organized corporatively are human, and they share both the greed and the altruism that characterize most human beings. But an objective view of corporate enterprise leads almost inexorably to the conclusion that the residual of corporate policies and actions that are sheer acts of good will and restraint and which represent genuine long-range sacrifice of corporate interest in favor of the social interest would represent in dollar terms an infinitesimal fraction of total profit.

I shall not go into the many arguments pro and con as to whether business should or should not be altruistic. I have come to the view, however, that corporate power is so potent and so pervasive that voluntary social responsibility cannot be relied upon as a significant form of control over business. The power of business, allied with that of organized labor and exercised through control over the media and influence over government, overwhelms the weak reed of voluntary social responsibility. It may even exceed the power of democratic government. It has become an open question whether business is responsible to the society or whether the society is subservient to business. And it must be clear to all that the urgent social objectives of our time such as racial justice, pollution abatement, conservation of natural resources, and product quality cannot be left solely to voluntary social responsibility.

This kind of strong language was not found in my book of 1953. I was then skeptical and cautious but hopeful about voluntary social responsibility. My experience and observation since then have led me to the conclusion that the social responsibility concept is of minimal effectiveness and that an economy that serves the people can be built in America only if corporate enterprise is brought under social control on terms such that the public and not the corporations control the controllers.

NOTES

1. The preceding section is based on: Howard R. Bowen, "Human Values and the Corporation," in *The Corporation and Social Responsibility,* Proceedings of a Symposium held at the University of Illinois at Chicago Circle, April 20–21, 1967, pp. 13–14.

2. *Christianizing the Social Order* (New York: The Macmillan Company, 1914), p. 156.

3. Andrew Carnegie, *The Gospel of Wealth and Other Timely Essays,* ed. Edward C. Kirkland (Cambridge, Mass.: Harvard University Press, 1962).

4. Boston: Small, Maynard & Company, 1914.

5. "The Changing Basis of Economic Responsibility," *Journal of Political Economy,* March, 1916, pp. 209–29.

6. Chicago: University of Chicago Press, 1926.

7. For a more complete list see my *Social Responsibilities of the Businessman* (New York: Harper & Brothers, 1953), pp. 265–267.

8. The following is a sampling of recent books on the subject: Morrell Heald, *The Social Responsibilities of Business: Company and Community, 1900-1960* (Cleveland: The Press of Case Western Reserve University, 1970); Harold L. Johnson, *Business in Contemporary Society: Framework and Issues* (Belmont, Calif.: Wadsworth Publishing Company, 1971); John J. Corson, *Business in the Humane Society* (New York: McGraw-Hill Book Company, 1971); John D. Rockefeller, 3rd, *The Second American Revolution* (New York: Harper & Row, Perennial Library, 1973); Neil W. Chamberlain, *The Limits of Corporate Responsibility* (New York: Basic Books, 1973); Neil Chamberlain, *The Place of Business in America's Future* (New York: Basic Books, 1973); John Kenneth Galbraith, *Economics and the Public Purpose* (Boston: Houghton Mifflin Company, 1973); James W. McKie, ed., *Social Responsibility and the Business Predicament* (Washington, D.C.: The Brookings Institution, 1974).

9. Bowen, *op. cit.,* pp. 41–42.

10. *Ibid.,* pp. 41–43, 164–176. These proposals were somewhat related to the later development of worker representation in the management of the major enterprises of Jugoslavia.

11. James W. McKie, ed., *Social Responsibility and the Business Predicament* (Washington, D.C.: The Brookings Institution, 1974), p. 15.

12. Milton Friedman, *Capitalism and Freedom* (Chicago: University of Chicago Press, 1962), p. 133.

13. Bowen, *op. cit.,* pp. 14–21.

14. Cf., Howard R. Bowen, *The Business Enterprise as a Subject for Research* (New York: Social Science Research Council, 1955.)

15. When a company is sold as a going concern the purchase price, which often includes payment for intangibles, is included on the balance sheet of the acquiring company.

16. Bowen, *op. cit.,* p. 68.

17. *Los Angeles Times,* 1 February, 1975, Part I, page 2.

WILLIAM LETWIN

Social Responsibility of Business in an Insurance State

The social responsibility of business depends in part on the obligations that the laws at any time and place impose on firms and businessmen. Contemporary Western governments—often described as guardians of the Welfare State but more exactly epitomized as operators of the Insurance State—impose many legal burdens of a characteristic sort on businessmen among others. Under the dominion of governments that do so much to protect many citizens, what additional responsibilities are incumbent on business? To answer this question we must first consider the general scope of business responsibilities, next determine what responsibilities are imposed by the typical laws of an Insurance State, and thus discover what is left over to be done by firms and their executives.

THE SCOPE OF BUSINESS RESPONSIBILITY

When people talk now about the social responsibility of business, what they generally have in mind is a series of problems such as pollution and conservation, honesty in advertising, reliability of products, the right to work, and participation in management. Those problems or their ancestors have been with us for a long time, as has business, which makes it an interesting question why they should command more attention just now, if indeed they do. Certainly they are being attacked with impatient abandon, in the spirit of a surgical nurse who believes that any germ in the operating room will cause a fatal infection. I do not mean to denigrate good housekeeping, an unusually satisfactory art, because we all understand its ends and endorse them more or less. The same cannot be said about cleaning up business. We do not understand just what that would entail; we do not agree about how to start; and worst of all, we are not even clear about the nature of the subject, wrapped as it is in hazy vagueness of ideas and imprecision of words.

Trouble starts because the subject has so misleading a name. This allegation might be rebutted by the argument that the *social responsibility of business,* more like all other names, is purely conventional, and that conventions of usage fully justify any name whatsoever. Certainly it would be misplaced enthusiasm to mount a campaign against the name *table* on the pretext that some substitute would more accurately express the essence of the objects to which it refers. Any name for a thing is as good as any other, once people have acquired the habit of linking the name and the thing. Nevertheless, conventional usage does not always assure common understanding, particularly when the words that compose a complex name (such as social responsibility of business) have cloudy meanings and when the thing to which the name refers is an abstract idea rather than a material object.

The *social responsibility of business* makes it sound as though a subject named *business* has or should have a certain responsibility. If not misleading, this suggestion is certainly imprecise. Business is not a person but an activity, and speaking precisely, responsibilities cannot be postulated of activities. It would be silly to talk about the responsibility of the activity of lifting or pirouetting, although we might sensibly discuss the responsibility of persons engaged in those activities. I suppose that most people who speak of the social responsibility of business are not using *business* as the name of an activity but as an abbreviated name for business firms or for the business sector. But this usage is still imprecise, because responsibility can only be postulated of an actor, a conscious deliberate being who can choose to do one thing or another, in short a moral being; and there is only one thing that fits this specification, namely a human individual. Thus a business sector, firm, or company are not moral beings and therefore cannot bear responsibilities. Only the people who are members of a business firm can have responsibilities, because it is they alone who make choices, although we loosely attribute those choices to the collective body on whose behalf they act. Such looseness is dangerous, because to confuse the action of human beings with those of collective bodies can lead to morally grotesque conclusions. At the end of World War I, those who said that "Germany" had committed atrocities concluded that 'Germany" should be punished, as for instance by reparations, not noticing that this affected German babies born after the war, who, though German, were not guilty. Another example is the recent misbehavior of that mystical entity known as *the presidency,* which bears an inscrutable relation to another one, *the White House*, which displayed such a talent during the Watergate affair for making statements. Whoever did wrong, it was not the presidency or the White House, but various natural persons who tried to cloak themselves by attributing their actions to abstract entities. There is no end to instances of this habit, which is always imprecise and sometimes pernicious.

I conclude that this first step in understanding the social responsibility of business is to recognize clearly that we should ask what is the responsibility—or rather, what are the various responsibilities—of all the human beings who are connected with the activity of business. And we should recognize that this includes all the human beings in society, since all are connected with the activity of business: all as consumers of what they or others produce; many as workers, managers, or owners; and most as participants in politics and government, which set the framework within which the activity of business goes on.

Another confusing term in the name of our subject is *responsibility*. It has at least three distinct meanings. First, a person is said to be responsible for an event in the purely factual sense of being its proximate cause. "Who is responsible for having lit the fire?" can be simply a way of asking who did it. Second, and rather more common in ordinary usage, responsible is used to indicate a moral duty. "Who is responsible for having spilled the milk?" strongly suggests that the person who did it should not have done it; it implicitly accuses the person of an act of vice, in particular of carelessness or wastefulness. Third, responsible is used to indicate a legal duty. Examples are the householder's responsibility to clear snow off his sidewalk, the parent's responsibility for acts of a minor, the citizen's responsibility for filing a tax return. The difference between the three senses of responsibility is emphasized by contrasting their consequences. Moral responsibility results in praise or blame, legal responsibility in reward or punishment, and mere factual responsibility in none of these.

Confusion arises among these three types of responsibility because many actions involve all three. For instance, if a person applies a match to a puddle of kerosene he is factually responsible for setting fire to the house; supposing he did it deliberately, he is morally responsible in both the criminal and civil senses. Lest responsibility be given a bad connotation by this example, we may also instance a man who leaps into a stormy sea to rescue a drowning swimmer. He is factually responsible for bringing the swimmer to shore; he is morally responsible for his act of courage, which merits praise; and he is legally responsible for the rescue, which may entitle him to a reward. Not only may the three forms of responsibility apply to a single action, but at least two forms must always apply together. As nobody can sensibly be called to account morally or legally, for something which he did not in fact do (or deliberately refrain from doing), it follows that moral responsibility also implies factual responsibility. The converse does not hold, because some actions are morally neutral and many are legally indifferent.

Yet although moral responsibility and legal responsibility often overlap, so that the same action may be both blameworthy and punishable, there is no society in which moral responsibility and legal responsibility are identical. The legislator may turn a moral responsibility into a legal one, as by translating the injunction, Thou shalt not kill, into a law against murder. Many laws in any community can be interpreted as expressing moral convictions, though some writers on jurisprudence seem to question such an interpretation.[1] But in no community could *all* moral views be converted into legal duties. A few theocracies may have aimed to do so, with the oppressive effects portrayed in *The Scarlet Letter.* Most communities recognize that it would be futile to legislate modesty or courage or spontaneity. Not only is it impossible for the laws to make people do everything morally desirable, but also the laws regularly require actions that are neither virtuous nor vicious. The rule that a will must be witnessed by two disinterested persons and the rule that cars must drive on the right do not result from the conviction that these are morally superior ways of doing things; they result rather from technical convenience or morally neutral conventions. And finally, the imperfect congruence of moral and legal responsibility is demonstrated by the fact that every state enforces some legal responsibilities that conflict with the moral views of some or many citizens. For all these reasons moral responsibility and legal responsibility never correspond exactly, neatly, or entirely.

What then are we to make of the position asserted by some businessmen that the whole responsibility of firms is to obey the laws, no more and no less? Is it tenable to hold that the entire social responsibility of business is to shoulder as gracefully as possible whatever duties have been imposed by the laws of the land? I believe it is not. Since the prevailing moral code is neither wholly nor exactly represented in the laws, the statement that a company is responsible only to the laws is tantamount to the assertion that a company is immune from *moral* responsibility. This implication might be defended on the argument that a company is not a moral being; lacking a conscience it is necessarily deaf to moral injunctions. This view, which some advance by way of accusing business and others to defend it, is a further reason to abandon the practice of regarding a business firm as a thing rather than as the name for a certain number of people related to each other in certain ways. Correctly considered, the firm consists of human beings, and as human beings they are unable to live in a moral vacuum. When a man moves from his activities as a father or a friend to those as a manager or laborer, he is not miraculously exempted from moral duties. "All's fair in love or war" (and, as some add, in business) reminds us that our proverb-making ancestors were barbarians.

We should translate the social responsibility of business into the more precise statement that persons engaged in the activity of business have responsibilities, some of which are imposed by the law, others by moral principle, and some, though not all, by both.

So we arrive at the third term of our formula, *social*, which needs analysis at least as badly as the other two. Social is that which pertains to society, and *society* is an abstraction. It is as intangible as *love, momentum,* or *business.* It cannot be apprehended by the senses but only by the mind. It is not the name of a thing, but rather a set of relationships. It is commonly used, in a loose way, to designate all of the people who live together in a particular country. And taking society in this colloquial sense, we might interpret the social responsibility of business as raising the question, What obligations (moral and legal) have all the human beings who are connected with business to all the human beings who live in the same country?

Recalling that all the people in any place are somehow or other connected with the activity of business, we can restate the question as, What obligations (moral and legal) have all the human beings to all the human beings? The question will be easier to cope with if we decompose it so as to ask, *What obligations (moral and legal) has any person to other persons?* That is the general question we should be discussing, if we seek clarity, when we talk about the social responsibility of business. It is not easy to answer, but at least it is easier to understand.

What responsibilities does any human being incur towards all others, as a result of being involved, one way or another, in the activity of business? Putting the question in this way leads immediately to some valuable inferences. First of all, it dispels the prejudicial implication that business is *they* and society is *we.* It reveals that the problem is really one of we and we. The true question is, What should I, when I vote, aim to do by way of altering the relations between myself, in my aspects as an employee, and all others? The true question, to put it another way, an imprecise way, is, What should society require of society? The responsibility is everyone's because everyone is involved in the intricate network of relations that we call society, and everyone is also involved in the processes of getting and spending that we call business.

The second advantage of our rerendering of the problem is that it emphasizes how very many kinds of relations need to be examined. For instance, to probe deeply we will be bound to inquire into the responsibilities of an employee to his own employer, other employers, his fellow employees, customers, noncustomers who he meets in the course of business, managers, insurers, suppliers, and so on. Similarly, we should examine the proper relations between the buyer of a product and the seller, the manufacturing firm, its employees, other buyers, persons to whom he may lend the product or in whose presence he uses it, and many others. And the range of relationships in question is greatly increased if we interpret society as including relations among all human beings on earth, wherever they may live and whether living now or yet to be born. Of course the whole array of topics so revealed is impossibly large.

It may seem that we could narrow the subject by concentrating on the responsibility of executives. As the executive is authorized to make decisions on behalf of the firm, decisions binding on many persons connected with the firm, it is not altogether perverse to translate the social responsibility of business into the social responsibility of executives. But to do so would be to imply falsely that executives, alone of all persons connected with the activity of business, have moral and legal responsibilities. Responsibilities of persons in authority, though special, are not unique. The commander who gives an order to shoot is responsible for the outcome; and so, in a different way, is the soldier who obeys the order. In other words, the responsibility of the businessman—strangely come to mean the head of a business, unlike lumberman, mailman, rag-and-bone man, or Frenchman, which stretch high and low—is a special case within the responsibility of business, and that in turn is a special case within the domains of ethics and law.

LEGAL RESPONSIBILITIES

What responsibilities have the laws placed on the several parties to business transactions? The laws to which I refer are the common law and statutes of America and England, echoed in other English-speaking countries, and paralleled in other democracies. Although I will review only a few segments of that body of law, what they disclose is a general tendency to relieve each individual of unfortunate consequences that may befall him by transferring the cost of those consequences to a large class of individuals. This will be recognized as the underlying principle of any insurance scheme. And because it is a prevalent tendency of our laws, we may speak of the onset of the *Insurance State.*

Consumer's Insurance

It is a commonplace among historians that modern Western history is one grand movement from laissez-faire toward interventionism. This summary, not more accurate than many other wide generalizations about human affairs, is often illustrated by the story of how caveat emptor, the original rule in a crude society, was superseded by the more civilized doctrine of implied warranty. The real story is vastly more complicated than that.

At the outset, say between 1000 A.D. and 1600 A.D., there was in England little laissez-faire and no caveat emptor. On the contrary, much business was closely regulated by government. Especially vigorous was regulation of common foodstuffs, particularly those which, even in a predominantly agricultural society, were bought rather than made at home.

Bread commanded the most careful attention. Public officials decreed from time to time the standard weight of the penny loaf, other officials inspected the product, and sellers caught skimping on weight or quality were punished. But man does not live by bread alone. The clerk of the market at Norwich in 1564, for instance, reported an inquest which determined that twelve bakers were selling underweight breads, and also that four named brewers "do brew their ale not wholesome for man's body, and that they have no taster" though they were bound by law to employ one, and that nine fishmongers "do sell their fish not well watered."[2] Medieval records, in England, France, and elsewhere in Europe abound in reports of cheating merchants and of the penalties to which they were subjected by municipal authorities and by the guilds which sternly regulated various crafts.[3] When the buyer ventured outside the range of common regulated goods, he still had ample protection, because the criminal law as well as the civil law came to his aid against the seller who misrepresented his goods. As a leading authority tells us,

> The false seller was not seen just as the breaker of a private contract; he was a malefactor commonly liable to punishment at the instance of authority as well as to a suit for compensation. Consumer protection is neither a modern invention nor an exclusively modern need. It was a part of the "criminal" law of local jurisdictions, offenses being seen as wrongs, trespasses, to the city or whatever it might be as well as to the party.[4]

The buyer was not, in all such instances, also the consumer of the product; and one may wonder just how much protection he "needed," inasmuch as the then-conditions of life did not make people very trustful; but need or no, the protection was there.

All that changed in time. By 1800 or so the doctrine of caveat emptor had come into operation. Little by little, judges adopted a rule that the buyer must assume legal responsibility for choosing goods that suit his purposes. There are several good moral arguments to sustain this principle of law. The buyer may be as well qualified as the seller to judge quality: good cooks know as much about meat as good butchers, and butchers as farmers. The buyer knows more about the particular use to which he means to put the article than does the seller: the hardware merchant may know about nails in general, but it is the carpenter who knows how hard is the wood, how heavy the hammer, and how steady his hand. Moreover, the buyer is as likely to be able to afford the loss as the seller: rich people buy many things from small tradesmen poised on the brink of bankruptcy. In any event, caveat emptor is one plausible way of arranging legal responsibilities as between buyer and seller, not in any sense the original way but not necessarily an immoral way. There is always a risk that an article that looks right will turn out to be rotten inside, weak, dangerous or otherwise faulty. Somebody has to bear that risk, and the rule of caveat emptor put it on the buyer, though he could shift it to the vendor by insisting on a warranty.

So far we have been looking at only a small segment of the chain that connects the beginning or production with the ultimate state in consumption. Before the seller stand the jobber, wholesaler, maker, his suppliers, their suppliers, as well as the employees and agents of all those; beyond the buyer are the consumers, who may include his family and guests, his employees, and his customers. For a while life was simple, because as long as remedy was sought within the law of contract, the buyer could proceed only against the seller. The buyer could not recover from the maker, nor the consumer from the seller, for want of contract between them.

All that has changed again, partly due to developments in the common law, partly by legislation. The former can be illustrated by the leading case of *Macpherson* v. *Buick,* decided in 1916 by the highest court of New York, the opinion written by Cardozo.[5] Macpherson had bought a Buick from a car dealer who bought it from the manufacturers. The car collapsed because a wheel was made of defective wood; the wheel had been made not by the Buick Company but by one of its suppliers; however, the Buick Company had not closely inspected the wheel, relying instead on the reputability of the wheel maker. The court awarded damages to Macpherson for injuries suffered when the car broke down. It reached its decsion by following a long line of decisions dating back to about 1800, in which manufacturers of "inherently dangerous" articles had been held responsible for damages occurring to the ultimate buyer and sometimes even to persons who used the goods though they had not bought them.[6] The massive shift culminating in *Macpherson* v. *Buick* was made possible or easier by evolution in the law of tort, which does not require the plaintiff to found his plea on a contractual relation with the defendant. Further evolution during the last half-century is indicated in the opinion of a high California judge. "A manufacturer," he held, "is strictly liable in tort when an article he places on the market, knowing that it is to be used without inspection for defects, proves to have a defect that causes injury to a human being." The thrust of this ruling is emphasized by the gloss of a legal scholar: "Not only a purchaser, mind you, not only a privy or relative or connection of a purchaser, but a 'human being' pure and simple."[7] We may conclude that the common law has not only demolished caveat emptor, has not only lifted responsibility from the buyer and placed it on the maker, but has stretched the maker's responsibility all the way forward to anyone injured by his fault.

Meanwhile legislatures have been at work to the same end. The British Sale of Goods Act, one specimen among many of this species, puts responsibility for faulty goods squarely on the seller. The British Consumer's Association maintains that the seller and manufacturer should be made jointly responsible, the buyer thus enabled to claim redress from either or both.[8] I see no reason to doubt that law, in all of the free world, is being pushed in that direction.

What will be the economic effect of this shift? Will it, as advocates of consumer protection imagine, benefit consumers at the expense of manufacturers? Will it, in other words, increase the utility that consumers enjoy by reducing the profits earned by shareholders? This is a dubious hope. Let us suppose that a manufacturer produces 1,000 barrels a day by a process which results in ten of those being faulty, and that selling them at a price of $5 each he makes exactly the standard rate of profit, the minimum at which it pays him in the long run to stay in that business. Suppose that the law now transfers from the buyer to him the legal responsibility for faulty goods. When the buyers now return the ten faulty barrels, he refunds $50, which reduces his gross earnings below the break-even point. In order to stay in business in the long run, he (like all his competitors) must now raise the price to $5.05 per barrel, in order to restore daily earnings to the break-even level of $5,000. From the standpoint of the consumer, the risk of his buying an unusable article, which was a risk of 1 percent, has been converted into an insurance fee of 1 percent, which guarantees him that should he get a bad barrel he will suffer no loss on that account. A 1 percent premium to ward off a 1 percent risk is fair insurance, but on the other hand it is compulsory insurance.

Of course the story is too simple. It assumes competitive markets and it assumes that long-run costs determine long-run prices and it assumes many other things, though these are reasonably plausible assumptions. But it omits an important alternative. After all, instead of swallowing the cost of the returned faulty barrels, the manufacturer may try to reduce the number of them by one means or another. Quality control inspection is one possibility, the one that courts tend to fasten on, though not the only one. But whatever method may be adopted, it will cost something, and that cost will be transferred to the consumer in the long run. So whether the manufacturer does or does not improve the reliability of the product, in the long run the consumer will pay for his freedom from risk by paying an insurance premium.

In short, although the legal burden has been shifted from buyer to seller, the economic burden has not been shifted in the same way. Instead, the economic burden has been shifted from a few unlucky consumers to all consumers, though it may be that in the process the total burden has been lightened.

Employment Insurance

Much current thinking about relations between employer and employee concerns the vague idea of "a right to a job." It is vague because it leaves various vital questions unanswered and even unasked. Does the right inhere in everyone who has a job or does it extend also to everyone who wants a job? Is it a right to some job, any job, or the correct job? Is it a right of an employee to continue in his present job, any job with equivalent pay, or only in a job of some sort with his present employer? On whom fall the obligations corresponding to the right: the present employer (but what if he goes out of business?), all employers in that industry, or the government? Is the right extinguished by misconduct of the employee, or by plain incompetence or inefficiency, or is it absolute? Does seniority confer a greater right (quite apart from contractual arrangements), or conversely, does an overriding right attach to people who—because of sex, youth or age, color, or whatever—have had the hardest time finding work and therefore have accumulated little seniority? And how does all this relate to a guaranteed annual wage; is the right to a job something beyond a right to a secure and decent income? All these questions are only a brief sampling to suggest how indeterminate is the asserted right in theory, quite apart from practical difficulties of establishing it by law.

Before turning to the present legal status of the right to work, it will be useful to review hastily its historical background. I take it that a right to work came to be asserted as against two features of economic life during what some describe as the Age of Laissez Faire and what might better be called the Age of Economic Liberalism, in any event the period that stretched, in the Anglo-American domain, from about 1750 to about 1900. The first feature was the employer's power, within the law, to hire whom he wished and dismiss when he pleased. The power seems especially harsh if one ignores the context in which it grew up. It was balanced by a power of the employee to enter and leave anybody's employment at will, a power equal at law if not always in fact. An employer might exercise his power captiously, so might an employee, some of both did. But as real wages rose and fell during the period, there must have been times when the employer was hard pressed to find as many workers as he wanted, even if at other times he could act a petty tyrant, knowing that there were plenty of unemployed eager to work for him. It is easy to forget also that economic liberalism came about as a reform of the bad old time, when activities of employers, employees, and everybody else had been subject to repressive control, exercised by feudal autocrats as well as by laws and customs which confined men, freemen as well as serfs, in town and country, to tight patterns of hierarchy and tradition. To emerge from all that into the fresh air of voluntary contract, mobility, and ambition was a blessing for man and master alike, achieved after centuries of chipping away at the old dispensation. Yet the new order had its disadvantages as well. Slaves, like cattle, are not allowed to starve, being too valuable to their owners. As a freeman has no owner, he may starve. His way to avoid starvation is to get insurance. He may insure himself by saving during the fat years or by joining mutual schemes, of which there are many possible varieties. Many demands of labor unions, from the beginning, can be interpreted as efforts to help workers find economic security.

Concurrent with the employer's power to dismiss (unlimited by law though subject to limitation by contract) was the onset of business cycles, which resulted in sharp unemployment every seventh year or so. A rural population habituated to periodic famines might have felt that periodic depressions were merely a new form, possibly even a milder form, of familiar disasters. But as death and birth did their work, the father's perils were forgotten and the son became obsessed with the chronic sore of worklessness. Some, who thought the disease was a congenital and incurable defect of private enterprise, profits, and factories, joined one or another branch of the radical opposition to liberalism. Others, who thought that the disease was inessential and curable, pushed the liberal state toward the Insurance State.

Considerable success has been achieved in covering risks arising from the business cycle. Unemployment compensation based on compulsory insurance schemes administered by government—financed by contributions from employees, employers, and taxpayers who belong to neither of those groups—has become a standard fixture in the free world. A rather more subtle way to ward off the risk of unemployment is by general policy to eliminate the business cycle. Policies of these sorts were officially initiated by the British "Employment Policy White Paper" of 1944. The Employment Act of 1946, statutory keystone of American contracyclical policies, although it deliberately shied away from the sacred formula of "full employment," came as close as possible to implying that this should be a prime objective of federal economic policy; and it is needless to add that similar declarations have been made by all well-conducted governments. Nor are these declarations merely pious, as is demonstrated by the constant readiness of governments during the postwar period to risk inflation in order to avoid unemployment. Overall policies to this effect have been supplemented, moreover, by particular rescue operations intended to save the jobs that would be lost if inefficient or unlucky firms went bankrupt. British governments have been notable rescuers: Mr. Edward Heath, a recent Conservative prime minister, bailed out a number of firms such as the North Clyde shipbuilders, even though he had declared the fixed intention of his administration to do no such thing. Mr. Harold Wilson's Labor government has done more of the same, though within a policy of exchanging public aid for a measure of public ownership.[9] On these broader and narrower fronts, then, governments act as though they believe there is a right to work. They act as though everyone who has a job or would like one should get one, at the expense, if necessary, of all those whose real income is cut by inflation, of all those whose real income will be cut by the additional cost of servicing a public debt increased by deficit financing, and of all those who pay the taxes which subsidize unprofitable businesses. When you make jobs that way, you do not make them free of cost. What you are engaged in is shifting the burden of unemployment from the few who would have suffered it to the many who pay to avoid it. The right to a job—so far as government enforces it by deficit and subsidy—is the name of an insurance scheme.

How far do the laws enforce the right to a job by placing a specific responsibility on the employer? Some hundreds of ticket clerks struck recently because British Airways proposed a shuttle service in which tickets would be issued by flight attendants. The professional ticketers felt that their rights to their own jobs were being infringed. Not a novel sort of protest, it is the core of many jurisdictional disputes. Nobody seriously believes that the laws should require every employer to keep every employee doing the same kind of work he was hired to do, even though that sort of work is no longer necessary. Neither do the laws require employers to retain in employment forevermore, employment of some kind or other, anybody whom they have once hired. But steps in that direction have been taken in Britain. An employee "wrongfully dismissed" can collect damages from his employer and may be reinstated in his job by order of the court. Any employee who is dismissed because of shortage of work must be compensated by his employer with "redundancy pay," the sum being determined, according to statute, in relation to his wages and length of service. As this rule does not cover employees who are temporarily put on part time, a new rule is being prepared which will require employers to pay every employee a guaranteed minimum wage. The same piece of legislation will also make the employer responsible for paying maternity benefits, for paying wages to workers while absent from work for union activities, for giving workers long notice of dismissal whatever the cause, and for providing any dismissed worker with a written justification of why he was dismissed.[10]

Under such rules the employer is gradually becoming the operator of a scheme of unemployment compensation for his employees. But let us be clear where the economic burden falls. For the employer these outlays newly imposed by law represent an increase in the cost of labor. All else being equal, he will therefore aim to use less labor and to produce a smaller output. So in the short run the cost of this unemployment compensation will be carried by (1) all potential employees of this firm, the demand for whose services has not been reduced, (2) all consumers of the product, the output of which has been reduced, and (3) all owners of the firm, the returns to whose capital have been reduced. In the long run, production will be readjusted by using more capital and less labor, which would aggravate the decline in demand for labor, increase the output of the product though not restore it to previous levels, and restore the rate of return to capital. And insofar as the rules apply to all employers, similar effects will be felt throughout the economy. Of course, the impact would be very much more complex than that, depending as it does on the degree of competitiveness in the economy, the rationality of managers, the extent to which these effects are altered and masked by improvements in technology, and many other variables. But the main lines can be taken as a reliable general prediction.

What all this tells us is that enforcing the right to work on employers, while it eliminates the risk of unemployment for people who are already employed, puts the burden on those who have never been employed and now experience greater difficulty in finding a job, on consumers, and on shareholders, many of whom are retired employees benefiting from private pension schemes. In short, an enforced right to work reduces the risks facing middle-aged workers by placing an added burden on the young and old and on all consumers, which latter class, of course, includes the middle-aged workers as well. People can rationally disagree about whether this kind of insurance is on the whole beneficial. They cannot rationally interpret it as nothing but a way of redistributing income from the wealthy employer to the impoverished employee. It is an insurance, though a curious one, in which the beneficiaries contrive with the aid of the law to transfer part of the insurance premium, no one can say exactly how much or little of it, onto the shoulders of persons some of whom are less privileged than themselves.

What if a private employer, fallen on bad times, were financially unable to carry out a legal responsibility to keep all his employees fully employed? If the right to a job is interpreted quite literally, as meaning security of work rather than of income, then three options are open. Government may subsidize the private employer, though indefinitely high and long subsidies are an expensive proposition. Government may nationalize the firm, though doing so cannot be expected to reduce the cost of keeping it going; on the other hand, nationalization has the merit that it squanders public money on public property rather than private property. Finally, government may allow the private firm to be closed down, while undertaking to provide its former employees with equivalent jobs in the public sector. Whichever of these three avenues is followed, government becomes the employer of last resort in each such bankruptcy. If it follows either the second or third, the public sector will sooner or later become the chief employer. It seems likely (though clearly not irreversible) that the right to work will tend to nudge the Insurance State towards socialism.

Environmental Insurance

Those who believe history is a movement as brisk and straight as a shark's surge toward its prey naturally believe that pollution is a phenomenon of today, before which virgin Nature had remained always unsullied, a condition to which men must now aim to restore her. The truth is far less gratifying. Pollution is as old as man and older. Animals of prolific sorts overgraze their feeding grounds, and having polluted that environment move on to another, or for want of food die off, polluting some other place in a different way. Anyone who believes that nonhuman animals are too wise to do such things will regret to hear of the *Cactoblastis cactorum* in Queensland, who starved "after they had denuded the countryside of the prickly pear which is their food and left the habitat bare of food for their posterity" and of many similar tragedies.[11] This may seem to be a problem of conservation rather than pollution, though I believe that distinction to be superficial. Call it what you will, it is one illustration among many to show that the innocent animals as well as quite a few plants were polluting Nature long before wicked man appeared on the scene. Ever since, pollution has been rife wherever men lived; medieval cities may have set the all-time record for dirtiness of every sort, but tiny villages and isolated homesteads anywhere a thousand years ago were polluted enough for practical purposes, that is, enough to make men's lives brief and tawdry. There may be more pollutants floating around the world just now than ever before, but it would be very difficult to establish that they cause earlier death and more suffering per capita now than ever before.

Public control of pollution is not a modern invention either. To illustrate its history, we may turn to the development of the law of nuisance in England since the Norman Conquest. In 1201 Simon of Marston recovered damages from his neighbor, Jordan the Miller, who raised his mill pool, which flooded Simon's field.[12] In 1608 William Aldred of Norfolk sued his neighbor, Thomas Benton, for building a pigsty next to Aldred's house, with the consequences that might have been expected. Benton put up the strong defense that "the building of the house of hogs was necessary for the sustenance of man: and one ought not to have so delicate a nose, that he cannot bear the smell of hogs ...," despite which Aldred won.[13] It would be tempting to parade many like instances, as showing the variety of things that men have done in their ordinary pursuit of lawful purposes which have inconvenienced their neighbors. All of them would show the same rule of law to be operating: whenever a man pollutes his neighbor's environment in a degree beyond what is an unavoidable consequence of living or what is customary at that time and place, the judges will step in to abate the nuisance or award damages. The core of the legal responsibility, as many judges put it (and put it still in many nuisance cases) was: "Every man must so use his own, as not to do damage to another."[14]

All this served well enough as long as the source of nuisance was relatively simple offenses caused by immediate neighbors. To this day the law reports of American state courts are full of nuisance actions brought against funeral parlors which intrude in peaceful residential sections, psychically polluting them with foreboding of mortality; and as often as not the plaintiffs win. But when the defendant is a large organization with a "public function," owning a great deal of fixed capital, it wins more often than not. Nuisance actions against airports, cemeteries, factories, and refineries—especially after they have been in place for a while, for only then do their effluents make themselves felt—do not succeed, for judges will not casually undo a way of life. On rare occasions, about an hundred years ago, a smelting operation might be stopped because it killed plants and animals in the vicinity, but in time it became rare even to award damages in such a case.[15]

Effective control of pollution, as it is now generated, requires legislation, international agreements, and discretionary acts of public policy. Those are now forthcoming, throughout the developed world at least, in large number. I do not propose to catalogue the legal responsibilities daily being placed on firms that emit smoke, carry crude oil in tankers, operate nuclear power stations, use water for cooling or acid for tempering, or are otherwise capable of making things less agreeable for some human being somewhere. I mean instead to show in what way public control of pollution constitutes a scheme of insurance.

Pollution is an inevitable outcome of all human activity. When we breathe we exhale carbon dioxide, which is a pollutant. When we move we turn potential energy into kinetic energy plus heat, which is usually a pollutant. When we work we inevitably make not only the intended product but also all sorts of by-products, which are pollutants. The by-products of a furnace are fumes and ash; of a lathe, shavings; of a cornfield, husks; and of an office, used paper. All such are pollutants because if not removed they would foul the working environment, and if removed they will foul some other part of the environment. So pollution cannot be eliminated, but only reduced, or concentrated in places and in forms that we find most tolerable.

If pollution is not controlled, there is a considerable risk that some individuals will suffer much more than most. People who live just leeward of a stockyard, downhill from a refinery, under the glide path of an airport are special victims of fate, always assuming they did not choose that fate deliberately. Assuming they have not brought it on themselves, anybody's sense of justice suggests that they deserve a remedy.

Various remedies are possible. The polluter may be legally required to stop his activity altogether, move it elsewhere, modify it so as to reduce pollution to a specified level, continue it and pay damages, or continue it and pay for moving the sufferers out of reach. The remedies have different consequences in detail but the same consequence in general. All of them raise the cost of producing the goods in question.

Who bears the additional cost? Not, as the naive suppose, the producers. Rather, in the short run the cost will be shared between the consumers (who will pay a higher price and get a smaller output) and the producers (who will earn a lower profit), in a ratio which depends on the long price-elasticities of demand and supply. In the long run, the cost will be born entirely by the consumers, who will get less of the product and at a price just as much higher as will cover the extra cost. And this is of course entirely just, since the consumers will now be buying not only the product as before but in addition a reduced amount of suffering from pollution. The decrease in suffering may well be worth much more than is paid to achieve it. Nevertheless, by insisting that pollution be controlled, government will have put a legal responsibility on producers and an economic burden on consumers.

This is clearly an insurance scheme, since the additional cost of reducing pollution is borne by *all* consumers, though the benefits are experienced by those relatively few who were previously exposed to pollution. If the consumers of the now more expensive products were the identical persons who had previously suffered from pollution, then it would be a straightforward case, in that those who paid for the insurance were equally at risk of needing it—though somewhat inequitable in that the amount of insurance premium paid by any person would be proportionate to how much of the product he bought rather than to his risk of suffering from pollution. But if some people are for one reason or another more exposed than others to pollution, then pollution control is another of those uncomfortable insurance schemes in which the people who must pay are not the same as the people who benefit. Worst of all, it cannot be shown as probable, much less certain, that the beneficiaries are in any way more needy than those who subsidize their benefits.

Some General Reflections on Insurance

Many other legal arrangements in modern states can be interpreted in the same manner as the foregoing. Limited liability of shareholders, the privilege of bankruptcy, employers' liability for negligence of employees, and no-fault car insurance are other items in a large and growing catalogue of schemes whereby one group of persons is insured at the expense of a different group.

It is emphatically not the case that all compulsory insurance schemes have this character. For instance, Federal Deposit Insurance in America is supported by all customers of banks and is, at least roughly, equally likely to benefit any one of them. Physicians' and lawyers' insurance for malpractice, where compulsory, is like that too. So would retirement benefits under compulsory schemes be, if the benefits paid out were not, as so often they are, subsidized by current tax revenues, which makes them partly a compulsory redistribution of income from younger generations to an older one. Perhaps compulsory insurance schemes always tend to attract a degree of public subsidy, but many seem to be reasonably self-contained.

Neither do I mean to suggest that the modern state is concerned exclusively with insurance. Much of its budget goes that way, especially if we consider defense establishments as the most popular form of insurance. But most of the laws are still mainly concerned with the ancient activity of governing rather than the rather more recent activity of purveying public goods. Nevertheless, the balance has been shifting. It may be an exaggeration to speak of the Insurance State, for every state does many things, but it is a pardonable exaggeration if it captures the prevailing spirit of government.

In this analysis of how the Insurance State Operates, the reader may have detected a faint reservation about its merits.

Some people wish to avert certain risks. Fear is more or less natural and prudence is more or less admirable. It is therefore right to wish to avert some risks, and even if it were not right it would be a desire harmless enough to be indulged. If people form private associations to insure themselves against those risks which as individuals they wish to avoid, that can be endorsed as desirable or at least tolerated as an amiable weakness.

Yet there surely are some few who positively enjoy taking risks. Their more temperate brethren should, I believe, let such people indulge their tastes, at least insofar as the risk seeker is not carrying others unwillingly with him, is not, let us say, a bus driver gaily swinging along a winding mountain road. Certainly, if the others should be permitted to have insurance, he should be permitted not to have it.

An argument commonly made against allowing anyone to do without insurance is that when misfortune strikes them the uninsured will throw themselves on the mercy of the community, and even were they too proud to appeal for help, sympathy would force the rest of us to volunteer it. On such reasoning some firms require employees to carry a minimum of life insurance, medical insurance, and private pension insurance. These and many similar arrangements are not magnanimous displays of generosity so much as ways in which the austere members of a group defend themselves against claims by the more casual. So might a father force his son to save, for fear that otherwise he might require subvention, which the father would be unable to refuse. So does the state (or the public) require all to buy unemployment compensation. Another ground for the policy, of course, is the belief that insurance is so good for people that they should be made to have it, especially those who least want it. Subjecting people who are morally mature to such compulsion, paternalistic in the strict sense of the word, would be justified if those who impose it could present credentials certifying their superiority. At best, then, compulsory insurance makes the lighthearted behave as though they were earnest; at worst it treats them like children; and the whole effort turns into farce when, as often happens, somebody else really foots the bill.

Another ground for reservations about compulsory insurance is familiar, the possibility that a person insured against all unfortunate consequences of his actions may get careless. This point, recently made by the London Solicitors' Litigation Association in its evidence to the Royal Commission on Personal Injuries, as an objection to the proposal for no-fault compensation to victims of accidents, has been made many times before in many contexts.[16] I cannot point to any persuasive evidence that it is true, but intuition suggests that many people would restrain themselves if they knew that they would have to pay for the consequences of inattention. Were this not probable, it would be futile to hope that punishment, blame, or cost could ever influence the conduct of any human being; in which case it would be futile for us to consider gravely the social responsibility of business. In other words, when we set out to consider this question at all, we necessarily assume that men's actions can be influenced by the legal and moral responsibilities placed on them, from which it follows that we must expect some diminution of personal carefulness to result from the typical legal arrangements of an Insurance State. Though this disadvantage may be more than offset by various benefits, it may not be, and in any event it should be reckoned in striking the final balance. One possible implication, for instance, is that where the risk of private loss to the owner, director, and manager is minimized by such legal devices as limited liability bankruptcy, and public subsidies to failing firms, managers may become less careful, not only in the sense of being willing to take greater risks (to the detriment or advantage of the public, according to luck) but also of becoming more prone to negligence. The Insurance State expands the legal responsibilities of its subjects with the ironical result of perhaps making them act less responsibly.

MORAL RESPONSIBILITIES

For anybody except a duly authorized guide to instruct others in their moral duties, they being sane adults, is an impertinence. What any individual ought to do in a given situation must depend on his moral principles and habits—inevitably somewhat peculiar to himself, especially in emphasis and modulation, though far less idiosyncratic in basic substance than is commonly supposed—and on his judgment of particularities in the situation, which is apt to differ markedly from the judgment of others. The substantive components of ethical behavior, comprising principles and their application to cases, are more or less private to each person. Others may exhort, criticize, advise, which may influence, illuminate, or confound; but nobody can solve another's ethical dilemmas by presenting him with authoritative judgments.

Happily, on the other hand, moral conduct can be rationally analyzed in very broad terms that elicit broad procedural principles, impersonal in that they apply equally to everyone, whatever his individual substantive views and style. One of these broad principles is that moral responsibilities arise as to each and every relation that a human being has to any other. Lest this statement be misinterpreted as the fundamental maxim of a specific moral doctrine, that of universal benevolence, two qualifications must be appended. The *kind* of moral responsibility one person owes another depends on the kind of activity which at that moment links them; the *intensity* of responsibility depends on the closeness, morally speaking, of the two.

What meaning we should attach to the first qualification will become clearer as we consider some instances. The activity of being parent to a young child involves moral responsibility to support the child and foster its ultimate independence. Although opinions differ as to exactly what these responsibilities entail in general, and judgments differ even more as to what is required for this particular child at this moment, wide agreement exists about the parent's moral obligation in the abstract. By contrast, the activity of judging in a court of law imposes moral responsibilities of a totally different sort. The judge is not to provide for the litigants' needs or foster their eventual maturity but rather to resolve their dispute in a disinterested manner. Again, the activity of taking part in a contest puts on the contender a moral responsibility specific to that activity, which is to act fairly, even beyond the quasi-legal responsibilities imposed by the rules of the game. The tennis player who deliberately loses a point in order to compensate for a linesman's miscall in his favor is carrying out his moral responsibility, going beyond his legal responsibility of which the linesman is arbiter. The contestant's duty is not to foster the well-being of his opponent, not to take a disinterested view as between himself and the opponent, but to play decently.

Should business executives fashion their general moral behavior in accordance with any of the above models? Certainly not. An executive does not in the course of business stand in relation to anybody as parent to child, because his customers, employees, stockholders, suppliers, and all the rest are mature adults, not presumed to require sustaining and educating, especially by him. An executive is not, in general, a judge as between litigants. Neither is he a contestant, except possibly in relation to competitors, certainly not in relation to customers, employees, and the like. As buyer and seller he is linked to others by the activity of exchange, in which the basic moral responsibility is not to deceive the other—though what constitutes deception, in the moral sense, is a large question, full of shoals and rapids. Besides engaging in exchange, a business executive acts as a ruler, exercising authority over his subordinates. The community that he governs consists of free men who come together voluntarily to pursue a common purpose, which is, however, only one among all the ends at which each individual participant aims, and not the most important one. The executive's moral responsibility in this activity is to command in a way that properly balances the obligations he places on participants with the various other ends they wish to pursue in the rest of their lives. This is easier to say generally than to spell out in particular, but that is true of all abstract principles, which does not invalidate them or impugn their usefulness. Again, a further activity of the executive is to manage on behalf of the owners, which involves the moral responsibility of a trustee. To sum up, the moral responsibilities of an executive are of diverse types, according to the many different types of activity in which he necessarily engages. We should not chastise him if he makes moral decisions different than the ones we would have made; we should reprimand him if he feels dispensed from moral obligations (on the ground that business and morality do not mix); and we should criticize him if he confuses the kinds of moral obligations appropriate to his various activities (as, for instance, by supposing, perhaps in misguided generosity, that he owes parental care to his employees).

The intensity of one's moral responsibility to others, given a certain type of responsibility, depends on their proximity. If I consider that I have a moral duty to aid people in need, and knowing that my capacity to aid is limited relative to the needs that exist, it is reasonable that I should distribute aid, in that order of priority, to dependents, friends, associates, and last of all to people I do not know. An opposing view is that we should not consider the suppliant's proximity but the extent of his need. But to discover and accurately estimate the distribution of need over the whole world is a task beyond anybody's capacity, and therefore those who wish to aid in accordance with need will often be making a gesture only, well-intentioned but impractical as compared to aiding those whose circumstances are known to the benefactor as part of his immediate world. It is divine to love all men equally; we must confine ourselves to the mortal's obligation to give what limited help we can in ways which will make it of some real use to the recipients.

Executives who wish most fervently to do right feel oppressed by the terrible weight of moral calculation required to ascertain the impact of their actions. What effect, they feel they must consider, will their decisions about smoke control have on Siberian peasants or about pricing policy on citizens of Madras? If an American company has decided to make philanthropic contributions, what amount should be directed toward improving the education of Australians? Such questions cannot be laughed away on the brutal premise that far-off people are too inferior to matter, but they may have to be deliberately overlooked on the argument that obligations closer to home have a prior claim. This was one of the most telling objections to the U. S. foreign aid program during the 1960s, and if the government of the U. S. A. was rightly accused of trying to operate on too wide a horizon, then business executives can conclude a fortiori that they should not—because they cannot—hold themselves morally responsible to everyone throughout the world. The general principle that people incur just as much moral responsibility when engaged in business as in any other part of their lives would be self-destructive if it were interpreted as allocating to each person a burden far beyond his power to bear.

Many abstract questions about ethics and business become more vivid if examined in their bearing on an episode such as the thalidomide case. Who was morally responsible for the deformation of thalidomide babies? A case can be made out against every sort of person who was involved. The firm which developed and originally marketed thalidomide did so, it has been said, without testing it enough. Some scientists in that company, it has been said, expressed doubts about the product's safety; but if they failed to publicize those doubts, once the firm decided to produce thalidomide, then they morally implicated themselves by their silence. In certain countries, apparently, sale was licensed by public agencies; the licensing authorities, and their employees, can be said to have moral responsibility greater than that of the firm, since the firm proposes but they dispose. Other firms made the product on license; they are morally responsible for not having conducted their own tests, for accepting the assurances of a clearly interested party. Wholesalers and retailers sold the stuff; although it may not be feasible for them to test all products they sell, they cannot totally shed moral responsibility by claiming that it is convenient for them to remain ignorant, cheaper to rely blindly on assurances of the makers. Doctors prescribed the drug, which was not obtainable otherwise; can it be held that the doctors' moral responsibility to his patient is exhausted by his reading the advertising literature of the pharmaceutical manufacturer? And what about the women who took the drug? If the patient's moral responsibility for his own actions is fully satisfied by following the prescription of a doctor, then a solidier would morally be justified in following any command issued by an officer. Hesitant as I am to pronounce on so tangled a case, I am inclined to believe that all those parties were jointly responsible, though not equally responsible if, as has been alleged, information about the danger was suppressed willfully and in bad faith, and if, as many would say, deliberate deception is more culpable than normal carelessness, and if patients are in some sense entitled to rely on physicians.

Looking forward, we might ask what the thalidomide case should tell us about the moral responsibility of the producer who has reason to believe that his product is dangerous, although he cannot exactly specify the danger. If the product is also capable of being beneficial to some and pleasurable to others, it would be a loss to suppress it. Surely he must adequately inform prospective buyers that the danger is there. When is that moral responsibility discharged? Not merely when he has labelled the bottle "Danger," since every container ought to bear that label, whatever its contents. Dangerous to whom and how is what we wish to know, but the answer is often a very long story that can only be told accurately in highly technical terms. The moral responsibility, as distinct from the legal responsibility, for honest labelling is obviously a very perplexing problem. So are all moral responsibilities of business when it comes to their practical detailed implementation. Perhaps as firms now employ legal experts to advise them about their legal responsibilities, they will begin to employ moral experts. As moral understanding, unlike legal knowledge, is possessed by every person and therefore by every executive, and as moral expertise, unlike legal expertise, is not taught in accredited professional schools, the better solution may be for firms to organize fuller discussion of their moral responsibilities, perhaps under the stimulation of a consultant, whose function would be not to advise but to question.

CONCLUSION

One puzzle about the social responsibility of business, as I indicated at the outset, is why the subject generates such intense interest now. It is not at all new, but has deeply concerned people for many centuries; it only seems new to us because it has recently acquired a new name, which beguiles and confuses. Translate the novel name and the continuous substance emerges. It is the ethical and legal responsibilities of all participants in the economic life of any community toward each other, according to their several specific relations in the process of production and consumption. These responsibilities have been pondered and pronounced upon through the ages, remaining more or less stable for relatively long stretches of time, altering relatively quickly at other times. Possibly now is a time when such relations are changing quite quickly, though we should mistrust that impression, for speed of change tends to be exaggerated by those who are living through it, just as it tends to be underrated by those who observe it from a distance. The earthworm fleeing from a bird considers itself to be whizzing along at top speed, but an artificial satellite looks to us as though it is traversing the sky at a stately snail's pace. Such general reflections do not disprove that ours is a time of rapid change. If it is, that may explain why the perennial problems of ethics and law seem so perplexing and exciting.

The long history, within which current concerns are an episode, if perhaps a hectic one, exhibits a distinct drift for the time being. As far as Europe is concerned, and the widespread civilization which has emanated from it, that history can well be divided into three stages: feudal autocracy, liberalism, and the Insurance State. The first lasted many centuries, changing all along, though not evenly through time, nor uniformly as between its several characteristic institutions, nor yet concurrently in various countries. The second was brief, a century or two at most, Adam Smith at its center chronologically, during which voluntary contract (within a necessary but skeletal framework of law) was installed after much struggle as a pillar of freedom and rights. The third began to start about a hundred years ago. What we are going through now is not the beginning of something quite different but rather the maturing of an infant rather advanced in calendar years. That is why I think our time is not one of crisis and explosion, despite the loud cries of anguish that fill the air.

Many characteristic legal responsibilities now placed on persons in their business relations with each other emphasize universal insurance of various sorts, compulsory on all members of certain groups, economically incident on many who imagine themselves to be untouched by it. Moves to extend the scope of compulsory public insurance to new areas are constantly being made in many countries. Despite misgivings that I have expressed about such arrangements, it would be hard to say that they are unpopular, that they cost more than they are worth, or that they will necessarily debase the imagination, initiative, and moral sensitivity of the people. And although for the time being the drift toward the Insurance State should be expected to continue, it would be contrary to everything we know about human beings to suppose that this is the last stage of human relations. The long-range future of humankind will be different, but no prediction about the next stage is trustworthy.

The moral responsibilities of persons in their business relations with each other, on the contrary, have not been altered by the coming of the Insurance State. Conventional views about what most needs to be examined and emphasized in the moral realm do of course change with time, but they are relatively little influenced by the current condition of the laws. Many moral quandaries that beset businessmen today are remarkably similar to those explored by medieval casuists, as are also the solutions independently reinvented every day by thousands or millions of people. What has changed, and happily so, is the view that ethics is alien to business. Fewer people now believe that, though many still believe that the ethics of business is different from ethics at large. This view animates much of the present eager search for truth about the social responsibility of business. I do not believe that the truth about the subject is separate and special from the truth about ethics generally. But the truth about that is difficult to apprehend, to discuss, and most difficult to apply correctly to the complexities of any human situation. If it were not so difficult we would have solved those problems by now, and if we ever do we will cease to be human.

NOTES

1. See, for instance, the famous debate between H. L. A. Hart, "Positivism and the Separation of Law and Morals," *Harvard Law Review,* vol. 71 (February, 1958), pp. 593–629, and Lon Fuller, "Positivism and Fidelity to Law...," *Harvard Law Review,* vol. 71 (February, 1958), pp. 630–672.

2. R. H. Tawney and E. Powers, ed., *Tudor Economic Documents* (London: Longmans, Green and Company, 1931), pp. 127–128.

3. See, for instance, Joan Evans, *Life in Medieval France* (London: Phaidon Press, 1957), pp. 47–49.

4. S. F. C. Milson, *Historical Foundations of the Common Law* (London: Butterworths, 1969), p. 276.

5. 217 N. Y. 382, 111 N. E. 1050.

6. See E. H. Levi, *Introduction to Legal Reasoning* (Chicago: University of Chicago Press, 1949), pp. 7–19.

7. E. Cahn, *Confronting Injustice* (Boston: Little, Brown Company, 1966), p. 26, commenting on *Greenman* v. *Yuba,* 27 Cal. 697 (Sup. Ct., 1962).

8. *Which?,* November, 1974, p. 322.

9. The most dramatic instance perhaps was his government's decision to prevent the nationalized British Steel Corporation from closing down certain plants, which provoked its chief executive to declare on February 7, 1975, that it would not be able to compete with foreign steel makers.

10. See the Consultative Document on employment protection issued by the Department of Employment, October, 1974. Cf., the Employment Protection Act 1975, and the amended Redundancy Payments Act 1965.

11. A. Allison, *Population Control* (London, 1970), pp. 53 ff.

12. Selden Society, vol. 62, p. 160. See the brilliant study by Joel F. Brenner, *Legal Policy and Social Costs* (University of London, Ph.D. dissertation, November, 1972), especially chap. 3 on which I have drawn.

13. *Aldred's Case* (1611), 9 Co. Rep. 57b, at 58b.

14. So Lord Holt in *Tenant* v. *Goldwin* (1705), 2 Ld. Raym. 1089, at 1092.

15. See Brenner, pp. 81 ff. Cf. *Rose* v. *Socony,* 54 R.I. 411, 173 Atl. 627 (1934).

16. *Sunday Times* (London), December 29, 1974, p. 2.

HARVEY BROOKS

Scope of Business Responsibility in the Assessment of Technology

Industry is the main instrument for the introduction of new technology into social use and for the widespread deployment of existing technology. Even when funding for the introduction or application of technology comes from government, the work is most frequently performed by industry, and much of the responsibility for the assessment of the impact of projects devolves upon industry itself or upon profit-making engineering consulting firms and similar organizations. For research and development alone, industry accounts for nearly 70 percent of performance,[1] but this probably understates its role in the total innovation process and in the implicit assessment of the social impact of technology, because it does not include engineering and design for production or the technical marketing and application engineering and consulting services that are an integral part of the introduction and dissemination of technology into the economy.[2]

This essay is concerned with the changing role and responsibilities of industry in regard to the social assessment of technology and what this may mean for the future posture of industry with respect to technological innovation. It will be my thesis that of all the issues falling under the rubric of "business and society" this is probably the most important and will have the most far-reaching consequences for the institutional evolution of business and of its relationships to the public and the political system. In the past the process of technological innovation in the private sector has been thought of as largely autonomous, with the market providing sufficient guidance to determine priorities in R and D and the allocation of investments for new products and services. Technological laissez-faire, or *laissez-innover,* has survived much longer than economic laissez-faire but is now under severe attack. What I shall attempt to do is to examine the forces which are eroding technological laissez-faire and to predict what new equilibrium may emerge from the present tensions.

TECHNOLOGY ASSESSMENT

In a certain sense technology assessment (TA) is a new label for a very traditional activity of industry when considering the introduction of a new product or service. The traditional aspects are technical feasibility and market analysis. Can the product be manufactured? Will it work? What will it cost? Does it fulfill a public or private need, and is there a large enough potential market for the firm to recover its initial investment in development, manufacture, and testing the market? Can it be sold at a competitive price that will yield a profit?

In its modern usage, however, technology assessment deals with those aspects of a proposed technology which cannot readily be subjected to tests of market acceptability or economic efficiency. In economic terms we are concerned not just with the primary benefits to consumers and producers—with the expected consumer and producer surpluses—but with the externalities, the social costs and benefits, including many which are difficult to reduce to a common economic measure. Technology assessment is aimed not at the corporate balance sheet but at an overall hypothetical social balance sheet, and it goes beyond the assumption that what is good on the average for both the firm and its customers is necessarily good for society as a whole.

Thus technology assessment as it is now defined focuses attention on the secondary and unintended consequences of the application of technology, on what are sometimes called second- and third-order effects, on its impact on interests and values other than those involved in the transaction between buyer and seller—the public affected by pollution, the workers not employed as a consequence of automation, the hazards to bystanders created by products after they are used and disposed of, or the secondary benefits of public transportation in reducing congestion for residual auto users. More and more such issues are feeding back to the producers and generators of technology, who are thus compelled to consider much more than the mere market acceptance of their activities.

The new issue raised by TA is: What is the responsibility of the corporation, and indeed the individual technologists who work for it, for the remote and perhaps unintended consequences of their activities? How much should they be expected to foresee these consequences and to bear their costs when their responsibility can be identified? Is it sufficient merely to obey the rules established by government to contain these consequences, or is it necessary to anticipate and forestall undesirable consequences not yet apparent to the political system? Should corporations wait for society to make the rules; should they make new rules through voluntary agreement; or should they take the initiative in proposing new rules to government, based on their superior knowledge of the technologies with which they deal? What is the responsibility of scientists or technologists within an industry when they become aware of evidence, however tentative and uncertain, that points towards potential public hazards arising from the activities of their industry? Should they disclose such evidence to the public or to appropriate officials, regardless of economic consequences or of the possibility that the evidence is in error? Should such "whistle-blowers" among scientists and engineers in industry be protected from economic sanctions by their employers when they reveal information of possible adverse economic consequence to their industry that involves matters of public health or safety? Should technical employees be personally liable for damages when involved in the design of a product or process which is subsequently proved to be hazardous to the public? Is "engineering malpractice" a concept that should be recognized by the courts, analogously to medical malpractice? If so, what does it embrace?

The above are some of the issues now being raised by the new form of TA. We have witnessed in the last ten years a rapid transition from an era of euphoria about technology to one of suspicion and distrust of technology and of the industry which generates and applies it. Whereas new technology was once considered innocent until proved guilty of harm beyond a reasonable doubt, now it is presumed guilty until its harmlessness has been established with high confidence. The burden of proof has shifted away from those wishing to block the introduction or application of technology onto those wishing to promote it, and the cost of assembling the evidence to prove innocence in advance of any sales is borne largely by industry and thus ultimately by the consumers of its products. This is the new fact of life with which business must live, and I doubt if it will change much in our lifetime.

THE CHANGING ENVIRONMENT

The change in the climate towards technology has come about partly as a result of changing public attitudes and expectations, but also as a result of the change in the character of technology itself and of the growth of scientific knowledge that has enabled us to deal more confidently with hitherto unforeseeable consequences of the application of technology. The problem is particularly acute now because the political climate has changed much more rapidly than the technologies themselves and the institutions which manage them. A few years ago it used to be fashionable to exclaim over the rate of technical progress and bemoan the fact that social change could not keep up with it. To a degree this is true, but by and large the lag of technology behind social expectations is much more obvious than the reverse. Although the air of our cities is in most instances cleaner than it was five or ten years ago, the social demand for clean air has far outstripped our progress in attaining it. The federal inter-state highway system launched in 1956, which was acclaimed politically as a triumph of intelligent planning and rational design,[3] is now looked upon by many as a social disaster and has been brought almost to a halt, especially in metropolitan environs. The automobile, once the very symbol of progress, is now pointed out as the prime symptom of the degeneration of our society. The space program, launched with a remark-able consensus among the public and politicians, is now looked upon by many as a peculiarly frivolous form of public conspicuous consumption in the midst of world poverty and social injustice at home. Nuclear power, the great hope for the liberation of man in the euphoric 1940s, is now the target of a growing public crusade against its further development. DDT, the miracle chemical of World War II and the savior of millions of lives in the postwar period, has now been banned in most developed countries, except for very limited uses.

In assessing these changes, it is difficult to disentangle changing psychological and emotional predispositions from changes in the actual objective assessment of these technologies based on growth of scientific knowledge about the consequences of their deployment. By their very nature the secondary or "higher order" consequences of a technology do not appear until it has been applied on a substantial scale, and for this very reason they were hard to foresee when it was introduced. At the beginning the primary benefits greatly exceed the risks or secondary costs, and the secondary problems, or for that matter the secondary benefits or advantages, do not become apparent until the technology is well esta-blished with many vested interests behind it. Often, as in the case of the automobile and the highway system, a whole new pattern of life is bound up with the technology—a pattern which cannot be reversed now without great economic dislocation and even personal hardship, although it would have been relatively easy to choose a different pattern originally. The role of the automobile in urban air pollution was not established scientifically until 1952,[4] and evidence of adverse effects of urban air pollution, except in a few special situations like Los Angeles, did not begin to be brought forward until the late 1960s.[5] Initially, much of the evidence was incon-clusive and open to question, leaving legitimate scope for skepticism among those whose economic interests or habitual living patterns were likely to be adversely affected by regulation of automobile emissions. It is possible that the political movement for drastic regulation of auto emissions was as much motivated by ideological animosity towards big business as by well-informed concern for public health.

Similarly, it was only in the late 1950s that the sensitivity of chemical analysis had increased to the point where the ubiquity of DDT in the environment could be established with confidence, and even today a connection between DDT and adverse effects on human health—except in rare situations of acute accidental exposure—has not been scientifically demonstrated.

In some cases completely new scientific results have suddenly changed the assessment of an existing, well-established technology. A dramatic recent example is the case of freon, which is used in aerosol spray cans and as a refrigerant in air-conditioners and refrigerators. The production of freons and related chlorofluorocarbons is an $8 billion industry employing about 250,000 people. About half the world's production is in the United States.[6] Theoretical calculations indicate that freon released at the ground will diffuse slowly upwards into the stratosphere and will act as a catalyst for the destruction of ozone, reducing its total amount in the stratosphere. This in turn will permit more of the sun's ultraviolet rays to reach the surface of the earth, increasing the incidence of human skin cancer and possibly producing adverse effects on the rate of growth of crops. The present effect is small—less than 1 percent of the average ozone concentration—but it will become very large if present rates of increase of freon production continue for another decade. The effect is also global in the sense that the effects of local production of freon will spread quickly over the entire stratosphere. More recently it has been shown that the fumigant methyl bromide, whose use in agriculture is growing more rapidly than the use of freon in aerosols, is an even more potent disturber of the ozone cover.[7] Since this is a new field of research, it is not unlikely that other even more subtle effects of human activity on the stratosphere may be discovered.

These predictions are the result of a very sophisticated theory, but one sufficiently based on laboratory measurements, so that it has a high probability of being correct. New corroborative evidence in support of the theory seems to be appearing daily. Yet it could not possibly have been foreseen when the freon industry was developing. What was attractive about freon among many alternatives was that it was nontoxic and therefore especially safe for human use. A technology assessment when it was first being considered would have been very unlikely to have foreseen the stratospheric effects, whose recognition was made possible only by very recent advances in fundamental atmospheric chemistry and the computer modeling of atmospheric structure, in part stimulated by concern over stratospheric effects of the SST.[8]

Many other examples can be cited in which rather subtle effects have been discovered that throw doubt on the safety or freedom from environmental hazard of major industries. In most of these examples it would have been difficult to foresee the effects now believed probable, especially in a general climate of opinion where new technology was generally presumed harmless and where therefore there was little economic or political incentive to undertake research looking for subtle and often rather esoteric consequences of the use of a new chemical.

Another recent example is that of polyvinyl chlorides (PVC).[9] This is a class of chemicals used as the basis of many plastics and is produced in the amount of about 2.2 million tons annually. It represents a potential health hazard to 1.5 million workers engaged in the manufacture or processing of PVC, and possibly to many others who live in the vicinity of plants where PVC is present. Yet only in May, 1970 was the first evidence presented by a foreign scientist of a possible connection between PVC exposure and the occurrence in rats of a rare form of cancer of the liver, angiosarcoma. In retrospect one can fault the chemical industry for not having carefully tested a chemical to which so many workers were exposed, but this is the wisdom of hindsight asserted in the light of the new attitudes towards the burden of proof discussed above.

In both the freon and PVC cases the first reaction of scientists in the industry was one of disbelief and denial, and indeed the initial evidence in both cases was quite speculative and uncertain. How could one justify the threat to an industry providing the livelihood of hundreds of thousands of people on the basis of such speculative evidence? In each instance technical uncertainty provided plenty of legitimate scope for the interpretation of evidence to fit institutional, professional, or political presuppositions. Much higher standards of proof are expected by those whose institutional interests or political values are adversely affected by the findings than by those who are indifferent to the outcome or who take a "better safe than sorry" stance towards environmental or occupational health. Yet hundreds of thousands of people were probably placed in jeopardy by failure to act immediately on this suspicious evidence and by failure to follow it up with an intense research program to settle the toxicity of PVC one way or the other. Unfortunately, the problem was further complicated by the fact, often true in such cases, that for low levels of exposure the carcinogenic properties of PVC are very long delayed. Thus it was only in January, 1974 that the first cases of angiosarcoma attributable to PVC exposure were reported. It was not until April, 1974 that the permissible occupational exposure for PVC was lowered from the existing standard of 500 ppm to 50 ppm by the NIOSH.[10]

In the freon case the theoretical discoveries were made by academic scientists and reported in the open literature, but in testimony to congressional committees, industrial scientists employed by industries engaged in the production of freon expressed great skepticism of the results, labeling them as pure speculation and "abstract theory." The industrial testimony implicitly assumed that any uncertainties in the assumptions or the models used by the scientists would be resolved so as to reduce the estimated effects, although there was actually no reason to believe that the uncertainties might not equally well operate in the opposite direction.

One of the problems in the environmental debate is the empirical observation that as time goes on new scientific knowledge has usually tended to increase estimates of the harm resulting from a given technological activity, while technological progress has at the same time usually resulted in a reduction of the estimated costs of controlling the hazard by abatement techniques. Thus in the example of automobile emissions, research has tended to substantiate some health damage from auto pollutants at very low levels, at least in especially sensitive parts of the population. After a very thorough review of all the evidence, a committee of the National Academy of Sciences was unwilling to recommend any relaxation of the existing standards, although these standards had been criticized at the time they were legislated as unreasonably conservative. At the same time the fuel penalties and purchase price of automobiles equipped with emission controls have come down steadily.[11]

Over the years standards for exposure to radioactive radiations have been lowered repeatedly in the light of new scientific findings, while methods of preventing exposure to radiation have become steadily more effective and less expensive. Recent work on the health effects of the oxidation products of sulfur dioxide emitted from coal-fired power plants has substantiated the fact that even present standards for SO_2 ambient levels may be too high because of their ultimate conversion to sulfates, and there seems little doubt that, with continued research and development, the cost of stack gas cleaning will come down and its reliability will improve, although there is much disagreement between industry and government experts as to how fast this will happen.

Examples such as this lend credence to the advocates of a conservative stance towards environmental and health standards, a stance based on the projection of scientific and technological progress rather than on current knowledge. The point I am making is that it is not only changing public expectations but also accelerating acquisition of knowledge about potential hazards as well as about the alleged or actual capabilities of technology that has led to the shift in the burden of proof of which I have spoken. Indeed, there is a kind of paradox in recent environmental legislation in that it posits much greater faith in the capabilities of technology to solve problems under sufficient pressure than the technologists themselves would believe. Furthermore the wishful expectations of lay people have sometimes proved more accurate than the scientific caution of technologists steeped in the issue. For example, savings in fuel consumption achieved with the newest catalyst designs have belied the gloomy predictions of industry specialists or oil company writers.

NEW LEGISLATION

The new climate for technological innovation and application has become well established by legislation, judicial interpretation, and administrative action. I need only remind the reader of a few recent examples to establish the point.

A little noticed and undebated provision of the National Environmental Policy Act, section 102c, has become the instrument for very broad new controls on technology.[12] The environmental impact statement, required by this legislation for "any federal action significantly affecting the quality of the environment," has permitted environmental groups through court action to delay, modify, or halt nuclear power plants and many other projects involving the application of technology.[13] A remarkable judicial history has grown up around this section in only six years of its existence. Its most significant effect has been to prevent federal regulatory agencies from restricting their review of projects under their jurisdiction to the limited domains of expertise or authority mandated in their legislative authorization. The Atomic Energy Commission was forced to consider thermal pollution as well as radioactivity from nuclear power plants. The proponents of power plants were forced to present consideration of alternative sources of energy, as well as the alternative of none at all. Although in theory an agency was not bound in its final decision by what was in an environmental impact statement, in practice the courts ruled that it had to show that it had made a "good faith effort" to weigh the trade-offs involved and that its decision could be plausibly deduced from the considerations presented in the environmental impact statement.[14]

The clean air amendments of 1970 mandated emission standards for light-duty motor vehicles, and established a timetable for their achievement, a timetable that has now been relaxed by at least four years and may ultimately not come into force before 1982 instead of 1975. Since 1970 the auto industry has spent $300 million a year on R and D and $200-$300 million a year on new manufacturing facilities just to implement the standards that have now been partially postponed.

The National Occupational Safety and Health Act has mandated a whole new set of standards for safety and health in industry, and the new mine safety act has established much more stringent rules for the safety of coal miners and their protection against respiratory disease.

A consumer product safety act and an enforcement commission have begun to create new ground rules for consumer products, with a much greater burden on the manufacturer to design his product to avoid hazard not only in ordinary use, but also in situations of possible misuse by the consumer. The burden has been shifted from consumer circumspection to the designer who must imagine all possible misuses of the product.[15]

The principle of negligence in tort liability in the courts has been replaced by a new principle of "strict liability." This means that in litigation regarding a manufacturer's liability for harm caused by his product, the focus of inquiry has shifted away from what the manufacturer should or should not have done or foreseen onto the product itself and its use in the environment for which it was intended. The question becomes one of whether the design of the product was reasonably safe for its environment, given cost and functional constraints.[16] It is the product and the technology that are on trial, not the behavior of the manufacturer in a particular instance; such a trial thus becomes a technology assessment of the product, with the burden of proof on the designer and the manufacturer.

Legislation now in the works will require assessment of a wide range of chemical products before they can be introduced into the environment or put on the market. Already elaborate certification is required for the use of new pesticides, with a new certification required for each different use, and the burden of proof to establish both efficacy and environmental safety resting on the producer.[17]

New legislation on water pollution states as its ultimate objective "zero discharge" into waterways by the 1980s, and in the meantime mandates the use of "best available" abatement technology by all potential polluters discharging into waterways, irrespective of how much a particular installation improves overall water quality.[18]

Much of this legislation, and the associated litigation, pays little attention to the cost implications to consumers entailed by the standards which are mandated. Essentially, the mandate is to avoid all risks that technology can make avoidable almost irrespective of cost, although this varies from case to case. The test becomes the technical feasibility of abatement rather than a balancing of costs against benefits. The political and judicial climate is thus one which resolves technical uncertainties on the side of health, safety, and environmental purity. It is assumed that industry and its employees will resolve technical uncertainties in the way most advantageous to their institutional and professional interests, and that therefore government and the judicial system must provide a countervailing pressure, which will resolve uncertainties in the opposite direction.

RESPONSE OF INDUSTRY

The response of industry to this new climate has been for the most part a defensive one. Not only has it resisted new legislation and regulation, but its scientists and engineers have been highly skeptical of the scientific basis on which the new regulations have been predicated. In most cases this skepticism may have been justified in scientific terms, but people in the environment of industry have failed to appreciate the difference in perspective from which scientific evidence is viewed by themselves and environmentalists. Industry tends to demand scientific proof that the regulations are really necessary and that the costs of meeting the standards are justified to a high confidence level by the benefits to health or the environment. To industry the costs are real and the benefits highly speculative. The environmentalists, and their viewpoints when accepted in legislation and court action, demand scientific proof that the regulations are *not* necessary and can be relaxed only with a high degree of confidence that no deleterious consequences will follow. Thus the auto industry and its critics mostly talk past each other, assessing the same scientific evidence with entirely different standards of proof. From a scientific point of view, I find myself sympathetic to both sides, for the disagreement is much less frequently one over scientific fact than one might be led to expect from the fury of the arguments. More often it is simply a question of each side in the argument demanding much lower standards of proof in support of its viewpoint than that of the other side.

The attitude of industry is based on economic rationality. In its own assessment everything has a price, including the degree of cleanliness of the environment and the health and safety of its workers. This is indeed a correct perception, and the actual behavior of large numbers of people in the use of technologies like the automobile supports the notion that society has implicit ways of attaching a price to such values as human life or clean air.[19] But when we attempt to make these values explicit in the political process, the trade-off approach becomes less acceptable. Thus the firm tends to overestimate rational economic factors and underestimate political ones in its decisions. It treats politics as something exogenous to its decision-making process, something possibly to be manipulated, but not to be taken seriously as one of the parameters of the market of the same significance as consumer preferences. What is rational and right is what makes sense in terms of past standards and expectations of the public as evidenced by the past market for the firm's goods and services. To the business person and the technologist politics is basically irrational, an aspect of the environment only to be taken into account when actually embodied in existing legislation and court decisions. It is my impression that corporate planning until recently has seldom attempted to anticipate the political environment ten or fifteen years hence, even when it was prepared to project sales and technology this far ahead on the assumption of an invariant political environment. As a technologist myself, I find myself irresistibly drawn towards such an attitude and must continually pinch myself to avoid excluding politics from my forecasts of technology.

In my opinion most business resistance to regulation or to unfavorable assessment of its products or processes is quite sincere, based on rational appraisal of the objective situation in terms of its own experience and bureaucratic habits. I am not one who believes that business is in conspiracy to mislead and defraud the public. But, like all other bureaucracies and professions, business's capacity for self-deception is greater than it appreciates, and this is nowhere more apparent than in its assessment of the political environment or in its interpretation of highly uncertain technical evidence.

HOW CAN BUSINESS IMPROVE ITS RESPONSE?

One must begin by asking what *improvement* means. It could be interpreted narrowly to mean long-term profitability or rate of return, or it could be interpreted more broadly to mean greater responsiveness to public expectations and social values, including but not limited to those expressed through the market. Even in the narrow terms of the first definition, I believe that business response could be improved. There is nothing more disruptive of business profits than abrupt changes in the environment brought about by politically inspired regulation following a public crusade, and yet many of these events do cast their shadows and can be anticipated, perhaps even forestalled. What makes it difficult for business to respond to these signals is that it is often unprofitable in the short run for a single firm to do so, especially if its competitors are not forced by law or other collective coercion to do the same. The competitive disadvantage of socially more "responsible" behavior is, however, frequently overestimated. Among paper companies, for example, it appears that those with the most advanced pollution control are also the most profitable. Of course, it is hard to know which is cause and which is effect in this instance, but in a changing political climate the least polluting plant may likely be the one with the greatest long-term ability to survive and grow.

One can classify the past responses of business to political regulation as follows: (1) active-defensive, (2) passive-responsive, and (3) active-anticipatory.

As I have suggested above, the active-defensive mode of response has been the most common. The industry denies the need for regulation and questions the facts or analysis on which it is premised. It argues that self-regulation is doing an adequate job and employs institutional advertising to state its case to the public. Its actual response to criticism, however, frequently tends to be cosmetic, to present the appearance of reform with little of its substance. Business will lobby to the bitter end against regulatory legislation and will contest any legal challenge to its activities in the courts. It will shroud the activities criticized in secrecy. This strategy has proved increasingly unrewarding in recent years and has usually ended by creating greater public antagonism than existed before. There is little question that the attempt of General Motors to discredit Ralph Nader boomeranged and probably resulted in earlier and more stringent regulation of auto safety, as the industry itself soon recognized by adopting a more cooperative attitude towards safety regulation. I do not mean to imply that industry should never oppose regulation, but it should do so only with great caution and with greater recognition of the sincerity of its critics and better insight into their assumptions.

The passive-responsive mode is one in which industry is prepared, and announces its willingness, to live by the rules established by political authority, but without anticipating them or trying to do better than the standards set by law. It does what is necessary to comply with the law but no more, and it avoids trying to resist regulation by lobbying or public relations. This is, perhaps, the view that would be espoused by Milton Friedman in response to advocates of social responsibility of business. The main social responsibility of business in this view is to maximize its long-term profitability within the ground rules established by law. There are many arguments in favor of this view. If business does more than the rules require, it is assuming a quasi-political function, just as much as if it lobbies against a proposed regulation. In effect it is collecting a tax from its employees and stockholders to carry out a political purpose decided upon unilaterally by its management.

There are, however, certain difficulties with this mode. One of the most serious is the constant appearance of new knowledge which bears in one way or another on the social costs of the company's products or operations. A purely passive mode would dictate that the company wait for this knowledge to be discovered by others and to be embodied in regulations before it made any response. Only if required by law to demonstrate the efficacy or safety of its products before they could be marketed, as in the case of prescription drugs or chemical pesticides, could a firm justify the funding of research aimed at assessment of the social impact of its activities. As the experience of the auto industry has shown, however, this passive strategy can be extremely costly. A law or a regulation can be put into effect almost overnight, but technology can respond only slowly. If technological planning fails to anticipate regulation based on new knowledge, the company is likely to be faced with expensive crash programs to alter its technology.

A second related point is the danger that legislation and regulation are likely to be inconsistent or based on an inadequate appreciation of the technology that is being regulated. Most environmental regulation has been put into effect with little consideration of its economic cost or the potential social return from alternative investment of the same funds. A company knows its own technology best and what the possibilities for change are. Regulations based on the research of outsiders may be less rational and even less effective than those informed by intimate knowledge of all aspects of the technology to be regulated. This argues strongly for company-financed or cooperative industry-financed research, aimed at monitoring and exploring the possible social costs and consequences of its activities and the possibilities for mitigating them. Such research would be aimed at anticipating regulation, whether by bettering current standards for reducing social cost, or merely by being technically prepared to respond quickly to new ground rules, or to argue for modification of the rules to achieve the same benefits in a more economical but equally effective way. Such research may, of course, be unduly biased to the advantage of the industry. It cannot be a substitute for technical monitoring of the industry by an outside agency, and there is also the danger that it might permit the industry to "snow" regulatory agencies with mountains of slightly misleading facts.

The final mode, the active-anticipatory, was foreshadowed in the discussion of the preceding paragraph. It involves a more aggressive pursuit of the mitigation of social costs, with the possibility even of lobbying for more stringent government standards as the technical possibility of meeting these standards at reasonable cost develops out of its own active research program.

There are hazards to such a strategy, quite apart from the fact that it can be quite expensive and risky. The expense can put the firm that follows this strategy at a disadvantage relative to its competitors, although in some cases the expense may be shared on an industry-wide basis, provided it is organized so as to conform with antitrust principles. It may involve second-guessing the political process, and it could have the effect of merely accelerating the application of more stringent regulation by calling attention to problems that might otherwise have lain dormant in the public and political consciousness. The industry position might simply become the point of departure for more stringent standards. On the other hand, an active industry program in assessing its own impacts could over time improve the political climate for regulation and disarm the public mistrust which has been generated by past industry behavior in the active-defensive mode. Furthermore, active industry participation in the assessment of its own activities may avoid the creation of cumbersome and less effective bureaucracies in government to do the same kinds of assessment.

Industry cooperation in the setting of performance standards and safety criteria for its products is much more widespread than is generally appreciated by the public. The American National Standards Institute, a cooperatively industry-financed organization with a budget in excess of $30 million annually, establishes voluntary standards for many industrial products. The American Society for Testing Materials and the American Society of Mechanical Engineers also establish voluntary standards, which in many cases are recognized by government regulatory agencies. This process could well be extended more broadly to less product-oriented standards and criteria, such as ambient standards for various atmospheric contaminants inside and outside the plant or safety standards on the production line.

A number of industrial associations such as the American Petroleum Institute, the American Paper Association, and the Atomic Industrial Forum are beginning to finance cooperative research that deals not only with the general product problems of their industry but also with environmental impacts and product safety. This trend will probably continue and perhaps should be encouraged by some kind of tax advantage if it satisfies certain criteria of public availability and relevance to benefits which are primarily to public safety and environmental quality rather than to the specific consumer of the product.

On balance my own position comes out intermediate between the passive-responsive and the active-anticipatory strategy. Perhaps it should be labeled *passive-anticipatory.* It should fall short of active political involvement in the advocacy of regulation and standards or the influencing of legislation, but should actively seek to anticipate new regulations and constraints on the introduction and application of the particular technologies within the domain of the firm.

PERSONAL VERSUS CORPORATE LIABILITY

J. T. Bower has suggested that corporate decision making with respect to social cost issues may never sufficiently reflect the public interest.[20] Individual decision makers are more responsive to short-term goals determined by their careers in their organizations than they are to broader social issues or even to longer-term corporate goals. The reward system in corporations, as in most bureaucracies, is usually based on quite short-term considerations, whether they be immediate feedback from the market, technical proficiency, or the ability to be persuasive. Yet enlightened corporate policies promulgated by top management are meaningless unless they are reflected in the measures actually used to evaluate the subunit manager's performance. In Bower's words, "Clean air is a great corporate objective, but meaningless unless plant managers are forgiven the higher costs involved." The problem is one that is common to all hierarchical organizations, not just private corporations. It is the reward and penalty system that serves to ally individual self-interest with organizational goals; it is only through this mechanism that organizational policies can be implemented. The problem is that the feedback of the reward system must be more immediate than the actual achievement of the corporate goals which it is designed to support.

In response to this problem Bower, along with others, has proposed that the principle of limited liability in corporations be modified to make certain employees personally liable for certain kinds of deficiencies in performance that contribute to the adverse effects of corporate activities. Again, in the words of Bower, the goal is to "provide mechanisms that will modify the stakes of decision makers and planners, public as well as private, so that their career values are more closely associated with the stakes of society." The partial removal of the protection of limited liability from the individual corporate officer has already occurred with respect to many corporate regulations in the financial field, for example, in securities regulations, antitrust law, and conflict-of-interest policies. The Outer Continental Shelf Act, as amended in 1969, provides for a prison sentence for individual employees found negligent in connection with oil spills, and even the 1899 Rivers and Harbors Act, recently rediscovered by environmentalists, provides for mandatory sentences for individual employees found responsible in connection with the pollution of waterways.[21]

The converse side of the same issue has to do with the protection of public or corporate employees who engage in "whistle blowing," that is, who disclose to the public or to public authorities corporate activities or conditions which they believe to be harmful to the public interest. Industrial scientists are reluctant to challenge conspiracies of silence within their firms, or even within an industry, for fear of economic sanctions against them. Such sanctions can operate not only within one firm, through loss of job or failure of promotion, but a whistle-blowing scientist may become blacklisted for employment throughout a whole industry. It is asserted, for example, that chemists who were members of the Manufacturing Chemists' Association failed to disclose knowledge they had as early as November, 1971 that PVC caused cancer in experimental animals, and that fear of reprisals was a major factor in their silence. Whether or not such sanctions actually occur, the fear of them is a real deterrent to disclosure of information which might affect a firm's business unfavorably, even though disclosure may avert a public harm.

Of course, the ethical issue is not as simple as the more enthusiastic advocates of whistle-blowing, such as Ralph Nader, would have us believe. Frequently the first evidences of adverse effects are very uncertain, and many of them may later prove to be unfounded. When premature disclosure of such evidence might result in the loss of millions of dollars worth of business, or of thousands of jobs in an industry, the decision to disclose or not to disclose highly speculative or uncertain scientific information involves a difficult choice between evils. It is easy to accuse the scientists in the PVC case of irresponsible suppression of information or complicity in a conspiracy of silence now that the suspicions aroused by the earliest evidence have been confirmed and extended. But the initial experiments were actually methodologically suspect and corresponded to ambient levels of PVC much greater than existing plant standards called for. The consuming public has often borne costs in the name of safety or public health that a more rational evaluation of trade-offs and probabilities might not have indicated, but reasonable people will always differ on this because the scientific evidence is almost never conclusive at the time the choices have to be made. Whistle-blowing on safety or environmental issues within the firm could easily become a mode of harassment or blackmail to achieve an undeserved promotion or to avoid being fired for other reasons. With a large public disposed to believe the worst about corporate activities, an individual employee could have a leverage which would destroy the social discipline of a corporation or a public bureaucracy beyond the point of organizational viability, especially if the individual is not accountable for disclosures which are later shown to have no factual basis.[22]

Similarly, the opening up of individual employees to damage suits in connection with environmental damage or product safety, if permitted to go too far, could equally destroy the integrity of organizations and lead corporate managers to the same kind of bureaucratic pusillanimity which is popularly identified with the civil service. If mistakes are penalized and initiative never rewarded, the cautious and conservative type of manager will soon become dominant in the organization. The possibility of individual liability could thus paralyze innovation within the firm, much as regulation has apparently eroded management competence in many regulated industries such as railroads and utilities. Moreover, the assessment of individual blame may be very difficult and probably unjust in most cases. It can only be justified for its deterrent effect, but even this may be minimized if it becomes possible for certain key decision makers to take out "malpractice insurance" paid for by the firm, directly or indirectly.

Regardless of the pros and cons of individual liability and protection for whistle-blowers, I believe these are both new elements in the corporate environment that are going to have to be reckoned with in the future. They appear to me to be the next likely step in a trend towards shifting the burden of proof onto technology. Already the coal mine safety act contains a provision prohibiting discrimination against a miner who has reported unsafe conditions to the administrator of the act or testified in a proceeding related to the enforcement of the act. This is very likely to become a pattern for other safety and environmental legislation. It is something to which corporate policy makers and business school educators will have to give careful attention. Rather than opposing such legislation across the board as a matter of principle, it would be wiser to try to define what might be sensible limits, both as to the individual liability of employees and managers and the degree of legal protection to be afforded to whistle-blowers. For example, how should liability be related to organizational authority? Should a firm injured by an employee's disclosures have any recourse if the evidence on which they were based can be proved false or misleading?

For the most part self-employed professionals who deal directly with the public are not permitted to hide behind organizational anonymity. Indeed the situation has become notorious in the case of medical practitioners, as evidenced by the growth of malpractice insurance premiums. One could well ask why should salaried professionals in corporations or government bureaucracies be relieved of the ethical accountability required of their self-employed colleagues? If this increases the risks and insecurities of the salaried professional, perhaps those who bear these risks should be compensated accordingly. On the other hand, it must be recognized that, as in the case of medical malpractice, the consumer ultimately bears the cost of personal as well as corporate liability; experience with medical malpractice suggests that insured risks may be much more expensive than uninsured.

Individual accountability of salaried professionals is likely to enhance the role of professional societies and similar organizations in the assessment of technologies to which their expertise relates. Specialized professional organizations such as the Manufacturing Chemists' Association may become less exclusively identified with the economic interests of the industry which they serve and assume a more independent role as the conscience of their technology. Legislation will also have to resolve the question of the degree to which the risks of individual liability can be shared or insured. Experience with medical malpractice insurance tends to suggest that insured risks are ultimately much more costly to the consumer. The professional societies, and perhaps legislation, will also have to establish standards consistent across a wide range of professions as to what is and is not legitimate whistle-blowing.

THE IMPACT ON INNOVATION

All the trends which I have described raise a question about the future of technological innovation. Will regulations, controls, prohibitions, and individual liability make firms and technologists so supercautious that technological innovation will disappear? The danger of this certainly exists. In his thoughtful statement appended to the NAS report, *Technology: Processes of Assessment and Choice,* Dr. Morris Tannenbaum makes the following comment:[23]

> Of course, the purpose of new assessment mechanisms is to produce changes which will guide technology in socially desirable directions. However, the assessment mechanisms themselves will have second-order consequences. To the extent that assessment can define the social requirements of new technology at an early stage, this could encourage private investment. However, to the degree that new assessment mechanisms create new uncertainties, this could discourage private investment in areas which are at the focus of assessment activity. These may be the areas where innovation is most important and private participation most desirable.

For "assessment mechanisms" in this statement one should include all the changes in legislative and judicial climate that we have outlined above. Each must be itself assessed not only in the light of its capacity to protect the public from harm, but also in the light of its impact on the innovation process itself, and particularly on those directions of innovation which may have the potential for greatest net social benefit such as, say, fertility control methods, or life-saving pharmaceuticals, or chemicals used to increase food production or improve nutrition. The difficulty of assessment of the assessment process itself lies in the fact that while each assessment or regulation by itself may not be enough to significantly discourage innovation or make its risks economically unacceptable, the combination of many measures could be more than additive in its effects and thus bring innovation to a halt. If the public insists on more and more rigor with respect to unforeseen risks to its own health and safety, we may very well have to invent some social mechanism that helps to protect firms and individuals against the risks of unforeseeen scientific findings that suddenly change the social assessment of an activity in which a high investment had already been made. Indeed it may be argued that the more government policy increases the economic risk associated with privately financed innovation, the more government may be forced to step in to finance and direct the innovation process, and it is not clear that government is sufficiently responsive to market forces to make this an efficient alternative.

NOTES

1. National Science Foundation, *Databook,* NSF 74-3, National Science Foundation, January, 1974, p. 32.

2. H. Brooks, *The Government of Science* (Cambridge, Mass., M.I.T. Press, 1968), chap. 10, esp. p. 261.

3. L. H. Mayo, "The National Highway Program and Motor Freight Carrier Development: A Technology Assessment Perspective," Program of Policy Studies in Science and Technology, The George Washington University, March 22, 1969, chap. 3.

4. A. J. Haagen-Smit, "Chemistry and Physiology of Los Angeles Smog," *Industrial Engineering Chemistry,* vol. 44 (June, 1952), p. 1342.

5. W. R. Ahern, Jr., "Health Effects of Automotive Air Pollution," in *Clearing the Air, Federal Policy on Automotive Emissions Control,* eds. H. D. Jacoby and J. D. Steinbruner (Cambridge, Mass.: Ballinger Publishing Company, 1973).

6. M. B. McElroy, N. D. Sze, S. C. Wofsy, "Freon Consumption: Implications for Atmospheric Ozone," *Science,* 14 February, 1975, pp. 535–536.

7. M. B. McElroy, S. C. Wofsy, Y. L. Yung, "The Chemistry of Atmospheric Bromine," submitted to *Geophysics Letters,* April, 1975.

8. Climatic Impact Committee of the National Academy of Sciences, *Environmental Impact of Stratospheric Flight* (Washington, D. C.: National Academy of Sciences, 1975).

9. Federation of American Scientists, *Professional Bulletin,* vol. 2, No. 8 (November, 1974), p. 1.

10. *Ibid.,* p. 4.

11. Committee on Motor Vehicle Emissions of the National Academy of Sciences, *Report by the Committee on Motor Vehicle Emissions* (Washington, D.C.: National Academy of Sciences, November, 1974).

12. F. R. Anderson, *NEPA in the Courts, A Legal Analysis of the National Environmental Policy Act* (Baltimore, Md.: Johns Hopkins University Press, 1973).

13. A. W. Murphy, "NEPA and the Licensing Process: Environmentalist Magna Carta or Agency Coup de Grace," *Columbia Law Review,* vol. 76, No. 6 (October, 1972), p. 963.

14. *Ibid.,* p. 978.

15. A. S. Weinstein, A. D. Twerski, H. R. Piehler, W. A. Donaher, "Product Liability: An Interaction of Law and Technology," *Duquesne Law Review,* vol. 12, No. 3 (Spring, 1974), pp. 425–550.

16. *Ibid.,* p. 437.

17. C. Djerassi, C. Shih-Coleman, J. Dickman, "Insect Control of The Future: Operational and Policy Aspects," *Science,* 15 November, 1974, pp. 596–607.

18. Federal Water Pollution Control Act, Amendments of 1972, Public Law 92-500.

19. C. Starr, "Benefit Cost Studies in Sociotechnical Systems," *Perspectives in Benefit Risk Decision Making,* NAE-COPEP, Summary of a Colloquium, April 26-27, 1971 (Washington, D. C.: National Academy of Sciences, 1972), pp. 17–42.

20. J. L. Bower, "On the Amoral Organization," *The Corporate Society,* Robin Marris, ed. (London: Macmillan, 1974), chap. 6.

21. Federation of American Scientists, *op. cit.,* p. 5.

22. Phillip I. Blumberg, "Corporate Responsibility and the Employee's Duty of Loyalty and Obedience: A Preliminary Inquiry," *Oklahoma Law Review,* vol. 24, No. 3 (August, 1971), pp. 279–318.

23. Statement of Morris Tannenbaum, Appendix B, in *Technology: Processes of Assessment and Choice,* report of the Committee on Science and Public Policy, National Academy of Sciences, to the Committee on Science and Astronautics, U.S. House of Representatives, USGPO, Washington, D. C., July, 1969, pp. 148–150.

PART 4

Business and Society: State of the Art and Program for the Future

In order to make sense of the important conceptual issues so basic to the business and society field, the conveners considered it essential that its contours be sketched by one who was closely involved with the field yet who could be objective about it. We sought a person who possessed sufficient detachment to be able both to position the field in the context of American higher education generally and of professional business education specifically and to offer informed judgments concerning its likely future directions. In his essay, Earl F. Cheit performs this vital task in two ways: by a retrospective examination of the development of the field and by a prospectively oriented assessment of its likely course. Cheit analyzes the reasons for the mixed, and often emotional, responses that recent work in business and society has stimulated within the academic and the business worlds, responses characterized by enthusiasm for the relevance, popular appeal, and innovativeness of the work and, at the same time, by skepticism regarding its theoretical and methodological vigor and unease with its seeming lack of an agreed-upon common core of subject matter. Ironically, the same attributes which have led to its being praised, have also caused the field to be damned.

Cheit points out that, in common with other new fields, business and society, at its outset some twenty years ago, "had to take the leftovers" of issues and concerns that older and more firmly established groups in the nation's business schools had not already arrogated to themselves. Cheit notes that in the intervening two decades the field has achieved somewhat greater coherence and design, dealing with business as an institution and drawing upon the older and better-established liberal arts disciplines to examine the direction and ends of business activity, but is still inevitably at the crux of that perennial "source of tension in education—namely that between the useful and liberal arts." He posits four functions performed by course work in business and society: it offers some practical skills; it provides institutional studies; it analyzes environmental relationships; and it seeks to develop those energies of mind needed to direct business activities.

Cheit also traces the development of business education in the United States from the period of the late nineteenth century, and notes that "practical" education soon replaced "broad" education as the key objective of most business schools during the first half of the twentieth century. In the period 1959-63, counterpressures emerged and business education underwent a period of critical introspection from which a number of influential studies resulted. These studies stressed the importance of including environmental courses and research in the educational activities of business schools. Cheit outlines contents of the pioneering early courses in business and society and traces the growth and development of curricula in the field in the past twenty years. Relying upon a detailed study by George Steiner of present-day business and society course offerings, Cheit notes that

> they are unified by no single theory, they use various disciplines, but comprise no discipline. In this sense they have a special kinship to their home, the business school. An applied field looking to an unusual problem rather than toward an internal discipline with a theory has always been in trouble in the university.

He concludes that while business and society struggles in the "shadows" of eight disciplines, "it performs a function none of these disciplines alone can perform—effectively to put business activities in their environmental context."

Regarding the future of the business and society field, Cheit anticipates increased growth and emphasis within the business curriculum as a result of five factors: an expanded interest in the institutional aspects of business; enhanced public expectations concerning the role of business and the way these have forced managers to analyze their decisions in societal terms as well as in the more traditional economic terms; the drive within American education to bring together the useful and the liberal arts; the gradual replacement in the business and society field of abstract and speculative research on corporate social responsibility by empirical studies that are of interest to both the university and business; and, finally, the failure of the field to become a discipline, an event which has produced advantages as well as disadvantages. He concludes by observing that an aspect of education of future managers—that dealing with the environment in which they will work—can influence how adequately managers perform. That is what the [business and society] field is all about.

As can well be imagined, Cheit's essay generated considerable discussion at the workshop/conference. Key among the issues were:

1. If business and society is not already a discipline, could it become one and, more importantly, *should* it become one?

2. Should future research efforts in the field concentrate upon theory building, methodological refinement, and empirical studies rather than upon conceptual exploration of basic philosophical issues?

3. What should be the relationship between the business and society field and the pertinent academic disciplines such as economics, political science, law, history, and sociology?

4. To what extent should the field maintain an explicitly normative focus rather than an objective empirical orientation?

5. What backgrounds and qualifications are necessary for teachers in the business and society field?

For Joseph McQuire, business and society is not a discipline but a focus which deals with two types of issues, the one positive and the other normative, in an attempt to answer the question: How does and how should the business enterprise behave to serve the public welfare? He foresees with concern more emphasis on narrower issues, which can be addressed with greater methodological rigor, and a neglect of the essential substantive and philosophical questions that have been of such importance to the field in the past. Clarence Walton expressed similar views, particularly a worry that an emphasis on the immediate (and readily researchable) issues of the day could convert the field into something "very close to a kind of sophisticated journalism." Others, including William Frederick, Lee Preston, S. Prakash Sethi, and Frederick Sturdivant, stressed the need "for research . . . for careful, methodologically sound research," and considered business and society's failure to coalesce into a discipline to be a debility rather than a strength. Sturdivant saw the field as moving increasingly in the direction of a "usefulness" that is "beyond the broader philosophical constructs into empirically verifiable and testable questions involving the kind of research" that will have greater utility to both the operating manager and the policy analyst. Sethi felt the development of theoretical and methodological bases to go along with the present institutional base would add "precision, articulation, and measurement" to the "philosophical" thrust of the business and society field today. Raymond Bauer took a somewhat intermediate position.

> There is no salvation in being exclusively empirical or exclusively wise, or being exclusively disciplinary, or exclusively responsible and responsive to particular situations.

It seems to us, furthermore, that the business and society field has reached a point where scholars can begin to cut into many of the basic conceptual and philosophical issues the field has dealt with in the past and can do so with more rigorous methodology, bringing to bear where necessary tools from other social science disciplines.

C. West Churchman, on the other hand, wondered whether business and society had the exclusive mandate to explore the relation of business to society and whether the management scientists, the organizational theorists, and the macroeconomists might also have some claim on this area of inquiry. Steiner proposed the development of some consensus or common core of basic issues for teaching, and Harvey Brooks suggested that rather than being too broad in its focus, business and society with its stress upon the corporation and business failed to draw sufficiently from parallels which, in his view, exist in all the professions, since "each specialist, or each specialized occupation, is somehow expected to be responsible for everything else in society." George L. Bach feels that classroom work in business and society should first

> teach *its* kind of sensitivity to problems and, secondly, emphasize a process or a way of thinking about problems, not anticipating or inventing problems, and concentrate on how one finds the *right* analytical concepts and the *right* analytical tools that are going to be useful.

Neil Smelser suggested that, despite the fact that it lacks "a coherent paradigm, or a theoretical and methodological set of canons that people agree on and within which they do their research," business and society was a "field," measured by two important criteria: it is concerned with a more or less systematic accumulation of social problems and people teaching it give themselves a label.

Not surprisingly, the above questions concerning the nature and directions of teaching and research in the business and society field constituted a leitmotif during the workshop/conference. Louis B. Lundborg, retired Board Chairman of the Bank of America, emphasized the importance of exposing high-level executives to the problems and issues stressed in business and society, all the while recognizing, as an "inescapable fact of life," that what graduates may learn on the *conceptual* level at this time they will be unable to use except on a *functional* level. Milton Moskowitz, a business journalist, emphasized the need for the scholars in the field "to deal with the data . . . to pay attention to what goes on."

In the concluding session, Melvin A. Eisenberg wondered if it might not be essential to the education of business leaders that management education be restricted to the graduate level after the matriculants had received a classical liberal arts education. Many of the participants responded that this would be fine if the liberal arts faculties and disciplines were doing their jobs. Indeed, the failure of the liberal arts to play this role was one of the reasons in the first place for the emergence of the business and society field within schools of business administration.

Let us not leave this brief introduction to the Cheit paper without a few comments on management education generally. Certainly, one of the major challenges confronting society today is that of how to make the corporation, society's dominant economic institution, into a better instrument for carrying out the economic and broader social tasks which society has now assigned to it. One of the problems encountered in trying to achieve this end is that the means which the society at large employs to communicate its expectations to the corporation often produce a message that is badly garbled or even misdirected. In the long run, the only way in which genuine corporate reform can occur and the social challenge met is for the thinking of managers to be changed. It is here, of course, where the schools of management and business administration play their crucial roles. If we are to have a new corporate response to society's challenges, we must also have a new response from higher education. The tendency on the part of liberal arts faculties either to ignore business or to decry it and all it stands for is not likely to produce the healthy adaptation by the corporate sector that is required. It seems likely, therefore, that most of the work in business and society will remain in the professional schools of management.

We should be as interested in education *about* business and management as we are in education *for* business and management and as concerned with instilling a zest for business (to borrow Whitehead's phrase) as with affording an opportunity for basic training. Many schools of management are not now achieving these ends. The image of the manager created by some observers as the "servant," "agent," or "employee" of the "owner" in order "to make as much money as possible," describes a singularly unzestful career, and not just for the young. Yet many business schools, by ignoring the really challenging issues in society, instill or reinforce that image. Zest for life derives from challenge, and the most challenging issues in society today are not to be found in a business career if we exclude business from academic respectability, from its links with the humanities and social sciences, and from all goals and values except the economic.

Schools of management have an obligation to their students to stay at the forefront of knowledge and an obligation to the community as a whole to be the leaders, not the followers, in matters having to do with management training; norms and standards of management behavior; awareness of social trends and forces; changing values, attitudes, and ideologies; and innovations in organization and management techniques. If we remain in the passive role or the follower's role and hand on to our students only that which is already being done in the business world, or that which was being done the last time we looked, we have failed on every count. This is not to say that we should be unaware of what is now going on or that we should look only to the future and ignore the present and the past. It is to say that the schools are more than just channels for the transmission of conventional learning or current history. If the schools can adjust their goals to include these matters, if they can begin to relate the challenging issues of society to business, if they can help to communicate to the great corporations the new expectations that society has for them, and if they can help the corporations to respond appropriately to these new demands, there should be no shortage of zest in a business career.

EARL F. CHEIT

What Is the Field of Business and Society and Where Is It Going?

Although in the abstract higher education gives its most approving rhetoric to the idea of innovation, people who profess for a living express much private skepticism about specific innovations. The evolving field of social, political, and legal environment of business is a case in point. In business schools all over the country, deans and faculty members who want to point with pride (for the benefit of faculty recruits, potential donors, visiting committees, student recruits, or foundation officers) customarily include, among things worth noting, "the innovative work going on in the exciting new field" of business and society (the shorthand phrase I shall use in this paper). And they do much more than point with pride. In growing numbers, business school faculties around the nation are requiring students to take the courses in this field. Journal articles and surveys of American Assembly of Collegiate Schools of Business (AACSB) describe the consequent growth of this new course work with approval.

An AACSB survey in 1968-69 reported that 77 of 154 business schools required course work in the field. The ratio is higher today. A 1974 survey of 174 graduate schools of business, shows that 60 percent required at least one course in this field for the MBA.[2]

But privately, in faculty debates about budget and personnel, one hears another side of this matter. There one hears the skepticism: the field of business and society is not really a discipline with a theory; most of it cannot qualify as hard social science; much of its writing has the popular appeal of journalism; the field sometimes reveals itself as a coherent way to scold businessmen; and, worst of all, when one examines the courses taught in different institutions, or even in the same institution, they vary so widely that the field cannot be well defined. It is easy to see why the planners of this workshop would, at the outset, pose the two questions: What is the, field of business and society, and where is it going?

I am pleased to acknowledge the assistance of Janet Messman in the preparation of this paper.

TAKING THE LEFTOVERS

One could argue that the salient characteristic of the field—its recent, rapid growth—is one reason why it lacks definition. Excluded from subjects by the jurisdictional claims staked by established fields, newer fields traditionally have had to take the leftovers, which often defy definition. Business and society is just emerging from that phase.

David Riesman, in his lectures on *Constraint and Variety in American Education,* points out that this is what happened to his own field, sociology. Sociologists, Riesman states, "until recently could not touch the economy which belonged to the economists and could not touch government and military affairs which belonged to the political scientists, but had to find their clientele among criminals, children, old people, immigrants, factory workers, small-town folk, and other relatively powerless groups whom no one else had laid claim to."[3]

Until recently, business school faculty members desiring to meet the upsurge in interest in this field could not touch the business firm, which belonged to managerial economics, nor advertising, which belonged to marketing. The firm's internal management had already been claimed by organization theory, its technology by the field of production, its big money matters by corporate finance, and its relations to government by the field of industrial organization.

As a consequence, business and society faculty members found their early subject matter among the leftovers, subjects no one else had laid claim to: social responsibility, business ethics, environmental problems, ideology, consumerism, minority opportunity and business development, conceptual foundations of business, the social control of enterprise, the role of business in the political process, and business as an institution.

I taught one of those courses in 1959, and whatever else its virtues, clear definition of subject matter was not one of them. Nor could I include the kind of inspiring statement of purpose that described two courses I recall from graduate school. In those days, the head teaching assistant in Economics 1A and 1B would tell his crew: "In the first quarter, it's marginal cost equals marginal revenue. In the second quarter, it's savings equals investment. If the students learn both, you've succeeded." We may never reach such an admirable level of clarity in the teaching of business and society, but there is certainly more unity and definition in the field today than in the days I first taught at Berkeley.

COLLEGIATE EDUCATION FOR BUSINESS

Important as better, clearer definition is, we should recognize that its attainment will not make the field or its courses less difficult for a faculty to deal with or less controversial. Indeed, even if the field becomes more satisfyingly theoretical and reveals itself in well-received quantified forms; even if its writing becomes less readable, and on the whole less scolding; business and society will remain a focus of tension for reasons that grow directly out of the way collegiate education for business and the business environment have evolved. Mostly by default, the field of business and society has become a primary source of teaching about business as an institution; by design, it seeks to analyze and evaluate society's growing expectations of business, as well as the responses of American business to those expectations; and finally, because it draws upon liberal arts disciplines to consider the direction and ends of business activity, it deals directly with the oldest source of tension in education—namely, that between the useful and the liberal arts.

Business and society has important practical objectives, to be sure, but in my view, its most significant function derives from its attempt to deal with what Alfred North Whitehead once called "the key fact in education, and the reason for most of its difficulties," namely, the problem that "necessary technical excellence can only be acquired by a training which is apt to damage those energies of mind which should direct the technical skill." Ideally, business and society seeks to develop in students the analytical framework, an understanding of the processes of problem solving, and the sensitivity essential to people who will have leadership responsibilities in the next decade.

What is the field of business and society? I have outlined my answer by listing four functions performed by the course work. It provides institutional studies; it analyzes environmental relationships; it develops skills; and by use of all of these combined, it seeks to develop those energies of mind needed to direct business skills. I can complete my answer best by reviewing the developments that shaped the field and assigned these functions to it.

HISTORY OF BUSINESS EDUCATION

Historians of business education set its "pioneer" period from 1881 to 1900 when the first three schools of commerce were established—the Wharton School of the University of Pennsylvania in 1881 and the schools at the University of California at Berkeley and the University of Chicago in 1898.

The earliest influential interest in instruction in business came from men of wealth who began contributing to higher education following the Civil War. These men who gradually replaced the clergy on boards of trustees took an active interest in incorporating business concerns into higher education where they sought broad education, not vocational training.

Joseph Wharton's $100,000 gift to the trustees of the University of Pennsylvania easily resolved the conflict between useful and liberal by providing for a "liberal education in all matters concerning Finance and Commerce." Only two of the first five professorships—accounting and mercantile law—were vocational or professional. In a letter written shortly after his gift, Wharton wrote that

> [we aim to produce] educated young men with a taste for business, vigorous, active workers, of sturdy character and independent opinion, having a lofty faith in all things good, and able to give a reason for the faith that is in them.[4]

The Wharton School did not lead directly to a business career, and historian Edward Chase Kirkland observes, "Probably the Wharton School was in the light of modern educational practice largely a device to give students at the University of Pennsylvania a major in history and the social sciences."[5] Historian Kirkland also notes that

> Wharton was particularly impressed by the plight of young men who inherited wealth. Since they could not be reclaimed by hard work, as their fathers had been, higher education of the right sort was the answer.[6]

The education Wharton (and later, Stanford) sought to make possible was not be narrowing, like the apprenticeship system, nor was it to be of the kind offered by the proprietary business colleges, where one could learn accounts. These men envisioned something loftier, institutions of higher business learning, not mere teaching about trade.

But by introducing trade—this most practical of the useful arts—into universities, these early businessmen brought into sharp focus Aristotle's question about the difficulty of deciding which should have priority: virtue, the useful, or the higher knowledge.

At least some early American businessmen believed that the useful could be combined with virtue and higher learning through the study of business. Their view, and their actions in promoting it, eventually engaged two of America's most famous scholars—Thorstein Veblen and Alfred North Whitehead—in thinking and writing about the place of business schools in higher education.

For Whitehead, the business school as a new development in university activity was part of a natural evolutionary process.

> It marks [he wrote in 1928] the culmination of a movement which for many years past has introduced analogous departments throughout American uni-

versities. ...The conduct of business now required intellectual imagination of the same type as that which in former times had mainly passed into those other occupations [law, clergy, medicine, and science]. The justification for a university is that it preserves the connection between knowledge and the zest for life...[and] in the modern complex social organism, the adventure of life cannot be disjoined from intellectual adventure.[7]

For Veblen, the combination of useful (or pecuniary, as he called it) and higher learning threatened to undermine rather than enhance intellectual life. The thought that the captains of industry would become arbiters of taste, not only in the outside world, but on the campus as well, was more than distasteful to him. This effort, he wrote, tends to make "a gainful occupation . . . the first requisite of human life . . . and the vulgar allow it uncritically to stand as the chief or sole end that is worth an effort."[8]

It means a more or less effectual further diversion of interest and support from science and scholarship to the competitive acquisition of wealth...an endeavor to substitute the pursuit of gain and expenditure in place of the pursuit of knowedge, as the focus of interest and the objective end in the modern intellectual life.[9]

Although critical of other professional schools, Veblen was most concerned about the colleges of commerce, because, he argued, "they do not draw from the results of modern science nor do they aim, as do other professions, to serve the community." By training masters of gain, they would serve only the individual in private gain. Thus the colleges of commerce would create a bias hostile to scholarly and scientific work.

Looking ahead from the early 1900s, Veblen saw that the business schools must develop in one of two ways. Either they would not be adequately funded to perform the expensive job required to serve business, in which case they would turn out to be little more than a "pedantic and equivocal adjunct to the department of economics," or they would do what is necessary to service business fully and this would require great expenses for faculty, facilities, travel, and operations. This type of college of commerce, he wrote, would be too expensive and "would manifestly appear to be beyond the powers of any existing university."[10]

"So," he wrote, "the academic authorities face the choice between scholarly efficiency and vocational training, and hitherto the result has been equivocal.'' Some have tried to become schools that ''serve business traffic,'' but these have only succeeded in becoming ''a cross between a secondary school for bank clerks and traveling salesmen and a subsidiary department of economics.''[11]

Those options may seem a bit harsh, but there is no question about the general direction the schools were to take. The early start toward broad education for business quickly took a practical turn in response to a rapidly growing demand for a new form of business instruction which would meet the more practical needs of business.

By the time the University of California and the University of Chicago began their schools of business in 1898, faculty members in economics departments were eager to teach (and were indeed teaching) applied aspects of business administration.

Another force for practical instruction was the evolution of professional accounting. According to Pierson, in his Carnegie-sponsored study *The Education of American Businessmen,*

> the founding of N.Y.U's School of Commerce, Accounts, and Finance in 1900 can be directly traced to the decision reached by the New York State Society of Certified Public Accountants in 1899 that a school was needed to supply students of accounting with the knowledge necessary to pass the C.P.A. examinations.[12]

Shortly after the turn of the century, all business schools, says Pierson, ''regardless of origin and announced purpose'' began to move in the direction of the practical curriculum, teaching specific business practices and skills. By 1906 the Wharton School had become career directed, as did Chicago, Berkeley, and Harvard (which was graduate only). In short, during the period from the turn of the century to World War I, business schools turned enthusiastically to the practical curriculum, and began to grow.

This practical orientation attracted practical faculty members who worked to meet the needs of the business community. Much as Veblen had predicted, they and their schools grew away from the academic community. Pierson observes that it ''became difficult to tell whether the accounting instructors in these schools were primarily teachers who had an accounting practice on the side, or primarily practicing accountants who wanted to keep their hand in the teaching profession.''[13] Aware of this deficiency, many persons sought to maintain curricular balance between the liberal and the useful. But they were the exceptions, and although their influence was substantial in individual institutions, overall it was relatively small. Thus, although the great growth of business schools did not occur until after World War I, their directions and the basis for their vocational emphasis were being created very early in their history.

After World War I the overriding concern of business schools was their phenomenal growth. Relative to all undergraduate degrees, business administration accounted for about 1 percent until 1915; it rose to almost 17 percent by 1950, the post-World War II high. It was a spectacular rise of a small field, often with tenuous relationships on campus, to become the single most populous major for men. By the academic year 1949-50, one in seven undergraduate men was enrolled in business administration. It was as if business schools were trying to catch up with the historic growth rate of business itself. Enrollment figures made clear that business administration had become a major part of American higher education.

RECENT EVOLUTION

In retrospect, it seems fair to say that during a long period of their development, business schools came closer to Veblen's vision than to Whitehead's. But in recent years, schools of business have moved closer to Whitehead's view of their historic role and function, and the revival by the field of business and society of those broader concerns stated in Joseph Wharton's gift is one important reason. That revival began in the mid-1950s, as American business schools began what Clark Kerr then described as a search for their souls.

Most professional fields have experienced periods of examination and self-criticism, but probably none so concentrated a period of critical introspection as business administration in the five years between 1959 and 1964. Two comprehensive studies were published in 1959, *The Education of American Businessmen*[14] and *Higher Education for Business,*[15] sponsored by the Carnegie Corporation and the Ford Foundation respectively. The Institute of Higher Education at Columbia University, as part of its series on undergraduate professional schools, published *Liberal Education and Business* in 1963.[16] The next year the Committee for Economic Development issued a statement on national policy entitled *Educating Tomorrow's Managers,* which reviewed the above studies and others and relevant sections of the Robbins Report on Higher Education of Business Studies in Britain and offered a series of recommendations.[17]

These studies stressed the importance of including "environmental" courses and research in the work of business schools and pointed to examples of excellent work being done in several institutions. While the reports did not introduce the idea of this field, they did help reawaken interest in a role for professional business education that was broader than just vocational.

Gordon and Howell surveyed sixty schools—six graduate schools, thirty-three AACSB member and twenty-one nonmember schools offering graduate and undergraduate courses. At most institutions the view was expressed that the master's program should require work in the field of business environment. Four of the six graduate schools with solid core requirements offered courses which pointed in that direction. A fifth was planning to introduce a required course. The authors pointed out that

> Columbia, in the planned revision of its M.B.A. program, proposed to require the equivalent of three to four semester courses on the nonmarket environment of business, and its dean has strongly emphasized the need for stressing the philosophical and historical aspects of the role which business plays in American society.
>
> Of the thirty-three member schools in our sample offering both graduate and undergraduate work, only six required as much as a course on the legal, social, political, or intellectual environment of business. Only three of twenty-one nonmember schools has such a requirement.
>
> The kinds of courses required in this general area vary widely. Harvard requires a course on Business Responsibilities in the American Society which, according to the 1957–58 catalogue, seeks "to begin to familiarize the student with the economic-legal-political-social environment within which business decisions are made and the business process takes place, the impact of such environmental factors on the shaping of business decisions, and a recognition of the impact of such business decisions on the economy itself." This comes close to describing what we have in mind, with the qualification that in our view such a course should strongly emphasize the element of change in the environment of business. Actually, the Harvard course seems to be confined largely to the economic environment of business, with particular emphasis on national policy relating to competition and to economic stability.
>
> Carnegie Tech requires a semester of Government and Business in the first year and, what is more interesting, a course on Ideas and Social Change in the second. Tulane requires a course in Business and Society, in the teaching of which a sociologist and a philosopher have participated. Northwestern requires a course in Social Problems in Administration.
>
> A number of other schools require some sort of course in Public Policy, Government and Business, or the like. It is fair to say, however, that few schools require courses with the breadth and the kind of intellectual challenge that are needed by students who have a good chance to become leaders of the community."[18]

In discussing courses offered in Master's programs, Pierson pointed out that the work "introduces students to some of the ends a society seeks in its relations with business enterprises and some of the means (through law) which it has devised to carry out these purposes."[19] He observed that "it is not surprising that the specific topics covered by these courses show little similarity."[20] The focus at Chicago was on the legal and economic principles underlying the public control of business, and at Carnegie Tech it was on legal institutions and procedures resulting from industrial and social changes. Professor Leland Hazard described the course at Carnegie Tech as follows:

> Obviously it was not within the scope of our course on Ideas and Social Change to teach rules of law. Nevertheless it was important to examine, as we did, a few cases. They were selected to point up that most difficult, and at the same time most illuminating, situation in which one of two equally innocent persons must suffer. . . . We spent some time on the necessity for procedure in law. . . .
>
> The employment of several novels in the course was not a pretense at literary criticism. . . . Neither was there a pretense at history, philosophy, or theology. Of course it was necessary to skirt these fields in order to develop the proposition that law arises not in mystery but rather in the ebb and flow, in the very flux, of life.[21]

Gordon and Howell expressed the hope that framework courses dealing with the changing social, political, legal, and intellectual environment of business would take the place of the more narrow business law courses and that courses offered under the titles of Government and Business and Public Policy toward Business would be incorporated into the broader framework course. The changing environment within which business must operate is a key to their thinking.

Their "Suggested Professional Base or 'Core' for Undergraduate Business Students" included a course entitled Legal Environment of Business. Their proposed Master of Business Administration program recommended a course in the Legal, Social, and Political Environment for both those with or without an undergraduate major in business.

> The aims would be twofold: first, to impress on the student the multifarious and changing ways in which business interacts with its institutional environment, and second, to develop in him a sharpened interest in and a sense of responsibility for the kind of society in which he will live and work.[22]

Pierson suggested an undergraduate curriculum that included under "business foundation subjects" a course entitled Political and Legal Factors in Business, and under "functional business subjects," a course entitled Business Policy and Social Responsibility.

George Leland Bach's chapter in Pierson's book pointed out that the "role of the manager . . . will be more and more that of a man with many masters, and it will behoove him to be sensitive to the pulse of the whole community."[23] He saw this as a continuation of forces that have been actively working over the last fifty years. He stated strongly "the need for the manager of tomorrow to understand, and be sensitive to, the entire economic, political, and social environment in which he will live and in which his business will operate and be judged.''[24]

Bach proposed a two-year M.B.A. curriculum, which he noted ''is representative enough of the thinking at a number of prominent graduate schools to picture some important trends now discernible in graduate education.''[25] It would include a full-year required course on the place of business and the businessman in the economic, political, legal, and social environment. This would come in the second year when it could utilize the analytical tools gained in the first year. He described the course as one which would try

> to understand the reasons for government intervention in and regulation of business. It would look intensively at the political and legal processes in democratic industrialized societies and at the role of business and businessmen in relation to other organized groups. It would try to force students to think through thoroughly problems of business ethics and social responsibility and their own systems of social values.[26]

The reports revealed that the better graduate programs had established a leadership position in this field. Though not called Business and Society, their early courses evolved into the current core course work in the field today. Professor George Steiner reports that UCLA was developing course work in this field for some twenty years. Originally a small seminar called Enterprise Philosophy, it is now a required M.B.A. course called Business and Society, Professor Bach at Stanford and Professor Lodge of Harvard report that their current offerings stem from earlier courses long part of the curriculum. So it is not surprising that the major reports found models at Columbia, Harvard, Carnegie Tech, Cornell, Berkeley, and similar institutions. Their early work, in effect, provided a base for the case made by the foundation reports for providing both for undergraduates and M.B.A.'s, required courses in business environment.

In the twenty years since the major studies were begun, the field has grown rapidly. Growth was slow during the first ten years, but has been rapid since, especially in the past five years. The causal relationships are not easily established, but it seems reasonable to conclude that reports had a significant, though delayed, impact.

Today, virtually every business school in the country offers course work in, or with the objectives of, the field of business and society. The courses are extraordinarily diverse. An unpublished draft of a *Directory of Corporate Social Policy Courses in Graduate Business Schools and the Professors Who Teach Them,* prepared in October, 1974 by the National Affiliation of Concerned Business Students, presents one perspective of the field we are describing. Based on data from 190 United States colleges and universities, this directory lists approximately 660 courses, 670 faculty, and 65,000 students (day and evening)! The following fourteen universities and colleges are shown as offering concentrations in the field: Boston College, University of California at Berkeley, Columbia University, University of Detroit, Harvard University, Louisiana Technological University, University of Nebraska, University of New Mexico, New York University, State University of New York at Buffalo, Northwestern University, University of Pennsylvania, University of Pittsburgh, and the University of Washington.

WHAT IS THE FIELD OF BUSINESS AND SOCIETY?

Now we ask of this field: What is it? One can answer in two ways: first, by the content of those courses; second, by their functions, which we referred to earlier.

George Steiner has developed a fairly good measure of what is being taught through his collection of course outlines in the field. His analysis of these outlines for the three year period 1971–1973 produced three major groupings.

First are courses which are concerned solely with business social responsibilities. Included in this group are courses with such titles as "Business Responsibilities in Society" and "Social Responsibilities of Business." There are comparatively few courses that seem to focus solely on business social responsibilities.

Second are courses which are concerned with the broad range of interrelationships between business and society. They have titles such as: "Business and Society," "Business and Its Environment," "Administration and the Social Order," and "Environment, Management and Organizations." Courses such as these seem to be growing in number relative to the other two groupings.

Third are courses that are subsets of the second group. Here are found courses in "Business and Government," "Legal Environment of Business," "Marketing and Society," "Cultural Aspects of Administration," "Ethics and Morality in Business," "Minority Enterprises and Minority Economic Development," "Modern Capitalism," and "Business and Selected Social Problems."[27]

Because these courses deal with a rapidly changing environment, a wide scope of subject matter is relevant. In response to our queries, faculty members at major graduate schools pointed out that the particular emphasis of the course is most often a reflection of the background and training of the individual teaching the course. The available resource literature is voluminous. Reading assignments are rarely the same in different courses. Course material changes frequently.

In an earlier analysis Steiner bears out what most of us would expect, namely, that the field of business and society relies on a mixture of orientations. He identifies eight.[28]

1. *Economic orientation* (these tend to have a macroeconomic focus).
2. *Philosophical orientation* (emphasis is on culture, values, religious roots, ethics, and ideologies).
3. *Legal orientation* (emphasis on government control).
4. *Marketing orientation* (often traditional marketing material with new emphasis on broader social issues).
5. *Historical orientation* (Historical business-society relationship).
6. *Urban orientation* (emphasis on the great city problems which beset the nation).
7. *Governmental orientation* (public policies toward business are the main theme).
8. *Eclectic orientation* (the most important category. According to Steiner it includes the above approaches and subject matter ranging "from the roots of the private enterprise system to current changes in social values, business social responsibilities, government-business interrelationships, consumerism, pollution, and so on.").[29]

Professor Steiner noted a distinct trend for these courses to be required of all students—a trend we have observed earlier in other studies. In this trend we see the traditional way in which faculties give their stamp of importance to a particular field.

The second approach to the question What is the field? is to examine its functions. The courses in business and society perform three very important functions. First, they provide the institutional studies essential to a practicing profession. Second, they offer an analysis of the total environment within which the institutions of business function. Third, they develop the skills necessary for dealing with the problems of the relationship of business institutions to the broad society in which it functions. Perhaps the most important aspect of these courses is that these combined approaches are concerned with business leadership, the development of those energies of mind needed to direct the technical business skills.

The Morrill Act of 1862 assumed that the practical would be taught in a manner which would always put it in this "liberal" context. Its stated purpose was to "promote the liberal and practical education of the industrial classes." But the assumption that technical subjects would be taught in a liberal manner was not borne out by actual practice.

This was one of the reasons for the *Statement Concerning Curriculum Standards IVb,* prepared for presentation to the Standards Committee, AACSB from the Committee on Curriculum and Standards, Division of Social Issues in Management, Academy of Management.[30] The statement is an argument for a special course in business and society, taught within the business school as a necessary part of the curriculum. Its drafters contend that a course in one of the underlying disciplines and taught outside the business school will not do, nor will a course built around one of the functional areas such as marketing. In their words, "Although several different courses could alternately meet the requirements of integration, courses that only inferentially or peripherally deal with the subject matter are no effective substitutes for the shaping of student thought and effort around the integrative process."[31]

Every professional field has had to struggle with Whitehead's problem, with the concern that it was developing the skill but not the energies of mind needed to direct it. The field of business and society has provided one important answer to that concern. The courses have the apparent defects noted at the outset—they are unified by no single theory, they use various disciplines but comprise no discipline. In this sense they have a special kinship to their home, the business school. An applied field looking to an outward problem rather than toward an internal discipline with a theory has always been in trouble in the university. Business struggles in the shadow of economics. Mr. Steiner's survey shows that business and society struggles in eight shadows— ranging from history to economics. But it performs a function none of these disciplines alone can perform—effectively to put business activities in their environmental context.

This is what the major reports said was needed. The C.E.D.'s report put it most succinctly: the objective of business education should be to develop the qualities for business leadership, which, in addition to analytical capacity, include imagination, mental vigor, and an "understanding of human behavior and of social, political, and economic forces."[32]

When MIT started its School of Industrial Management in 1951, Institute Administrators called together a small group of company presidents to seek their advice in planning for this school whose students would become business leaders. One of the participants at the meeting later recalled that in response to the question of what should be taught, the company presidents came to easy agreement on a four-part answer. They agreed that students should not be taught how to run a company. They thought there was little likelihood that this could be done in any case, and there was little chance of doing it in school. The faculty would probably not know very much about it, and what was known could better be taught and learned on the job.

The company presidents urged three areas of study. Because significant changes would occur during their working lives, students first would need to know and understand these changes in the context of history and the business environment in order to be effective in a business career.

Second, the presidents advised that students should know the essential leadership skills of writing and speaking effectively.

Finally, the students should be taught something about how human beings behave—why they do what they do. In fact, they agreed that this should be the core of any management program.[33]

Like the Chrysler Airflow, this model of business education was ahead of its time for general acceptance. Today it is a moderately good fit for the work in many schools of business administration, thanks to, among other things, the growth of the field of business and society.

WHERE IS THE FIELD GOING?

But where, I am asked, is business and society going? For practitioners, that question means, Will it become a discipline or continue to be a field which draws on other disciplines? It also means, Will research and writing continue to be dominated by interpretive essays or will it become more empirical and theoretical?

My view is that thus far business and society has benefitted from not being a discipline. To be sure, there are some disadvantages in that situation. As I noted earlier, a subject field that cannot qualify as a discipline with a central theory has historically been in trouble in a university. Pulled in different directions, the field may disintegrate. It lacks a theoretical construct that gives its courses uniformity and generates deductive and predictive power. Therefore it cannot generate the research to show whether its predictions are borne out by experience.

The advantages of not being a discipline are significant, however. The field has been open to a variety of disciplines in selecting its faculty. Indeed, many institutions, like my own, have sought a variety of disciplinary approaches. Not bound by disciplinary structure and received methods, the field has not generated solutions seeking problems. Instead, it is working with problems, some of them left over from the disciplines, other new ones that are growing. If the field continues to develop this way, and I hope it does, its growth will continue. Liberal arts students and students in other professional fields will continue to be attracted to its subject matter.

Younger faculty members drawn to this field are changing it, however. Their research is more empirical, their growing concern is theoretical constructs. Their success could transform this field into a formal discipline. But I doubt that this will happen, or should happen, very soon.

For deans, the question Where is business and society going? also means Will it continue to grow, or has it reached its peak? One might suspect that the combination of its recent rapid growth and the current recession would produce a leveling off of interest in the field of business and society. Earlier this year the *Wall Street Journal* reported some signs that "social responsibility fades as a matter of corporate concern."[34] Despite these signs that for some, short-term profit looms larger than longer-term goals, I believe the more important signs point to continued growth. That view comes from the survey of deans of schools accredited by the American Assembly of Collegiate Schools of Business. In 1974 they were asked to indicate the major trends in their schools in the next ten years. Of the 163 deans queried, 101 responded. They predicted that curricular areas dealing with social responsibility would receive greatly increased emphasis in the future, more than any other curricular area. The report states:

> Although there is considerable difference of opinion by deans on the directions which the business curriculum will take in the next ten years, there is general consensus that the curriculum will respond to the apparent needs and desires of the business environment. Emphasis will be placed on providing useful management skills and the ability to solve the social and environmental problems facing the modern executive. Historical emphasis on skills in the functional operations of business and the ability to apply economic theory will lessen, while students will spend much more time studying such topics as the social responsibility of business, business ethics and morals, the role of women in management, consumerism, and problems of racial minorities. The concern for practicality will result in more internship programs, increased study of international business, and involvement with various specialized programs. Emphasis will continue on developing skills in the behavioral and quantitative sciences.[35]

This expectation of growth in the field is generally corroborated by other surveys and informed guesses. I am inclined to agree. My view is based, not on the opinions of the deans, but on five (somewhat overlapping) developments reflecting the nature and content of the fields, subject matter, and some of the currents in higher education.

First, the proposition that a mature professional school must be responsible for dealing with its own institutions is becoming firmly established, not for the purpose of excluding others from study, but because a professional school has an obligation and a capacity to do so. This means that the important institutional aspects of business must be dealt with in an analytical way in the business school. That important institutional material, both domestic and international, is growing, and the field of business and society will grow with it.

During the period of vocational emphasis in business education, the curriculum was too busy dealing with the functions of business to be concerned with the institutions of business. There were exceptions, to be sure, and there were specialized courses in business history. But for the most part, business schools became expert at dealing with the functions of business, not with an overall assessment and interpretation of business itself. Martin Mayer notes in his recent book, *The Bankers,* that

> Milton Friedman and Anna P. Schwartz could write a monetary history of the United States from 1867 to 1960 without paying much attention to any bank or banker, resting the entire analysis on events external to banking.[36]

The view that banking is neutral, and "if government pushed certain buttons, banks would necessarily respond in a predetermined way" makes an uncomfortable fit to current facts. Indeed, Mayer's book is devoted to showing that this assumption is false, that there has been a revolution, due to technical and structural changes, which makes banks prime movers, not responders.

Business schools were open to change. Many of them introduced courses dealing with new institutional forces—for example, those of the labor movement. Business school courses dealt with the history of labor institutions, their role, and style, but curiously, often did not do the same for business institutions. But no longer. Today, required courses in business and society introduce students to the institutions of business.

The second reason I expect growing emphasis on this field is that the public expectations of business continue to grow, as do the importance and variety of business responses. Whether or not we reach the stage of understanding projected by an important UCLA study of professions,[37] namely, that professions are in some sense held responsible for the important environmental aspects of their activity, clearly our expectations of them are rising. There is a growing realization that managers of large institutions have the scope of significant choice, and that this choice influences people and communities. As Carl Kaysen has observed in his essay, "The Corporation, How Much Power? What Scope?", a large business organization manifests this power through choices open to it in "prices and price-cost relations, investment, location, research and innovation, and product character and selling effort."[38] The choices made by managers have impact in particular markets and sometimes on the economy as a whole. Because of this range of significant choice, business behavior is judged by more than economic efficiency. Additional criteria are being applied, among them stability, equity, and what Kaysen calls "progressiveness." Even the power and scope of choice itself is increasingly seen as a problem because, given its impact, the decision has the characteristics of political decision, but without the essential characteristic of political participation.

The importance of these issues is not likely to decline, either in the larger society or in the business school. They have become the main subject matter of courses in business and society, much as Pierson and Gordon-Howell hoped they would.

A third reason for predicting growth in this field stems from the first two and is reflected in the newer relationships being developed between professional schools generally and colleges of arts and sciences. Colleges of arts and sciences are in trouble, partly for labor market reasons, partly because of the lack of a coherent view of a liberal education. Things may change, but in the near future their ability to help business schools combine the useful and the liberal seems to be limited. In the meantime, the business schools are growing rapidly and are strongly motivated to work at that job. They are at a stage in their development where they are confident enough to assert more jurisdictional control over their subject matter. They feel little need to emulate economics departments and a declining urge to develop an indigenous administrative subject matter. Business is important enough and its context is highly important.

That context has become more important than ever. We tend to think of professionals as persons who enter into a single client relationship. But professionals in business, or engineering, or agriculture, or forestry, are increasingly drawn to the center of society's major problems: growth, war, food supply, the environment. Allen Rosenstein, in his remarkable work, *A Study of a Profession and Professional Education,* makes a strong case that education for these fields cannot discharge its responsibilities merely by offering students elective choices. The responsibility is the preparation of students to understand and discharge the obligations of a profession.[39]

One way to achieve this would be that assumed by the land-grant legislation—teaching the skill in a liberal manner. Except for the University of Chicago, not many schools have tried or succeeded in this approach. Therefore it will be in course work in business and society where this function is performed. Its main role will be that of bringing together the useful and the liberal. That job is far from done.

My fourth reason for predicting continued growth is that after a long period of rather abstract writing and speculating about corporate social responsibility (to which I have contributed at least my share), understanding of this concept is being advanced by new relationships between business and the university and by some new approaches. Among the latter, the various projects begun by the National Affiliation of Concerned Business Students have the great advantage of modesty and directness. I believe they can produce significant long-term effects in the relationship between business and education for business, as can the kind of empirical research being done by Harvard Professor Raymond Bauer on corporate social responsiveness and other newer, if less ambitious, approaches to social responsibility.

Finally, I believe the future of this academic field is secure and will be one of growth, because the environmental issues are becoming ever more important and complex, and therefore the concern with what a business organization is, what it can and cannot do, what its basic responsibilities are is more important than ever. The economic downturn has not made these issues less important; it has increased their importance. The recession has produced lawsuits dealing with fair employment and promotion whose organizational consequences will be profound. It also brings home the fact that in large organizations environmental issues are becoming the most important.

At a recent conference in Berkeley, Louis Lundborg, retired board chairman, Bank of America, reported that a Bank of America study of the causes of business failure revealed that small business—of the mom and pop variety—fails because of the problem of money management; the medium-size enterprises—the $1 to $10 million sales volume—get into trouble primarily because of the problems of managing people; whereas in the very large enterprises—those reaching into the Fortune 500 group —the main problem is their relationship to the larger society. What is at issue is their credibility, their impact, their legitimacy, their ability to lead.

These issues are not likely to decline in importance off campus, and studies dealing with these issues are not likely to decline on campus. This is a fairly recent development.

Eighteen years ago, in his paper on the soul searching of business schools, Clark Kerr concluded:

> Finally, if the world is to be saved at all, it will not be saved by the schools of business. This is not because business managers are not important. On the contrary, the most crucial human factor in an industrial society may well be the business manager. It is rather because how adequately they perform does not depend primarily on how well they have been selected and how well they have been trained, but rather on the environment within which they work and on who can survive and prosper in that environment.[40]

That was true two decades ago.

Today, the environmental issues have grown in importance and a field has developed to deal with them. The field of business and society accepts the conclusion but not the premise. It moves from the premise that an aspect of education of future managers—that dealing with the environment in which they will work—can influence how adequately managers perform. That is what the field is all about.

NOTES

1. American Association of Collegiate Schools of Business, *Teaching Load—Class Sizes and Admission and Degree Requirement, 1968-69,* Part 4 (St. Louis, Mo.: AACSB Statistical Service, 1969).

2. Andrew Mann, "The Ethics Puzzle," *MBA,* vol. 8, No. 8 (September, 1974).

3. David Riesman, *Constraint and Variety in American Education* (New York: Doubleday Anchor Books, 1958), p. 91.

4. Edward Chase Kirkland, *Dream and Thought in the Business Community 1860-1900* (Ithaca, (N.Y.: Cornellf University Press, 1956), p. 96.

5. *Ibid.*

6. *Ibid.,* p. 98.

7. Alfred North Whitehead, *The Aims of Education and Other Essays* (New York: The Free Press, paperback ed., The Macmillan Company, 1967), pp. 92-95.

8. Thorstein Veblen, *The Higher Learning in America,* American Century Series (New York: Hill and Wang, 1957), p. 145.

9. *Ibid.,* p. 149.

10. *Ibid.,* pp. 158-159.

11. *Ibid.,* p. 159.

12. Frank C. Pierson and others, *The Education of American Businessmen* (New York: McGraw-Hill Book Company, 1959), p. 36.

13. *Ibid.,* p. 41.

14. *Ibid.*

15. Robert Aaron Gordon and James Edwin Howell, *Higher Education for Business* (New York: Columbia University Press, 1959).

16. William M. Kephart et al., *Liberal Education and Business* (New York: Columbia University Press, 1963).

17. Committee for Economic Development, *Educating Tomorrow's Managers* (New York: CED, 1964).

18. Gordon and Howell, *op. cit.,* pp. 267-268.

19. Pierson, *op. cit.,* p. 251.

20. *Ibid.*

21. *Ibid.,* p. 252.

22. Gordon and Howell, *op. cit.,* p. 267.

23. Pierson, *op. cit.,* p. 323.

24. *Ibid.*

25. *Ibid.,* p. 325.

26. *Ibid.,* p. 334.

27. George A. Steiner, "What Should Schools of Business Be Teaching About

Social Responsibilities?" *Business Ethics and Social Responsibilities: Theory and Practice* (Proceedings of the Center Conference, March 28–30, 1974, Charlottesville, Va., University of Virginia Graduate School of Business Administration), p. 19.

28. George A. Steiner, "University Courses in the Business-Society Area," *Contemporary Challenges in the Business Society Relationship* (Los Angeles: Graduate School of Management, UCLA, 1972).

29. *Ibid.,* p. 23.

30. Committee on Curriculum and Standards, Division of Social Issues in Management, Academy of Management, *Statements Concerning Curriculum Standard IVb, American Assembly of Collegiate Schools of Business* (Unpublished manuscript prepared for presentation to the Standards Committee, American Assembly of Collegiate Schools of Business, December, 1974).

31. *Ibid.,* p. 3.

32. Committee for Economic Development, *Educating Tomorrow's Managers* (New York: CED, 1964).

33. Whether coincidental or not, MIT's first appointment in the School of Industrial Management was the historian, Professor Elting E. Morrisson.

34. *Wall Street Journal,* 11 January, 1975, p. 1. See also, *Wall Street Journal* editorial, 17 January, 1975, p. 10.

35. Glenn D. Overman, "Major Trends in Collegiate Schools of Business During the Next Ten Years," *AACSB Bulletin,* vol. 11, No. 1 (October, 1974).

36. Martin Mayer, *The Bankers* (New York: Weybright and Talley, 1974), p. 4.

37. Allen B. Rosenstein, *A Study of a Profession and Professional Education* (Los Angeles: Reports Group, School of Engineering and Applied Science, UCLA, 1968).

38. M. Gilbert, ed., *The Modern Business Enterprise* (Baltimore, Md.: Penguin Books, 1972), p. 380.

39. Rosenstein, *op. cit.*

40. Clark Kerr, "The Schools of Business Administration," *Proceedings of the American Association of Collegiate Schools of Business* (St. Louis, 1957).

Bibliography

PART 1: RATIONALITY

Ackoff, R. L. *Design of Social Research.* Chicago: University of Chicago Press, 1957.

——, ed. *Progress in Operations Research,* vol. 1. New York: John Wiley & Sons, 1961

——. *Redesigning The Future.* London: John Wiley & Sons, 1974.

——. *Scientific Method: Optimizing Applied Research Decisions.* New York: John Wiley & Sons, 1962.

Arensberg, Conrad and Kimball, Solon T. *Family and Community in Ireland.* Cambridge, Mass.: Harvard University Press, 1940.

Ashby, Ross. *Design for a Brain.* New York: John Wiley & Sons, 1966.

Beer, Stafford. *Platform For Change.* London: John Wiley & Sons, 1975.

Bell, Daniel. *The Coming of Post-Industrial Society.* New York: Basic Books, 1973.

——. *The Cultural Contradictions of Capitalism.* New York: Basic Books, 1976.

Bennis, Warren G. and Slater, Philip E. *The Temporary Society.* New York: Harper & Row, 1968.

Boulding, Kenneth. "The Grants Economy." In *Collected Papers,* edited by Fred R. Glahe. Boulder: University of Colorado Press, 1971.

——. *The Image.* Ann Arbor, Mich.: University of Michigan Press, 1956.

——. "Urbanization and the Grants Economy: An Introduction." In *Transfers in an Urbanized Economy,* edited by Kenneth Boulding, Martin Pfaff, and Anita Pfaff. Belmont, Calif.: Wadsworth Publishing Co., 1973.

Campbell, J. *Hero With a Thousand Faces.* New York: Meridian Books, 1956.

Churchman, C. W. *Challenge to Reason.* New York: McGraw-Hill Book Company, 1968.

——. *The Design of Inquiring Systems.* New York: Basic Books, 1971.

——. *Prediction and Optimal Decision.* Englewood Cliffs, N. J.: Prentice-Hall, 1961.

—— and Ackoff, R. L. *Psychologistics.* Philadelphia: University of Pennsylvania Press, 1946.

Dahl, Robert A. and Lindblom, Charles E. *Politics, Economics, and Welfare.* New York: Harper & Brothers, 1953.

Descartes, Rene. *Philosophical Works.* 2 vols. Translated by E. S. Haldane and G. R. T. Ross. New York: Dover Publications, 1955.

de Tocqueville, Alexis. *Democracy in America.* 2 vols. Translated by Henry Reeve, Rev. Francis Bowen, and Phillips Bradley. New York: Alfred A. Knopf, 1953.

Durant, Will. *The Age of Faith.* New York: Simon & Schuster, 1950.

Forrester, J. *Industrial Dynamics.* Cambridge, Mass.: M.I.T. Press, 1961.

———. *Urban Dynamics.* Cambridge, Mass.: M.I.T. Press, 1969.

———. *World Dynamics.* Cambridge, Mass.: M.I.T. Press, 1971.

Freud, Sigmund. *Group Psychology and the Analysis of the Ego.* Translated by J. Strachey. New York: Liveright Publishing Corporation, 1951.

Gershenson, D. E. and Greenberg, D. A. *Anaxagoras and the Birth of Physics.* New York: Blaisdell Publishing Co., 1964.

Goode, William J. *World Revolution in Family Patterns.* New York: The Free Press of Glencoe, 1963.

Grossman, Gregory. *Economic Systems.* Englewood Cliffs, N. J.: Prentice-Hall, 1974.

Heilbroner, Robert L. *An Inquiry into the Human Prospect.* New York: W. W. Norton, 1974.

———. *Business Civilization in Decline.* New York: W. W. Norton, 1976.

Hillman, James. *The Myth of Analysis.* Evanston, Ill.: Northwestern University Press, 1972

Hirsch, Fred. *Social Limits to Growth.* Cambridge, Mass.: Harvard University Press, 1976.

Hume, David. *A Treatise of Human Nature.* Oxford: Clarendon Press, 1946.

James, William. *Varieties of Religious Experience.* New York: Longmans, Green and Co., 1902.

Jantsch, Erich. *Design for Evolution.* New York: George Braziller, 1975.

———. *Self Organization and Planning in the Life of Human Systems.* New York: George Braziller, 1975.

Jung, C. J. *Psychological Types.* New York: Pantheon Books, 1959.

———. *Two Essays on Analytical Psychology.* New York: Pantheon Books, 1953.

Kant, I. *Critique of Practical Reason.* Translated by L. W. Beck. New York: Liberal Arts Press, 1956.

———. *Critique of Pure Reason.* Translated by Norman Kemp Smith. New York: Humanities Press, 1950.

———. *Fundamental Principles of the Metaphysics of Morals.* Translated by T. K. Abbott. London: Longmans, Green and Co., 1898.

Kuznets, Simon. *Modern Economic Growth: Rate, Structure and Spread.* New Haven, Conn.: Yale University Press, 1966.

————. *Quantitative Economic Research: Trends and Problems.* New York: Columbia University Press, 1972.

Leontief, Wassily. "Mathematics in Economics." In *Essays in Economics: Theories and Theorizing.* New York: Oxford University Press, 1966.

Leibniz, G. W. *Philosophical Writings.* Translated by Mary Morris. London: J. M. Dent & Sons, 1956.

Lindblom, C. E. and Braybrooke, D. *A Strategy of Decision Policy Evaluation As a Social Process.* New York: The Free Press, 1963.

Lindblom, Charles E. *Politics and Markets: World's Pllitical-Economic System.* New York: Basic Books, 1977.

Locke, John. *Essays Concerning Human Understanding.* Chicago: Henry Regnery Company, 1960.

Loucks, William N. and Whitney, William G. *Comparative Economic Systems.* New York: Harper & Row, 1969.

Marris, Peter and Somerset, Anthony. *African Business: A Study of Entrepreneurship.* London: Routledge & Kegan Paul, 1971.

————. *Family and Social Change in an African City: A Study of Rehousing in Lagos.* London: Routledge & Kegan Paul, 1961.

McClelland, David C. *The Achieving Society.* New York: The Free Press, 1967.

Mesarovic, E. and Pestel, Eduard. *Mankind at the Turning Point.* New York: E. P. Dutton, 1974.

Meadows, D. H. et al. *Limits to Growth.* New York: Universe Books, 1972.

Mill, J. S. *A System of Logic.* London: Longmans, 1965.

Monod, Jacques. *Chance and Necessity.* New York: Alfred A. Knopf, 1971.

Ogburn, William P. and Nimkoff, Meyer. *Technology and the Changing Family.* Boston: Houghton Mifflin Company, 1955.

Parsons, Talcott et al. *Family Socialization, and Interaction Process.* Glencoe, Ill.: The Free Press, 1955.

————. "Some Comments on the Pattern of Religious Organization in the United States." In *Structure and Process in Modern Societies.* Glencoe, Ill.: The Free Press, 1960.

———— and Platt, Gerald. With the collaboration of Neil J. Smelser. *The American University.* Cambridge, Mass.: Harvard University Press, 1973.

———— and Smelser, Neil J. *Economy and Society.* Glencoe, Ill.: The Free Press, 1956.

Polanyi, Karl; Arensberg, Conrad; and Pearson, Harry. *Trade and Market in Early Empires.* Glencoe, Ill.: The Free Press, Falcon's Wing Press, 1957.

Rawls, John. *A Theory of Justice.* Cambridge, Mass.: Harvard University Press, Belknap Press, 1971.

Scheler, Max. *Ressentiment.* New York: The Free Press, 1961.

Singer, E. A., Jr. *Mind as a Behavior.* Columbus, Ohio: R. G. Adams and Co., 1924.

———. *On the Contented Life.* New York: Henry Holt and Co., 1936.

———. *Experience and Reflection.* Ed. C. W. Churchman. Philadelphia: University of Pennsylvania Press, 1959.

Sorokin, Pitirim A. *Modern Historical and Social Philosophies.* New York: Dover Publications, 1963.

Stone, Christopher D. *Where the Law Ends.* New York: Harper & Row, 1975.

Titmuss, Richard. *The Gift Relationship: From Human Blood to Social Policy.* New York: Pantheon Books, 1971.

Vickers, G. *Value Systems and Social Process.* Baltimore: Penguin Books, 1970.

Weber, Max; Roth, Guenther; and Wittich, Claus, eds. *Economy and Society: An Outline of Interpretive Sociology.* New York: Bedminster Press, 1968.

PART 2: LEGITIMACY AND RESPONSIBILITY

Anshen, M., ed. *Managing The Socially Responsible Corporation.* New York: Macmillan Co., 1974.

Apter, David E. *The Politics of Modernization.* Chicago: University of Chicago Press, 1965.

Averitt, R. T. *The Dual Economy.* New York: W. W. Norton & Company, 1968.

Baran, P. A. and Sweezy, P. M. *Monopoly Capital.* New York: Modern Reader Paperbacks, 1966.

Barnet, Richard J. and Muller, Ronald E. *Global Reach: The Power of The Multinational Corporation.* New York: Simon & Schuster, 1974.

Bauer, Raymond A., ed. *Social Indicators.* Cambridge, Mass.: M.I.T. Press, 1967.

——— and Fenn, Dan H., Jr. *The Corporate Social Audit.* New York: Russell Sage Foundation, 1972.

Becker, Carl. *Freedom and Responsibility in the American Way of Life.* New York: Vintage Books, 1945.

Bell, Daniel and Kristol, Irving, eds. *Capitalism Today.* New York: Basic Books, 1971.

————. *The Coming of Post Industrial Society.* New York: Basic Books, 1973.

Berle, A. A., Jr. *The Twentieth Century Capitalist Revolution.* New York: Harcourt, Brace, and World, 1954.

————. *Economic Power and the Free Society.* New York: The Fund for the Republic, 1957.

————. *Power Without Property.* New York: Harcourt, Brace, and World, 1959.

———— and Means, Gardiner C. *The Modern Corporation and Private Property.* New York: Harcourt, Brace, and World, 1967.

Blumberg, Phillip I. *The Megacorporation in American Society.* Englewood Cliffs, N. J.: Prentice-Hall, 1975.

Boulding, Kenneth E. *The Organizational Revolution: A Study in the Ethics of Economic Organization.* New York: Harper and Brothers, 1953.

————. "Intersects: The Peculiar Organization." In *Challenge to Leadership: Managing in a Changing World.* New York: Free Press, for the Conference Board, 1973.

————. *The Economy of Love and Fear: A Preface to Grants Economics.* Belmont, Calif.: Wadsworth Publishing Co., 1973.

Cavanagh, Gerald F. *American Business Values in Transition.* Englewood Cliffs, N. J.: Prentice-Hall, 1976.

Chamberlain, Neil W. *The Limits of Corporate Responsibility.* New York: Basic Books, 1973.

————. *The Place of Business in America's Future: A Study in Social Values.* New York: Basic Books, 1973.

Chandler, Alfred D., Jr. *Strategy and Structure: Chapters in the History of the Industrial Enterprise.* Cambridge, Mass.: M.I.T. Press, 1962.

————. *The Visible Hand: The Managerial Revolution in American Business.* Cambridge, Mass.: Harvard University Press, 1977.

Cheit, Earl F. "The New Place of Business." In *The Business Establishment.* New York: John Wiley & Sons, 1964.

Clark, J. M. *Social Control of Business.* Chicago: University of Chicago Press, 1926.

Cochran, Thomas C. *Business in American Life: A History.* New York: McGraw-Hill Book Company, 1972.

Cohn, J. *The Conscience of the Corporations: Business and Urban Affairs, 1967–1970.* Baltimore: John Hopkins University Press, 1971.

Commoner, Barry. *The Closing Circle.* New York: Alfred A. Knopf, 1971.

Corson, John J. *Business in the Humane Society.* New York: McGraw-Hill Book Company, 1971.

Dahl, Robert. *After the Revolution?* New Haven, Conn.: Yale University Press, 1970.

Dahl, Robert A. and Lindblom, Charles E. *Politics, Economics, and Welfare.* New York: Harper and Brothers, 1954.

Daughen, Joseph R. and Binzen, Peter. *The Wreck of the Penn Central.* Boston: Little, Brown, 1971.

Dowling, John and Pfeffer, Jeffrey. "Organizational Legitimacy: Social Values and Organizational Behavior." *Pacific Sociological Review* 18 (January, 1975): 122-136.

Drucker, Peter F. *The Concept of the Corporation.* New York: John Day Company, 1972.

Edwards, Richard C.; Reich, Michael; and Weisskopf, Thomas E. *The Capitalist System: A Radical Analysis of American Society.* Englewood Cliffs, N.J.: Prentice-Hall, 1972.

Eisenberg, Melvin Aron. *The Structure of the Corporation: A Legal Analysis.* Boston, Mass.: Little Brown and Company, 1970.

Epstein, Edwin M. *The Corporation in American Politics.* Englewood Cliffs, N.J.: Prentice- Hall, 1969.

————. "The Historical Enigma of Corporate Legitimacy." *California Law Review* 60 (November, 1972): 1701-1717.

————. "The Social Role of Business Enterprise in Britain: An American Perspective. Part I." *The* [British] *Journal of Management Studies* 13 (October, 1976): 213-233.

————. "The Social Role of Business Enterprise in Britain: An American Perspective. Part II." *The* [British] *Journal of Management Studies* 14 (October, 1977): 281-315.

Friedman, Milton. *Capitalism and Freedom.* Chicago: University of Chicago Press, 1962.

Galbraith, John Kenneth. *The New Industrial State.* Boston: Houghton Mifflin Company, 1967.

————. *Economics and the Public Purpose.* Boston: Houghton Mifflin Company, 1973.

Gouldner, Alvin W. *The Coming Crisis of Western Sociology.* New York: Basic Books, 1970.

Green, Mark J.; Moore, Beverly C., Jr.; and Wasserstein, Bruce. *The Closed Enterprise System.* New York: Grossman Publishers, 1972.

Grossman, Gregory. *Economic Systems.* Englewood Cliffs, N. J.: Prentice-Hall, 1974.

Hacker, Andrew. *The End of the American Era.* New York: Atheneum, 1970.

Harrington, Michael. *The Other America.* New York: Macmillan Co., 1962.

Heald, Morrell. *The Social Responsibilities of Business: Company and*

Community, 1900-1969. Cleveland: The Press of Western Reserve University, 1970.

Heilbroner, Robert L. *The Limits of American Capitalism.* New York: Harper & Row, 1965.

———. *The Future of Capitalism.* New York: Macmillan Co., 1967.

———. *An Inquiry Into The Human Prospect.* New York: W. W. Norton, 1974.

———. *The Making of Economic Society.* 5th ed. Englewood Cliffs, N. J.: Prentice-Hall, 1975.

Hofstadter, Richard. *The Age of Reform.* New York: Vintage Books, 1955.

Hurst, James W. *The Legitimacy of the Business Corporation in the Law of the United States.* Charlottesville, Va.: University of Virginia Press, 1970.

Jacoby, Neil H. *Corporate Power and Social Responsibility.* New York: Macmillan Co., 1973.

Johnson, Harold L. *Business in Contemporary Society: Framework and Issues.* Belmont, Calif.: Wadsworth Publishing Company, 1971.

Kahn, H., ed. *The Future Of The Corporation.* New York: Mason and Lipscomb, 1974.

Levitt, Theodore. *The Third Sector.* New York: Amacom, 1973.

Lowi, Theodore J. *The End of Liberalism.* New York: W. W. Norton, 1969.

Lundborg, Louis B. *Future Without Shock.* New York: W. W. Norton & Company, 1974.

Manne, Henry G. and Wallich, Henry C. *The Modern Corporation and Social Responsibility.* Washington, D. C.: American Enterprise Institute for Public Policy Research, 1972.

Mason, Edward, ed. *The Corporation in American Society.* Cambridge, Mass.: Harvard University Press, 1959.

Maurer, J. G. *Readings In Organizational Theory: Open System Approaches.* New York: Random House, 1971.

McClelland, David C. *The Achieving Society.* New York: Van Nostrand Reinhold Company, 1961.

McConnell, Grant. *Private Power and American Democracy.* New York: Alfred A. Knopf, 1966.

McKie, James W., ed. *Social Responsibility and the Business Predicament.* Washington, D.C.: The Brookings Institution, 1974.

Meadows, D. H. et al. *Limits to Growth.* New York: Universe Books, 1972.

Nader, Ralph and Green, Mark J. *Corporate Power in America.* New York: Grossman Publishers, 1973.

————; ————; and Seligman, Joel. *Constitutionalizing the Corporation: The Case for Federal Chartering of Giant Corporations.* Washington, D.C.: The Corporate Accountability Research Group, 1976.

Nisbet, Robert. *Twilight of Authority.* New York: Oxford University Press, 1975.

Nozick, Robert. *Anarchy State and Utopia.* New York: Basic Books, 1974.

Parsons, Talcott. *Structure and Process in Modern Societies.* Glencoe, Ill.: The Free Press, 1960.

Perrow, Charles. *Organizational Analysis: A Sociological View.* Belmont, Calif.: Wadsworth Publishing Company, 1970.

————. *The Radical Attack on Business: A Critical Analysis.* New York: Harcourt, Brace, Jovanovich, 1972.

Polanyi, Karl. *The Great Transformation.* Boston: Beacon Press, 1957.

Preston, Lee E. and Post, James E. *Private Management and Public Policy.* Englewood Cliffs, N. J.: Prentice-Hall, 1975.

Rauschenbusch, Walter. *Christianizing the Social Order.* New York: Macmillan Co., 1914.

Rawls, John. *A Theory of Justice.* Cambridge, Mass.: Harvard University Press, Belknap Press, 1971.

Rockefeller, John D., 3rd. *The Second American Revolution.* New York: Harper & Row, 1973.

Sampson, Anthony. *The Seven Sisters: The Great Oil Companies and The World They Shaped.* New York: Viking Press, 1975.

Selznick, Philip. *Law, Society, and Industrial Justice.* New York: Russell Sage Foundation, 1969.

Senior, Nassau. *An Outline of the Science of Political Economy.* London: G. Allen & Unwin, 1939.

Shenfield, Barbara. *Company Boards: Their Responsibilities to Shareholders, Employees, and the Community.* London: G. Allen & Unwin, 1971.

Shonfield, A. *Modern Capitalism.* New York: Oxford University Press, 1969.

Silk, Leonard and Vogel, David. *Ethics and Profits: The Crisis of Confidence in American Business.* New York: Simon & Schuster, 1976.

Smith, Adam. *The Wealth of Nations.* New York: Modern Library, 1937.

Smith, Richard A. *Corporations in Crisis.* New York: Doubleday & Co., 1964.

Steiner, George A. *Business and Society.* New York: Random House, 1975.

Stinchcombe, Arthur L. *Constructing Social Theories.* New York: Harcourt, Brace and World, 1968.

Stone, Christopher D. *Where the Law Ends: The Social Control of Corporate Behavior.* New York: Harper & Row, 1975.

Sutton, Francis X. et al. *The American Business Creed.* New York: Schocken Books, 1956.

Tawney, R. H. *Religion and the Rise of Capitalism.* London: Murphy, 1929.

Thompson, James D. *Organizations In Action.* New York: McGraw-Hill Book Company, 1967.

Veblen, Thorstein. *The Engineers and the Price System.* New York: Viking Press, 1933.

Vernon, Raymond. *Sovereignty at Bay: The Spread of U. S. Enterprise.* New York: Basic Books, 1973.

———. *Storm Over the Multinationals: The Real Issues.* Cambridge, Mass.: Harvard University Press, 1977.

Votaw, Dow and Sethi, S. Prakash. *The Corporate Dilemma.* Englewood Cliffs, N.J.: Prentice-Hall, 1973.

Ward, Ben. *What's Wrong With Economics?* New York: Basic Books, 1972.

Weber, Max. *Sociology of Religion.* Translated by Ephraim Fischof. Boston: Beacon Press, 1964.

———. *The Protestant Ethic and the Spirit of Capitalism.* New York: Charles Scribner's Sons, 1963.

———. *The Theory of Social and Economic Organizations.* Translated by A. M. Henderson and Talcott Parsons. Glencoe, Ill.: The Free Press, 1964.

Index

6405052